M000114068

OVERWHELMED
by the *Spirit*

A Biblical Study on Discovering the Spirit

RANDALL A. HARRISON

Contents

ACKNOWLEDGMENTS

At the heart of this study is a lifelong endeavor to encourage both an active search for the empowering of the Holy Spirit among churches and ministers of the Gospel hoping to reach the world for Christ and a careful examination of the Scriptures to ensure that these Spirit-empowered ministries remain biblical in their focus. It is an effort to unite impassioned experience with solid biblical research. First-hand observation of ministry on three different continents (North America, Europe and Africa) leads me to believe that this is an uncommon marriage. Those who emphasize experience with the Holy Spirit are accused of neglecting serious biblical studies. Those who emphasize careful biblical investigation are accused of functioning in ministry without the empowering of the Holy Spirit. Regrettably, both accusations are often true.

I would like to express appreciation to some of those who have encouraged and helped me in my own personal search. First, I would like to thank those who played a part in my initial experience with the Spirit described in the first chapter of this book. I would like to thank Steve Stockley who organized the youth retreat where I came to Christ, Billy Long the anointed speaker at that retreat and all those who prayed for us. I would like to thank Rob Mitchell, whose miraculous healing at that retreat opened my eyes to the manifestation of God's power in our world today, for his help in recalling many of the details described in the first chapter.

Secondly, I would like to thank those who helped me in the detailed study of God's Word leading up to the publication of this book. I would like to thank Dr Howard Ervin and other faculty members in the theology department at Oral Roberts University for presenting solid biblical evidence for a Pentecostal position on Spirit empowering. I would like to thank Dr. David Bauer and the biblical studies department of Asbury Theological Seminary for introducing me to inductive Bible study methodology which serves as a basis for much of what is contained in this book. I would like to thank Dr Samuel Bénétreau of the Faculté Libre de Théologie Évangélique for his very helpful comments and suggestions on my doctoral dissertation entitled *L'Esprit dans le récit de Luc: Une recherche de cohérence dans la pneumatologie de l'auteur implicit de Luc-Actes* (*The Spirit in Luke's Story: A Search for a Coherent Theology of the Spirit of the Implied Author of Luke-Acts*). Much of the present work is taken from this dissertation. My thanks also go to Paul King and Craig Keener, two Sprit-filled scholars who encouraged me to write this book.

Finally, and most importantly, I would like to thank some of the members of my family who made it possible for me to complete my studies and write and publish this book. I would like to thank my daughter-in-law, Kim, for her labors in editing and for her frequent encouraging remarks. I would like to thank my brother-in-law, Jerry Dorris, for his help in getting it published. My greatest appreciation is reserved for my wife, Deanna, and children, Daniel, Christy and Rachel, who have encouraged me in this project for many years and spent countless hours discussing it with me. Many of our family decisions involving the sacrifice of time and money were made on my behalf and for the success of this book.

Chapter 1

Overwhelmed by the Spirit

"Randy, God has healed me! For the first time in my life, I am breathing through my nose!" Rob Mitchell's words took my breath away. It seemed impossible. And yet I knew his words had to be true. I had known Rob all my life. He had always been weak, always had difficulty breathing, always had asthma. Several times a year he was taken to the hospital and put on a respirator to help him breathe normally, but his breathing was anything but normal. If he was in the room, everyone knew it. His loud wheezing was a constant reminder of his illness. But on that April night in 1971, I could no longer hear him breathing. The wheezing was gone. Rob was healed and I knew it!

Rob had pediatric emphysema. Rob's mother was RH negative and he was born RH positive, a condition which can be fatal without treatment. Rob received a blood transfusion at birth to save his life. The transfusion caused his lungs to collapse, resulting in significant damage. This damage made it difficult for Rob to exhale. Rob quickly developed multiple allergies that made it difficult for him to inhale. The combination caused the audible wheezing, which was so familiar to all of Rob's friends and embarrassing to Rob. He hated silence because he and all of us were aware of his noticeably loud wheezing and his handicap.

Rob's parents spent thousands of dollars on treatment. Three times a week, he would go to the doctor's office to get shots for his allergies and breathe into a respirator. In the Fall and Spring, when his allergies were

1

worse, and when he was more tempted to participate in sports, Rob could have attacks when he simply could not draw enough oxygen into his lungs. Then he would be rushed to the hospital and put on a respirator. Rob felt as though he were more of a medical patient and burden to his parents, than a son. He was plagued with thoughts of suicide. "Wouldn't it be easier for me and my parents if God took me?"

Rob and I grew up together in church. We were crib kids together. We went to school together and both our families were faithful churchgoers. We heard stories from the Bible every week and believed them to be true. However, I don't remember ever hearing a clear presentation of the Gospel message and of my need for salvation. I had certainly never heard of God healing people today. I went to church to be with my friends. I was a pretty 'good' kid, a good student and hardly ever in trouble. One day the pastor of the church asked if I would like to participate in a special Sunday school class for kids who had not yet made a commitment to Christ and who were not members of the church. How could I refuse? I was a 'good' kid. At the end of this course, the pastor invited all of us to go forward in church and make a public decision for Christ, following him in baptism.

The next Sunday, at the end of the service, my sister Jan, who was two years younger than I and in the same Sunday school class, got up to go forward. I had been indecisive up to that point, but, being unwilling for my sister to get ahead of me in anything, I also decided to get up and go forward. Not long afterwards, I was baptized and joined the church. There was very little change in my life as a result of this decision. I had been told I needed to read the Bible. I started in Genesis and got half way through Exodus before getting too bored to continue. However, since I was a 'good' kid and didn't get into much trouble, no one worried about my spiritual condition.

Four years later, Steve Stockley, a new youth director in our church, decided to organize a youth retreat. All my friends were going, and I did not want to miss it. However, my parents did not have the money to pay for the retreat. I don't know if Steve had me in mind when he proposed an idea for enticing us to invite others to the retreat, but it was a great solution to my problem, and, in a very real sense, a godsend. For every invited guest we got to come to the retreat, he would take 20% off our cost. I made the calculation and found five other bored teenagers to sign up, three guys and two cute girls. My thoughts were not very spiritual.

Rob's biggest problem was not finances. His parents were always worried for Rob to be too far away from medical help. The retreat cabin in northeast Oklahoma was a twenty minute drive from the nearest town and did not even have a telephone. (Hardly anyone had a cell phone in those days.) It was also the time of year when allergies get worse, and a youth retreat would of course be filled with athletic activities. In the end, Rob was allowed to go because his parents had just purchased a portable respirator. Rob could take his most important medical treatment with him to the retreat.

On Saturday evening, April 3, 1971, we played capture the flag. Rob and I were on the same team. We made a long trek through fields and over barbed wire fences to sneak up on the back side of the enemy flag. Rob ran a diversion, pretending to make a dash for the flag, drawing their flag keeper away to capture him. As soon as the flag keeper ran after Rob, I ran and grabbed the unguarded flag and continued running across the dimly lit forest toward our team's side. The flag keeper realized his mistake and sounded the alarm. The entire enemy team converged on me in hot pursuit of the stolen flag. When I realized there was no way I could make it back to our side of the ravine without being captured, I hurled the flag as far as I could. It landed on the opposite side of the ravine and ended the game. There was some dispute as to whether it was legal in capture the flag to throw the flag, but it was already dark and time for a meeting with our special speaker.

Rob and I were elated. However, Rob was also in pain, a fact to which I was oblivious. I felt great. We had won, and I was sort of the star of the game. I was hoping my friends were impressed, especially the two girls I had invited. I certainly wasn't paying much attention to the speaker; I was thinking about the girls. Rob, on the other hand, was hurting and curled up in a chair, listening.

I believe that what occurred afterwards caused me to remember the speaker's words that night. Billy Long was a student at Oral Roberts University in Tulsa, Oklahoma, preparing with his wife Skipper to serve overseas. Billy grew up on a farm and used some unusual illustrations in his message. He said that a lot of people in church were like chickens with their heads cut off. Sometimes when you cut off a chicken's head, it can run around for a short while before it falls dead. It gives the appearance of being alive, but, in reality, it is dead. Many in church also give the appearance of being alive in Christ, but, in reality, they are spiritually dead. He also compared churchgoers to pigs. He said you can clean up a pig, put perfume on it and dress it in fine clothing. But, as soon as you release it, the pig will return to the mud, because it feels at home in the mud. People get cleaned up to go to church and act like Christians while they are there. But, when they get away from church, they return to their own ways. They look like Christians on the outside, but inside, in their hearts, what they want is mud.

At the end of his message, Billy asked all those who wanted to pray to go to the dorms. The meeting room was in the middle of a large T-shaped building, with a girls' dorm on one side and the boys' dorm on the other. The boys went to pray with Billy and the girls with Skipper. I did not go to pray. Rob did.

Back in the dorm, Billy noticed Rob's labored breathing and asked if he wanted to be healed. Rob's grandmother was a converted Jew turned Pentecostal and had often told Rob that she believed he would be healed one day. Rob raised his hands into the air and responded: "Yes, I want to be healed." Billy laid his hands on his head and prayed. The next thing Rob remembers is lying on his bunk and being able to breathe freely. He says, "It felt like I was able to suck all the furniture in the room into my lungs." He told his little brother, Mason, "I can breathe." Mason placed his head on Rob's chest to listen and just said, "Wow!"

I was also wowed by Rob's miraculous healing. I was overwhelmed by the power of God. Rob continued around the room telling everyone that God had healed him. As the news spread, chaos broke out. People did not know what to do in the presence of the living God. Some held hands in a circle and began to dance. Others shouted. Others cried with joy. Others ran to ring the dinner bell over and over for hours. The news had to be proclaimed. A decision was made to take Rob to town to call his parents and tell them the news. As many people as would fit crammed into a car to go share the good news.

In the midst of such pandemonium, shouting, talking, crying, rejoicing, I felt alone in the presence of God. It was as if the roof had been removed from that retreat center and God had come down right there among us. I became acutely aware of the presence of God and of my own selfish life. I lived to please myself, never thinking about the God who loved me and gave himself for me. Even the 'good' I did was only intended to cause others to think well of me. In that moment, I made a commitment to God. I said to him, "Wherever you want me to go, I will go. Whatever you want me to do, I will do. Whatever you want me to say, I will say." I met the Lord of the universe that night, and my life changed radically. From that day forward prayer became natural as I communicated with a God so near. Reading my Bible became a passion as the words leapt off the page to inspire my life. Sharing the Good News about Jesus became a priority, a necessity.

Our joy and passion for Jesus did not stop when we came home from the retreat. The desire to pray, read our Bibles and share Jesus with everyone around us helped to spark a revival in our high school and in our town of Tulsa, Oklahoma. We organized Bible studies and prayer meetings at school, in homes, and on the streets. We saw hundreds of young people turn to Christ. The story continues to this day. I would love to relate some of the stories since 1971 of how God has blessed me and many others with miracles, adventure, and a great sense of fulfillment in following his will and purpose in my life. But this book is not about me, or even about what God has done in my life. It is about the Holy Spirit, about his dealings in the lives of Jesus' first disciples and, ultimately, about what the Spirit wants to accomplish in and through the lives of his disciples today. With this in mind, let us return to the story of those powerful moments with God immediately following Rob's healing and introduce some of the important issues involved in the controversial subject of the Spirit's empowering.

The day after Rob's healing Billy Long led us in a Bible study. This time he had our full attention. Billy was Pentecostal and wanted us to understand our need for and how to receive the power of the Holy Spirit in our lives. He talked about a second experience, which we would need to be effective witnesses for Jesus Christ, and which he called the "baptism in the Holy Spirit." He showed us passages in the Gospels and in the Acts of the Apostles concerning this experience, passages which we will examine in later chapters of this book. We accepted without question everything he taught us. God had used Billy to do a miracle in our midst and to introduce us to the living God. As far as we were concerned, Billy taught the Word of God with God's authority. When he said we needed to receive the baptism in the Holy Spirit in order to be powerful witnesses for Jesus, we started praying to receive this baptism. After all, he was the most powerful witness for Jesus we had ever known. According to Billy, the gift of speaking in tongues is the sign that one has received this powerful second experience. So, we all prayed that God would also grant us this sign.

We prayed fervently and regularly for God to grant us this powerful gift of his Spirit. Many times we felt the presence of God in our midst. However, because Billy had told us to expect the gift of speaking in tongues as the sign that God had baptized us with his Spirit, we continued to pray for this blessing. Were we right to continue praying? About a month later, God specifically answered our prayers. Several of us were conducting evangelistic meetings in a small church in Avant, Oklahoma. While we were praying before the meeting, we again experienced the power of the Holy Spirit and began to speak in tongues. Were we now supposed to stop praying for powerful blessings from the Holy Spirit?

My experience would definitely be considered 'Pentecostal' or 'charismatic.' I hesitate to use these terms because they are often associated with so many stereotypes and views about the Holy Spirit which I reject. I am also a bit uneasy about beginning this book by relating my own personal experience, since some might be inclined to prematurely reject my conclusions on the false assumption that they are based on experience. As with all interpreters, including those who interpreted the Scriptures in the pages of the New Testament, experience has and does play an important role in my logic. However, I would like to assure my readers that I have taken painstaking measures to interpret biblical passages in context, with a particular emphasis on the literary context of the books which contain them. My readers will discover that this process has caused me to question both charismatic and non charismatic, Pentecostal and non Pentecostal interpretations of these passages.

Many others have discovered the Spirit in a similar manner. Since the Azusa Street revival in 1907, millions of Christians all over the world claim to have experienced the baptism in the Holy Spirit with the evidence of speaking in tongues. The *World Christian Encyclopedia* puts the number of Pentecostals/Charismatics in 2000 at over 500 million. That is roughly one quarter of all professing Christians in the world. Their number has multiplied more than 500 times in the last century. Between 1990 and 2000 there was an average annual addition of around 10 million adherents.[1] In 2006, 23% of the population of the United States and 56% of the population of Kenya considered themselves Pentecostal or charismatic.[2] Not all of these adherents would describe their Pentecostal experience using the same terminology. The definition of Pentecostal or charismatic experience varies considerably. But the trend toward an emphasis on the empowering of the Holy Spirit among Christians today is undeniable.

Evaluating Experience

How should we evaluate our experiences and the experiences of so many others? Certainly, we know that our experiences must be evaluated in the light of the teachings of Scripture. But we also know that experience can serve as

[1] David B. Barrett, *World Christian Encyclopedia: A Comparative Survey of Churches and Religions in the Modern World Volume I: The World by Countries: Religionists, Churches, Ministries*, Oxford University, New York, 2001, p. 4

[2] Laurie Goodstein, "Pentecostal and Charismatic Groups Growing," New York Times, Oct 6, 2006. Taken from "The Pew Forum on Religious Life, A 10-Country Survey of Pentecostals," http://pewforum.org/surveys/ pentecostal/, Oct 5, 2006.

a catalyst for correcting poor teaching, when the Scriptures have been misunderstood. Much of the New Testament is correcting a poor understanding of the Scriptures of ancient Israel in the light of the death and resurrection of Jesus and the experience of his disciples. For example, in Luke-Acts, the two-volume work by Luke, the apostles' teachings about Jesus—teachings held to be false by those who diligently studied the Scriptures at that time—are powerfully validated by manifestations of the Spirit. Despite all our desire and efforts to correctly handle the word of truth (2 Ti 2:15), our comprehension of the Scriptures remains incomplete. We are often compelled to reexamine the Scriptures, when faced with a new experience or a new insight drawn from the text of Scripture in order to determine if what was said to us is true (Ac 17:11).

On the other hand, just because someone is powerfully used by God, does not mean that their theology is correct. God uses imperfect people with imperfect doctrines. We must evaluate all teaching in the light of the Scriptures. Experience should not be the basis for Christian doctrine, but it can and should cause us to reexamine the Scriptures to verify what seems to be true in experience. On the weekend Rob was healed, we were not capable of such evaluation. We had just discovered the Spirit of God. We did not discover him through diligent study of the Word; he revealed himself to us through a powerful experience.

It is my belief that the disciples in Jesus' day came to know the Spirit in a similar manner. They recognized the powerful intervention of God through his Spirit long before they were capable of fully analyzing that experience in systematic theological terms. They understood that their experience with the Holy Spirit was the fulfillment of a prophetic end-time promise in the book of Joel (Ac 2:16), and that they were thus a part of that end-time community inheriting this promise. They could understand that they were beneficiaries of this promise because of their relationship with Jesus the Messiah, and that others needed to repent in order receive the same benefits (Lk 24:47-49; Ac 1:4-8; 2:38-39). They could also understand that, when Gentiles experienced a similar blessing, God had validated their entry into the same end-time community (Ac 10:44-48; 11:15-18). In the beginning, they were unable to make sweeping statements about what the Spirit always or even usually does, or how the Spirit always or usually operates in the life of a Christian. Neither their knowledge of the Old Testament, nor their understanding of the teachings of Jesus, nor their accumulated experience up to that point would enable them to draw such universal and definitive conclusions concerning the habitual and normative functions of the Spirit.

We must take this lack of experience and understanding into consideration when we come to interpret the Acts of the Apostles. We need to understand the narrative account of the early church in the light of its literary and historical context. I believe that one of the keys to this understanding is coherence. Luke's theology of the Spirit should be coherent. He should not contradict himself. I believe that both Pentecostal and non Pentecostal interpretations have failed to pass this test of coherence. Luke tells about believers who received the Spirit subsequent to their conversion, an idea which is difficult to reconcile with Paul's teaching on the subject (Rom 8:9). Pentecostal interpreters tend to redefine Luke's concept of receiving the Spirit to make it fit with Paul's theology. Non Pentecostal interpreters tend to interpret Acts through the theological lenses of Paul or John. Both groups introduce incoherent and anachronistic ideas into Luke's narrative. They assume the disciples were familiar with the teachings in Paul's writings before he wrote them.

The solution to this enigma is not found in harmonizing the writings of these two authors. Rather, we need to recognize that there was a certain progression in the early disciples' understanding of the Spirit's activities. The writings of Paul and John exhibit a more developed theology of the Spirit than what Luke describes in his account. We should not expect those who were just discovering the Spirit of God to fully understand and describe his workings. A theology of the Spirit must have developed with time. Forcing Acts to harmonize with Pauline theology, particularly with the concept of the reception of the Spirit at conversion (Rom 8:9), introduces incoherence into the narrative. The interpreter is forced to talk about exceptions[3] which do not fit logically into the narrative, or about conflicting sources which Luke has failed or refused to integrate into his own theology.[4] We do a disservice to these narrative accounts by trying to squeeze them into the mold of a more developed theology, such as we find in the letters of Paul. We are also in danger of losing important elements from Luke-Acts if we allow his message to be eclipsed by that of Paul or John.[5]

Some may argue that the most developed theology of the Spirit is found in the words of Jesus in the Gospel of John spoken before the writing of Luke-Acts. This is seen as evidence of an early developed theology of the

---

[3] Hull, p. 119; Marshall, *Historian*, p. 201; Stott, p. 17, 19-21; Turner p. 360.
[4] Oulton, p. 236; Scott, p. 89.
[5] James B. Shelton, *Mighty in Word and Deed: The Role of the Holy Spirit in Luke-Acts*, Hendrickson Publishers, Peabody, Mass., 1991, p. 2.

Spirit. I would reply that the disciples often did not understand Jesus' teachings (Lk 18:34) and that there is probably good reason why these teachings of Jesus in the Gospel according to John did not appear in the earlier synoptic gospels (probably several decades earlier). The disciples simply did not understand much of what Jesus taught about the Spirit. Jesus himself taught that the Spirit would "guide" the disciples into all truth (Jn 16:13), not that the disciples would understand all truth immediately after the resurrection. When Jesus "opened the minds" of his disciples so they could "understand the Scriptures," the text is probably referring to a few major subjects listed immediately after this reference (Lk 24:45-47). Like us, they still had much to discover about the overwhelming power of the Spirit.

Chapter 2

Arguing about the Spirit

Baptism and fullness: Diverging interpretations

From the moment I surrendered my will to the Lord and said, "Wherever you want me to go, I will go," I had a hunch that this commitment would lead me into overseas service. The hunch became a conviction and I began to prepare for missionary service. I met a beautiful young lady in college who also had a call to missions. Before we left to serve the Lord in Africa, we spoke in several churches to ask people to pray for us. One of those churches was the church in which I grew up.

This was my first opportunity to share my personal testimony in this church and relate how I had met the Lord during that youth retreat some six years earlier. Very few of the young people who had been at the youth retreat still attended the church, but many of the parents were still there. I remember pouring my heart out to this congregation, as I considered the possibility that others might be pretending to be 'Christian' as I had done before that weekend.

After the service a woman approached me with an enormous smile on her face. She pulled me aside to tell me that she had been placed on the committee to decide what to do about the young people after the retreat. I had to have her repeat what she said because I was clueless. I had no idea that a committee had been formed to talk about us. I did not know we were controversial. I had assumed that the church was rejoicing over our newfound faith in Jesus and our zeal to serve him. The woman went on to say that she felt compelled to read the Scriptures so that she could discuss the problem intelligently on the committee. When she read the Scriptures, she discovered her need for a Savior and gave her life to Jesus. She wanted me to know what the Lord had done in her life.

As you may have guessed, the controversial issue was not our faith or our zeal, but the "baptism in the Holy Spirit." The Pentecostal doctrine of the "baptism in the Holy Spirit" has been blamed, perhaps justly or perhaps unjustly, for causing difficulties and divisions in many churches around the world. I am glad that I lived in blissful ignorance of this controversy during my first few months of discovering the Christian life. Since that time I have dealt with these issues for more than three decades on three different continents.

When I interviewed for my first job in Christian service, I tried to be as honest as possible about my beliefs and doctrines. I certainly made no effort to hide my convictions. But, when I began teaching about a second experience with the Holy Spirit in an evening Bible study, the pastor asked to see me in his office. He requested that I only use *our* denomination's materials for teaching the Bible. I assured him that I was not using any other denomination's materials, only the Bible. He then informed me that the Bible was not a part of that denominational material and I must no longer teach directly from the Bible. I left his office in shock. Despite some knowledge of the controversy, I once again was caught off guard. I sought counsel from another pastor and quietly resigned from my position.

Lest you think that the problem resides solely in the camp of the non Pentecostals, allow me to share an experience I had in France. I had the opportunity to take a pastorate in a more 'charismatic' church. I was excited to work there because I thought that, in this group, I would not have to worry about offending anyone when I taught on the Holy Spirit. I was wrong. I was criticized by the church board for not being led by the Spirit in my preaching. "How can you be led by the Spirit," they asked, "when you teach the Bible in series and know weeks in advance the subject or chapters we will study?" I should "let the Holy Spirit guide" me moment by moment during my preaching. A visiting preacher, highly esteemed by the leadership of this church, told the congregation from the pulpit that we do not even need the Scriptures anymore because we have the Holy Spirit to guide us into all truth (Jn 16:13). I had to resign from this church as well.

The problem is also relevant in Africa. Most of my students in seminary can tell horror stories about self-proclaimed "prophets" who came to their churches and created havoc. Many of these "prophets" had very little or no biblical training and instigated very syncretistic movements, mixing biblical concepts with traditional African beliefs, sometimes even encouraging the use of fetishes or talismans. As a consequence, the division between 'Pentecostal' and 'non Pentecostal' churches has become even more pronounced. Each group characterizes the other with the worst abuses.

In our seminary in Côte d'Ivoire, we receive students from many different denominations. Every year I teach a course in which we discuss interpretations of the baptism in the Holy Spirit and the fullness of the Spirit. I have the students read and evaluate scholarly works from both camps. Our students have found it helpful to study and debate the various positions in a classroom setting. Having developed mutual respect and a certain amount of camaraderie, students are less likely to 'demonize' their opponents. They have seen each other's lives and service to the Lord. They know that their fellow students are sincerely committed to biblical principles and have also made many sacrifices for their faith. The students discover that the 'others' also base their beliefs on the Scriptures, that the interpretation of these expressions is not straight forward, that they do not have all the answers, that they may need to listen to others.

It was while I was in France that I began doing serious research on this subject. There were pastors on both sides of the fence who wanted to discuss the issues together. I was asked to speak at a pastors' gathering on the biblical basis for a Pentecostal, or charismatic, position. Following the meeting, I was asked to write an article on the subject for a pastors' journal.[1] I discussed the strengths and weaknesses of Pentecostal and non Pentecostal positions. Feedback for the article generated enough interest to produce a follow-up article in which I responded to rebuttals. Both articles have since been used in a seminary extension program to introduce students to the issues in question with regard to divergent understandings of the Holy Spirit. These events helped motivate me to do further research and to write a doctoral thesis on the subject. This book covers some of the same material, but hopefully in a more readable format. The following discussion contains much of the material from that first article.

---

[1] "La plénitude de l'Esprit," *Cahiers de l'école pastorale* 33, Sept. 1999, p. 8-10.

The Debate

The baptism in the Holy Spirit and the fullness of the Holy Spirit are some
of the most debated expressions among evangelical Christians. Viewpoints
vary considerably in the details. But, for the sake of simplicity, I will limit
our discussion to two basic positions. Evangelicals are divided between two
major opinions which I will call Pentecostal and non Pentecostal positions.[2]
In general, Pentecostals and Charismatics teach that baptism in the Holy
Spirit and filling with the Holy Spirit describe an experience or experiences
subsequent to conversion by which the believer is empowered for witnessing.
Non Pentecostals believe that the baptism in the Holy Spirit is an integral
part of conversion or just another way of describing conversion, and that the
fullness of the Spirit is an ongoing process after conversion whereby believers
become more and more filled with the Spirit as they submit to his guidance
and influence.

These positions are often held by partisans on both sides who have not
really examined the coherence of their position. This is completely understandable considering the complexities in the interpretation of these expressions. First of all, the two metaphors are not clearly defined anywhere in
Scripture. Their meaning is presupposed. The authors assume that their readers understand them without explanation. Secondly, the terms are used differently by Paul and Luke. In First Corinthians, Paul also uses the expression
'in Spirit' (*en pneumati*) in a phrase related to baptism, but the syntax of the
sentence and the context of the passage are dissimilar to the way Luke uses
the expression (1 Cor 13:13). Commentators disagree about how to translate
the expression in First Corinthians. In Ephesians, Paul uses the expression
'filled with the Spirit,' but also in a very different context. Luke adds to the
confusion by using two different Greek terms for the fullness of the Spirit.
Some interpreters believe these two terms to be entirely synonymous. Others believe we should distinguish between the two terms. Thirdly, the literary
context of Luke-Acts appears to provide conflicting information. The immediate context of the expression 'baptized in the Holy Spirit' in Luke's gospel appears to require a totally different meaning than that required by the

---

[2] I do not use the term to represent the official position of any Pentecostal denomination, but a
general consensus among Pentecostal and charismatic interpreters. I also do not intend to imply
that those holding the 'non Pentecostal' position described above, do not believe in 'Pentecostal'
experiences. Many who adhere to a 'non Pentecostal' position for the meaning of the expression
'baptized in the Spirit' do believe in the exercise of 'Pentecostal' gifts today.

contexts in Acts. In fact, I will argue that the intended meaning of the two speakers, John in the gospels and Jesus in Acts, is indeed different.[3] Finally, the expression 'baptized in the Holy Spirit' is not used in the Old Testament or in any known intertestamental literature. Hence, there is no obvious background information to guide our interpretation.

The Pentecostal position

The best arguments for the Pentecostal position are found in the literary context of Luke-Acts. The expressions 'baptized' or 'filled with the Holy Spirit' are used to describe typically 'Pentecostal' experiences with typically 'Pentecostal' results. The Spirit comes on the disciples in a 'Pentecostal' manner and they begin to exercise 'Pentecostal' gifts.

Expressions used by Luke to describe Holy Spirit experiences

Most of the references to being baptized or filled with the Holy Spirit are found in Luke's two-volume work: Luke-Acts. The noun form of the expression 'Baptism in the Holy Spirit' is not used in the New Testament. John the Baptist's call to repentance, in which he contrasts being 'Baptized with the Holy Spirit' with being baptized with water, is repeated in all four gospels. Luke is the only author to apply John's prophetic words to an actual experience. He does this twice in Acts.[4] With one possible exception, the expressions 'filled with' or 'full' of the Spirit are only used in Luke-Acts.[5] Luke also uses a number of other expressions to describe these Spirit experiences: *The Holy Spirit will come upon you* (Lk 1:35); *the Holy Spirit was upon him* (2:25); *the Holy Spirit descended on him* (3:22); *Jesus returned…in the power of the Spirit* (4:14); *The Spirit of the Lord is on me* (4:18); *I am going to send you what my Father has promised…clothed with power from on high* (24:49); *you will receive power when the Holy Spirit comes on you* (Ac 1:8); *I will pour out my Spirit on all people* (2:17); *you will receive the gift of the Holy Spirit. The promise is for… all* (2:38-39); *they received the Holy Spirit* (8:17); *the Holy Spirit came*

---

[3] I am not questioning either John the Baptist's inspiration or that of the author. Luke's purpose and how he uses John's prophecy resolves this apparent dilemma. See chapter 6.

[4] Mt 3:11; Mc 1:8; Lk 3:16; Jn 1:33; Ac 1:5; 11:16. 1 Co 12:13 contains 3 of the 4 same Greek terms, but not in proximity to each other and probably with a different meaning. See chapter 6.

[5] *pimplémi* Lk 1:15, 41, 67; Ac 2:4; 4:8, 31; 9:17; 13:9; *plérés* Lk 4:1; Ac.7:55; *pléroô* Ac 13:52; Eph 5:18.

on all who heard (10:44); *the Holy Spirit came on them as he had come on us at the beginning* (11:15); *the Holy Spirit came on them* (19:6). Since Luke is the one who uses these expressions, it makes sense for interpreters to look for the meaning of these expressions in Luke-Acts.

The reading of these expressions in context reveals that they are synonymous. They refer to the same events. Luke uses no less than six expressions to refer to the disciples' experience with the Spirit in Acts 2. They must wait for and receive *the promise of the Father* (Lk 24:49; Ac 1:4; 2:39). They will be *baptized in the Holy Spirit* (Ac 1:5). They will *receive power* when the *Holy Spirit comes on* them (Ac 1.8). They were all *filled with the Holy Spirit* on the day of Pentecost (Ac 2:4). Peter describes the event as the fulfillment of the promise that God would *pour out* his *Spirit* on all people (Ac 2:16-17). Finally, Peter tells his listeners on the day of Pentecost that they too can *receive the gift of the Holy Spirit* (Ac 2:38). Luke uses 2 expressions in chapter 8 to describe the same event: *receiving the Spirit* and the *Spirit coming upon* the believers (Ac 8:15-17). The episode in the house of Cornelius contains 4 expressions describing the same event: the *Holy Spirit came on* them (Ac 10:44; 11:15); the *gift of the Holy Spirit* was *poured out on* them (Ac 10:45); they *received the Holy Spirit* (Ac 10:47); and the experience recalls the promise that they would be *baptized in the Holy Spirit* (Ac 11:16).

Holy Spirit experiences and powerful phenomena

The reading of these expressions in context also reveals a very close relationship between these expressions and prophetic acts: prophetic words or manifestations of the Spirit's power resembling those of the Old Testament prophets. The angel of the Lord revealed to Zechariah that his son John would *be filled with the Holy Spirit even from birth* (Lk 1:15) and that he would operate *in the spirit* (Spirit[6]) *and power of Elijah* (Lk 1:17). Both Elizabeth and Zachariah prophesied after being *filled with the Holy Spirit* (Lk 1:41, 67). Jesus himself was *filled with the Holy Spirit* (Lk 4:1) and endued with the *power of the Spirit* before he started his ministry (Lk 4:14). The text he chose to describe his ministry of teaching and acts of power begins with

---

[6] The Greek term for spirit does not distinguish between a spirit and the divine Spirit. The NIV translation assumes that Luke is referring to the human spirit of Elijah in this passage. The Spirit of God fits much better in the context of Luke-Acts. Luke repeatedly refers to and makes allusions to Elijah stories in Luke-Acts with an emphasis on the power of the Holy Spirit in his ministry (Lk ch. 4, 7, 9, Ac 1). Luke also repeatedly associates God's Spirit with power as in this verse.

the words, *The Spirit of the Lord is on me, because he has anointed me to preach good news* and, to summarize the rest of the reference, to perform powerful acts (Lk 4:18-19). The disciples on the road to Emmaus describe Jesus as a *prophet, powerful in word and deed* (Lk 24:19). Peter summarizes the ministry of Jesus in a manner which recalls the words of Jesus in Luke chapter 4: *God anointed Jesus of Nazareth with the Holy Spirit and power...he went around doing good and healing all who were under the power of the devil* (Ac 10:38). Jesus assures his disciples that they will be *clothed with power from on high* when he sends the *promise of the Father* (Lk 24:49). He also promises them *power* for witnessing *when the Holy Spirit comes on* them (Ac 1:8). When the disciples are *filled with the Holy Spirit* they begin *to speak in other tongues as the Spirit* enables them (Ac 2:4). The Joel passage (2:28-32) cited by Peter to describe their Pentecost experience links the outpouring of the Spirit with prophecy, signs and wonders (Ac 2:16-22). Following this Pentecostal event, the story of the disciples' ministry in Acts is filled with powerful manifestations of the Spirit. Speaking in tongues and prophecy immediately follow the reception of the Spirit on two other occasions (Ac 10:44-48; 19:6). On another occasion the disciples pray that God will enable them to *speak the word with boldness* and that he will *stretch out* his *hand to heal and perform miraculous signs and wonders*. In response they were all *filled with the Holy Spirit and spoke the word of God boldly* (Ac 4:29-31). Healings, signs and wonders continued to accompany the disciples' proclamation.

Luke clearly uses manifestations of power to prove that Jesus and his disciples did effectively receive the outpouring of the Spirit. The link between these two themes is implicit throughout Luke-Acts and explicit in several important passages. After the outpouring of the Spirit at Pentecost and the manifestation of speaking in tongues, Peter explains the event in these terms: *this is what was spoken by the prophet Joel: 'In the last days,' God says, 'I will pour out my Spirit on all people...and they will prophesy'* (Ac 2:16-18). After the outpouring of the Spirit on the house of Cornelius Peter tells us that he and his companions *were astonished that the gift of the Holy Spirit had been poured out even on the Gentiles. For they heard them speaking in tongues and praising God* (Ac 10:45-46). Here speaking in tongues and praising God is presented as a clear sign of the outpouring of the Spirit, powerful enough to convince skeptics predisposed against the possibility of such an outpouring. The theme of God's power is utterly and totally linked to the outpouring of the Spirit in Luke's theology.

Holy Spirit experiences and subsequence

Pentecostals point out that on five different occasions in Acts there is a lapse of time between conversion and the outpouring of the Spirit on the same individuals. This is seen as evidence that the expressions 'baptized' and 'filled with the Holy Spirit' do not refer to conversion but to an event which is often subsequent to conversion, that is, to a second blessing.

1. On the day of Pentecost, the disciples of Jesus, already called 'apostles' (Ac 1:26), and others were *all filled with the Holy Spirit* (Ac 2:4). The disciples had followed Jesus for three years and testified about the resurrection. Luke writes nothing which would cause us to doubt the conversion of these disciples. Luke is the one who writes about the thief on the cross. Jesus said to him, "Today, you will be with me in paradise" (Lk 23:43). If salvation for this thief is assured, how much more can we be sure of the disciples' salvation? Jesus' instructions for his disciples before Pentecost were to wait until they were clothed with power from on high (Lk 24:49), not until they were converted or saved. Clearly, when Jesus' disciples were filled with the Holy Spirit on the day of Pentecost, they were experiencing something subsequent to their conversion, an empowering necessary for their witness (Ac 1:8).

    Some might argue that the Spirit had not yet been given and that this delay is an exception. The idea of the Spirit not yet being given comes from the Gospel of John (Jn 7:39). It is not an idea that one could draw from reading Luke-Acts. Luke uses the same vocabulary to describe the experiences of John the Baptist, Elizabeth and Zachariah at the very beginning of his gospel (Lk 1:15, 40, 67). Even in the Gospel of John, the Spirit appears to be 'given' immediately after the resurrection, not fifty days later (Jn 20:22).[7] Even if we were to agree that God withheld his Spirit exceptionally from the first disciples until the day of Pentecost, there are still four other episodes in Acts in which there is an apparent lapse of time between conversion and the Spirit experiences described by Luke.

2. Acts chapter 4 records the story of an unusual prayer meeting. After being jailed and then threatened not to speak about Jesus by religious

---

[7] This statement does not imply that Luke and John are in contradiction. However, they are obviously not writing about the same ideas, and John's phrase should not be used to describe Luke's theology.

authorities, the disciples pray that they will be able to speak God's word with boldness and that God would stretch out his hand to heal and do signs and wonders. Luke tells us that *the place where they were meeting was shaken. And they were all filled with the Holy Spirit and spoke the word of God boldly* (4:31). He uses the same vocabulary and verbal form (aorist passive of *pimplēmi*) that he used to describe the disciples' experience at Pentecost. Pentecostals disagree on whether this experience is evidence for multiple fillings. John Michael Penny believes that this example shows the possibility of having multiple experiences of being filled with the Spirit.[8] Howard Ervin, believing the fullness of the Spirit to be entirely synonymous with the baptism in the Holy Spirit, does not believe in multiple fillings. He points out that Peter is already described as being full of the Spirit in verse 8 of the same chapter (probably earlier the same day). Since Peter is not likely to have lost his 'fullness' in one day, he concludes that Peter and the other 120, who were all filled on the day of Pentecost, are not included among the 'all' who were filled with the Spirit at this prayer meeting; they were already filled. In his opinion the 'all,' in this verse (4:31) must refer to the 3000 converts on the day of Pentecost. Their filling is not mentioned in Acts 2.[9]

Regardless of their varied positions concerning a single filling or multiple fillings, Pentecostals agree that the experience occurs some time after conversion, and that it refers to a powerful experience with the Spirit and not a gradual process. The context of its use in Luke-Acts does not fit the concept of a gradual process. When Luke describes a person being filled with the Spirit, it is an event (Lk 1:41, 67; Ac 2:4; 4:31). The use of the adjective 'full' (Lk 4:1; Ac 6:3; etc.) could be understood to include a process, but this process must be assumed. There is no description in Luke-Acts of a process using fullness vocabulary.

3. After Phillip proclaimed the gospel and performed miracles in Samaria, Luke tells us that men and women believed and were baptized in the name of the Lord Jesus (Ac 8:5-16). The news that they had received the word of God reached Jerusalem and they decided to

---

[8] *The Missionary Emphasis of Lukan Pneumatology*, Sheffield Academic Press, 1997, p. 96-100.
[9] Ervin, p. 49-54.

send Peter and John to pray for them that *they might receive the Holy Spirit, because the Holy Spirit had not yet come upon any of them* (Ac 8:15-16). When Peter and John placed their hands on them, *they received the Holy Spirit* (Ac 8:17). This is a clear incident of a lapse of time between the Samaritan believers' conversion and their experience with the Spirit.

4.   In chapter 9, Saul is miraculously converted on the road to Damascus. He is blinded by the experience and must be led by the hand to follow the Lord's instructions to go into Damascus. After three days of praying and fasting, the Lord sends Ananias to pray for him that he might *see again and be filled with the Holy Spirit* (Ac 9:1-18). Again we see a clear lapse of time between his conversion and his experience with the Spirit.

5.   Finally, in chapter 19, Paul discovers some disciples and asks them, *"Did you receive the Holy Spirit when you believed?"* (Ac 19:2). They respond by saying that they had not even heard of the Holy Spirit. Paul asks a question about their baptism and discovers that they only knew John's baptism. Paul explains to them the Good News and baptizes them in the name of the Lord Jesus. Then Luke writes, *When Paul placed his hands on them, the Holy Spirit came on them, and they spoke in tongues and prophesied* (Ac 19:6). There is some question as to whether these *disciples* who *believed* were truly converted before Paul baptized them in the name of Jesus. But, even if we say that they were converted at that moment, their experience with the Spirit only occurs after Paul *placed his hands on them*. Even if this experience occurs only moments after their conversion, it is still a subsequent experience in Luke's account.

Pentecostals conclude from these five accounts that the disciples in the early church were baptized or filled with the Spirit in a second experience subsequent to conversion. The only clear exception is that of the household of Cornelius. Such an exception is easy to comprehend. In this episode, the author explains how the Jews, couched in prejudice against the Gentiles, needed visible proof in order to accept the possibility of salvation for the Gentiles (Ac 10:44-48). Only after witnessing the visible evidence of the fullness of the Spirit did they decide to baptize them in the name of the Lord Jesus. Presumably, their experience with the Spirit occurred when they believed Peter's message about forgiveness of sins through the name of Jesus. This apparently simultaneous Spirit experience does not create a problem for the Pentecostal position, since Pentecostals do not believe that all Christians must experience the baptism in the Spirit as a second blessing, subsequent to conversion. The Pentecostal position simply summarizes the conclusions drawn from the passages above. They believe that the Pentecostal experience described by Luke in the Acts of the Apostles is not equivalent to conversion. It is a separate experience which may occur simultaneously, but more often occurs subsequent to conversion. This conclusion is then applied to present-day experience. If the apostles and other believers in Jerusalem, Samaria, and the Gentile world were in need of a second experience, logic would imply that many other believers might also need a second blessing to be empowered by the Spirit.

Pentecostals draw a second conclusion from these accounts concerning how the early disciples discerned the fullness of the Spirit in the believer. Frequently in Acts, Luke informs his readers that the early Christians were able to discern the presence of the Spirit. There are numerous occasions where the reception of the Spirit is obviously discernable (2:4; 4:31; 8:17; 10:46; 19:6). There are also occasions where the lack of reception is noticed (8:16; 19:2). On one occasion, the proof of reception is explicitly given: Peter and those who came with him knew that the household of Cornelius had received the Holy Spirit, because they heard them speaking in tongues and praising God (10:45-46). Two other times speaking in tongues is mentioned immediately after the reception of the Spirit (2:4; 19:6). In the Samaritan account, the author does not mention which phenomena follows the reception of the Spirit, but there is something visible which entices Simon the magician to offer money in order to acquire the power to transmit the Spirit to others (8:18-19). In the account of Saul's conversion, only his healing is mentioned following Ananias' prayer for healing and being filled with the Spirit (9:17-18). The details of his being filled or any other phenomena which may have accompanied the event are not mentioned. But Paul himself informs us in 1 Corinthians 14:18 that he speaks in tongues. Since speaking in tongues is explicitly mentioned on three occasions immediately following the reception or filling with the Spirit, and it is easily implied on two other occasions, Pentecostals have traditionally concluded that speaking in tongues is *the* sign of the baptism in the Spirit. However, the arguments are not strong enough to retain fidelity among all Pentecostals or Charismatics. Many prefer to say that speaking in tongues is *a* sign among others.

Weaknesses in the Pentecostal position

There are three major weaknesses in the Pentecostal position on the baptism in the Holy Spirit. First, there seems to be some confusion in the use of vocabulary concerning Spirit experiences in Luke-Acts. Secondly, Pentecostals tend to ignore or not sufficiently explain the clear connection which Peter makes between the reception of the Spirit and salvation in his Pentecost speech. Thirdly, the Pentecostal emphasis on speaking in tongues as *the sign* of the baptism in the Holy Spirit goes beyond the biblical data.

Confusion in the use of vocabulary concerning Spirit experiences

There seems to be confusion among Pentecostals in the use of the expressions 'receiving the Spirit' and being 'baptized in the Spirit.' These expressions are used by Luke in referring to the Pentecost and Cornelius episodes. Jesus tells his disciples that they will be *baptized in the Holy Spirit* in a few days (Ac 1:5). A few days later Luke tells us that they were *filled with the Spirit* (Ac 2:4). Peter refers back to this event when he says that the Gentiles in Cornelius' household *have received the Holy Spirit just as we have* (Ac 10:47). This conclusion is most likely drawn because the Gentiles also spoke in tongues like the apostles on the day of Pentecost (10:45-46). Peter also connects the expression 'baptized in the Holy Spirit' with the Cornelius episode (11:16). These two expressions, 'baptized in the Holy Spirit' and 'receiving the Holy Spirit' describe the same experience in both episodes. It would be logical to conclude that the two expressions are completely synonymous. Pentecostals, however, distinguish between the reception of the Spirit at conversion and a later baptism in the Spirit. It is possible to conclude that the two events occur simultaneously in the house of Cornelius; however there is every indication that the disciples are not in need of conversion on the day of Pentecost. In the Samaritan episode, the believers 'receive' the Holy Spirit. There is no mention of being 'baptized' or 'filled' in this episode, which is obviously subsequent to their conversion (Ac 8:15-17). The Pentecostal interpreter usually refers to this 'reception' of the Spirit as a baptism in the Holy Spirit. Robert C. Cunningham, for example, exhorts his fellow Pentecostals to "refrain from using" the expression 'receiving the Spirit,' since the "believer receives the Spirit when he is saved" (Rom 8:9). He then explains, "It is true that in Acts, chapters 8 and 10 ... we read of people 'receiving the Spirit,' but in each case the context clearly shows this 'receiving' refers to the Pentecostal baptism."[10] Even though context appears to support a reference to a 'Pentecostal baptism,' this does not explain why Luke says that these believers *received the Holy Spirit* (Ac 8:17).

Logical connections to salvation language in Peter's message

A second major difficulty with the Pentecostal position is the clear connection between the reception of the Holy Spirit and salvation in Peter's speech on the day of Pentecost. The quotation from Joel which Peter uses both to explain unusual phenomena and to challenge his listeners to repent ends with the phrase: *everyone who calls on the name of the Lord will be saved* (Ac 2:21). The call to repentance at the end of his message appears to refer back to this promise: *Repent and be baptized, every one of you, in the name of Jesus Christ for the forgiveness of your sins. And you will receive the gift of the Holy Spirit. The promise is for you and your children and for all who are far off--for all whom the Lord our God will call* (Ac 2:38-39). It should also be pointed out that this call to repentance is a response to the impassioned appeal of Peter's listeners, *what shall we do?* (Ac 2:37). This is not an appeal to be filled with the Spirit in order to be more effective witnesses. This is an appeal for salvation, an appeal for reprieve from the consequences of having crucified Christ the Lord (Ac 2:36). Clearly the gift of the Spirit promised by Peter on the day of Pentecost is closely connected to conversion and salvation. Even if the gift of the Spirit is presented as an endowment of power for the apostles on the day of Pentecost, it is presented as a part of salvation for those who repent. Any clear presentation of Luke's theology of the Spirit must reconcile these two concepts.

Insistence on speaking in tongues as the sign of the baptism in the Holy Spirit

The third major difficulty of the Pentecostal position is an insistence on speaking in tongues as *the* sign of the baptism in the Holy Spirit. While there is evidence to suggest that speaking in tongues is a sign, there is not enough

---

[10] "Writing About the Person and Work of the Holy Spirit," *Conference on the Holy Spirit Digest: A Condensation of Plenary Sessions and Seminars of the Conference on the Holy Spirit in Springfield, Missouri, August 16-18, 1982*, vol. 1, ed. Gwen Jones, Gospel Publishing House, Springfield MO, 1983, p. 273.

evidence to establish a rule that all who are baptized in the Spirit must speak in tongues. Both times the expression 'baptized in the Spirit' occurs, the believers did speak in tongues. But two occurrences do not make a rule. Nowhere is it explicitly stated that those who are baptized in the Spirit necessarily speak in tongues. If we enlarge the number of occurrences to include expressions of being 'filled with the Spirit,' we discover that other proofs or signs also occur: prophecy, speaking the word of God with boldness, wisdom, signs and wonders, joy, etc. (Ac 2:17-18; 4:31; 6:3, 8, 10; 13:52).

The non Pentecostal position

The best arguments for a non Pentecostal position come from a synthetic presentation of New Testament theology concerning experiences with the Holy Spirit. In other words, events in the book of Acts are interpreted so as to not contradict clearer statements about the Holy Spirit in other parts of the New Testament. In Romans 8:9, for example, Paul ties possession of the Spirit to belonging to Christ. He states, *if anyone does not have the Spirit of Christ, he does not belong to Christ.* Therefore, reception of the Spirit must occur at the moment of conversion. How then can Luke, Paul's traveling companion, talk about believers 'receiving' the Holy Spirit at some point subsequent to their conversion? As we discovered above, the Pentecostal position, that what Luke really means by 'reception' in these passages is a *Pentecostal* reception of the Spirit, subsequent to an initial reception of the Spirit, is certainly not evident in Luke's use of vocabulary. John also closely associates conversion with the Spirit (Jn 3:3, 5). Non Pentecostals insist that the Scriptures must be congruent and that we must, therefore, interpret experiences in the Acts of the Apostles in a way which does not contradict this principle presented clearly in Paul's letter to the Romans and reflected in John's gospel.

Another Pauline text commonly quoted by non Pentecostal interpreters is 1 Corinthian 12:13. Paul states, "For in the one Spirit we were all baptized into one body" (NRSV).[11] They argue that, if we were all baptized in one Spirit, then every believer has received the baptism in the Spirit. Therefore the baptism in the Spirit must take place at conversion and there is no place for a subsequent baptism.

---

[11] NIV translates *by one Spirit* but places the possible translation *in one Spirit* in a footnote. I will discuss the translation of this verse in chapter 6.

Baptized in the Spirit and the reception of the Spirit

Non Pentecostal interpreters believe that the expression 'baptized in the Spirit' refers to the reception of the Spirit at conversion. God's normal way of operating is to give his Spirit to believers at conversion. Peter's promise in Acts 2:38 is often quoted as the 'norm' for Christian conversion and initiation: *Repent and be baptized, every one of you, in the name of Jesus Christ for the forgiveness of your sins. And you will receive the gift of the Holy Spirit.* The conclusion drawn is that God baptizes in or with his Spirit those who repent when they repent. After all, Peter's call to repentance is not addressed to disciples needing power for witnessing, but to those needing salvation (Ac 2:36-37). The gift of the Spirit in Acts 2 is clearly associated with salvation.

The need to reconcile two biblical authors, Paul and Luke, forces us to reconsider any apparent lapse of time between conversion and the reception of the Spirit in the Acts of the Apostles. It is necessary to present arguments for four of the five 'Pentecostal' episodes discussed above. No arguments are needed for the episode in Acts 4, because it involves believers being filled with the Spirit who had already received the Spirit. Most non Pentecostal interpreters adopt a combination of two explanations. On the one hand, there is evidence that, in some of these *Pentecostal* episodes, conversion did not actually take place until the moment of Spirit reception. On the other hand, special circumstances may have been in effect in some instances in Luke-Acts, where God made an exception and withheld the reception of the Spirit until a later time for some reason.

James Dunn believes that in each of the 4 episodes Spirit reception occurred at the moment of conversion-initiation. According to Dunn, the disciples did not acquire an authentic saving faith in the Lord Jesus until the day of Pentecost.[12] As proof of this assertion he cites Acts 11:17: "God gave them the same gift to them as he gave to us, *when we believed* in the Lord Jesus Christ."[13] For each of the other episodes, Dunn finds some detail which seems to indicate that the faith of the individuals concerned was insufficient or deficient for salvation and Spirit reception. The Samaritans "believed Phillip" (Ac 8:12) rather than believing "in Jesus," and therefore, their faith was probably an "intellectual assent…to the acceptability of what Phillip was saying" rather than "a commitment to God." Simeon's subsequent behavior demonstrated his deficient faith

---

[12] Dunn, p. 52.
[13] Dunn, his italics, p. 52. "*When we believed*" is Dunn's translation as in NRSV. NIV translates *who believed*. The aorist participle can be translated in a variety of ways.

(Ac 8:18-24).[14] Paul's three days of blindness is probably symbolic representing his incomplete conversion (Ac 9:8-9).[15] The disciples in Ephesus were not disciples of Jesus but disciples of John who still needed to be converted.[16]

Many non Pentecostal interpreters agree with Dunn's explanations for the apostle Paul and the Ephesian believers but find it difficult to accept his interpretations for the disciples at Pentecost and the believers in Samaria. Luke's vocabulary is too clear to doubt the conversion of these individuals. These interpreters prefer to speak of exceptions, where there is a departure from the norm established by Paul (Rom 8:9) and mirrored in Peter's call to repentance (Ac 2:38-39), due to unusual historical circumstances. John Stott, for example, believes that the Jesus' disciples received the Holy Spirit at Pentecost long after their conversion, because "they could not have received the Pentecostal gift before Pentecost."[17] *"Up to that time the Spirit had not been given"* (Jn 7:39).[18] He also believes that, to avoid a perpetuation of the schism between Jewish and Samaritan believers, God may have "deliberately withheld the gift of his Spirit from the Samaritan believers" until "the genuineness of the Samaritan's conversion" was "acknowledged and confirmed" by an apostolic delegation.[19]

Filled with the Spirit

It is difficult to determine a single non Pentecostal interpretation for the fullness of the Spirit. At the risk of oversimplifying non Pentecostal interpretations, we will identify two major trends. First of all, non Pentecostal interpreters have adopted a spatial understanding for the metaphor of being filled with the Spirit, emphasizing that there are degrees of fullness. Believers are more or less filled with the Spirit. Max Turner, for example, states that "this metaphor is used precisely to distinguish those whose lives are particularly marked by the work of the Spirit from ordinary Christians."[20] Thus, when the Jerusalem church was asked to choose seven men *full of the Holy Spirit and wisdom* (Ac 6:3), they needed to identify those "who stand out for their spiritual wisdom (with an inference that others have it in less re-

---

[14] Dunn, p. 65.
[15] Dunn, p. 75-78.
[16] Dunn, p. 83-87.
[17] Stott, p. 17.
[18] Stott, p. 32-33.
[19] Stott, p. 20.
[20] Turner, p. 169.

markable degree)."[21] Since there are degrees of fullness, fullness can increase or decrease, be lost or recovered and must be maintained. Paul's injunction to be filled with the Spirit in his letter to the Ephesians is especially important. Paul uses a present imperative indicating either a continuous, durative experience or a repeated experience.[22] While some non Pentecostal interpreters recognize Luke's use of this metaphor to describe an influx of the Spirit at specific moments,[23] most believe in the progressive nature of being filled. Alfred Kuen compares it to a water reservoir being filled by a tranquil source.[24]

Secondly, non Pentecostal interpreters tend to use other Pauline expressions to describe being filled with the Spirit. Max Turner compares the spiritual qualities of wisdom, faith and joy mentioned by Luke with the fruit of the Spirit in Galatians 5.[25] John Stott equates the concept of being spiritual as opposed to carnal in Paul's first letter to the Corinthians (3:1) with the concept of being filled with the Spirit.[26] Alfred Kuen sees equivalence with the expressions, *live by the Spirit* (Gal 5:16) and *walk according to the Spirit* (Rom 8:4).[27] Pauline expressions are used to describe fullness and the means for being filled are also Pauline: submission or yielding to the Holy Spirit (Rom 8:13-14). John Stott states, "An important condition of enjoying his fullness is to yield to him without reserve."[28]

Weaknesses in the non Pentecostal position

There are three major weaknesses in the non Pentecostal position. First of all, using the conclusions of one New Testament author to determine the interpretation of another is bad methodology. Each author should be understood in his own context before comparing the results with the ideas of other authors. The other two major difficulties are related to the first. Non Pentecostal interpreters tend to assume that Paul and Luke are using terms in an equivalent manner, despite the evidence that they use the terms differ-

---

[21] Turner, p. 410.
[22] Dana, p. 300; Wallace, p. 485; Robertson, p. 890.
[23] Henri Blocher, "La plénitude du Saint-Esprit," *Ichthus*, 17, 1971, p. 21-24. Turner, p. 167-68.
[24] Kuen, p. 121.
[25] Turner, p. 408-09.
[26] Stott, p. 38-39.
[27] Kuen, p. 130.
[28] Stott, p. 47.

ently. Finally, non Pentecostal interpreters, in their desire to reconcile Luke and Paul's ideas, do not give sufficient attention to the context in Luke-Acts.

Bad methodology: using Paul to interpret Luke

John Stott believes that "the revelation of the purpose of God in Scripture should be sought primarily in its *didactic*, rather than its *historical* parts."[29] The idea of subordinating one genre of Scripture (history) to another (epistles) is unacceptable. Craig Keener points out that such a methodology breaks the basic rules of biblical interpretation and runs the risk of compromising the doctrine of biblical inspiration, because "*all* Scripture is God-breathed and is useful for teaching" (2 Ti 3:16).[30] This infers that all of Scripture is didactic.[31] Much of the Bible is descriptive. These historical sections of the Bible are intended, not just to relate historical facts, but also to teach theology. Luke defines his own didactic purpose for his work in the first few verses; he writes his account so that his readers *may know the certainty of the things* they *have been taught* (Lk 1:4).

The theological nature of Luke-Acts has become increasingly apparent to biblical interpreters since Hans Conzelmann published his work, *Die Mitte der Zeit* (The Middle of Time), in 1954. His work showed that Luke is no longer viewed as "a somewhat shadowy figure who assembled stray pieces of more or less reliable information," but rather "as a theologian of no mean stature who very consciously and deliberately planned and executed his work."[32] Luke's theology is also very different from Paul's. I. Howard Marshall asserts, "There is no disputing that the theologies of Paul and of Luke are two different entities."[33] Luke discusses different subjects from different points of view. I am not proposing that we interpret Luke in such a way as to contradict Paul. However, Luke's theology is worthy of being investigated apart from foregone conclusions derived from Paul. By following Stott's recommendations, we risk losing impor-

---

[29] Stott, p. 8, Stott's italics.

[30] *3 Crucial Questions about the Holy Spirit*, Grand Rapids, Baker Book House, 1996, p. 186, Keener's italics. See his discussion p. 186-89.

[31] John Stott has qualified his position in response to such criticism in *The Spirit, the Church, and the World*, InterVarsity Press, Downers Grove, IL, 1990, p. 8. He writes: "I am not denying that historical narratives have a didactic purpose, for of course Luke was both a historian and a theologian; I am rather affirming that a narrative's didactic purpose is not always apparent within itself and so often needs interpretive help from elsewhere in Scripture." It seems evident from his conclusions that his methodology goes far beyond interpretive help and involves subordination.

[32] W. C, Van Unnik, "Luke-Acts, a Storm Center in Contemporary Scholarship," *Studies in Luke-Acts*, ed. Leander E. Keck and J. Louis Martyn, Philadelphia, Fortress Press, 1980, p. 23.

[33] Marshall, *Historian*, p. 220.

tant aspects of Luke's theology by forcing Luke to conform to Pauline thought.

Assuming the equivalence of terms used by Paul and Luke

The second major problem with the non Pentecostal position is that interpreters often assume equivalence in the terms used by Paul and Luke. We have already seen that some non Pentecostal interpreters feel free to equate various Pauline terms with the Lukan concept of being filled with the Spirit. None of these terms, the 'fruit of the Spirit,' 'spiritual,' 'live by the Spirit,' 'walk according to the Spirit,' are ever used in the same context with the expression 'filled with the Spirit.'[34] Non Pentecostal interpreters have assumed that these expressions refer to the same reality simply because it fits their theology.

It is also incorrect to assume that two biblical authors use the same terms in the same way. Terms have more than one connotation and must be interpreted within their literary context. For example, Paul and Luke both use the term 'to baptize' in the same sentence with the expression *en pneumati* (in, with or by the Spirit). All the uses in Luke-Acts refer back to John the Baptist's use of this expression and should probably be translated 'baptized in' or 'with the Spirit' (Lk 3:16; Ac 1:5; 11:16). There is no explicit reference to John the Baptist in the only place where Paul uses these terms together (1 Cor 12:13). Because the context is decidedly different, translators are divided on the meaning in 1 Corinthians.[35] D. A. Carson warns us not to make this expression into a technical term which always has the same meaning.[36] The expressions 'receiving the Spirit' and being 'filled with the Spirit' are also used by both authors. We must not assume that both authors mean to communicate exactly the same thing. They have different backgrounds. They are writing at different times to different readers in different situations. These last two metaphors are fairly generic and can transmit a variety of meanings.

Ignoring context in Luke-Acts

It is assumed by non Pentecostal interpreters that in Acts 2:28-29 Peter establishes the pattern and norm for the reception of the Spirit or baptism

---

[34] Luke does associate phenomenal joy, one aspect of the fruit of the Spirit mentioned by Paul (Gal 5:22), with being filled with the Spirit (Ac 13:52). This is not sufficient evidence for assuming equivalence between the Pauline and Lukan concepts.

[35] "in one Spirit" (NRSV, NJB), "by one Spirit" (KJV, RSV, NASB, NIV).

[36] *Exegetical Fallacies*, 2nd ed., Grand Rapids, Baker Books, 1996, p. 45.

with the Spirit at conversion. The context of Luke-Acts simply will not support this assumption. None of the accounts in Acts giving the details of Spirit reception and/or baptism conform to this pattern. The apostles were already converted when the Spirit was poured out on them (Ac 2). No details are given for the 3000 converted on the day of Pentecost. The Samaritans received the Spirit sometime after conversion (Ac 8). The household of Cornelius was baptized in the name of Jesus after receiving the Spirit (Ac 10). (If Peter established a pattern, baptism in the name of Jesus, another element mentioned in this 'pattern,' should also be included.) The Spirit came upon the Ephesian disciples after Paul laid his hands on them (Ac 19).

Even if we conclude that Luke only tells the details of Spirit reception when the events deviate from the norm, and that what we have in the Acts of the Apostles are all the exceptions, non Pentecostal logic is still inconsistent with the details of the story. If Spirit reception or baptism in the Spirit were assumed to occur at conversion in the book of Acts, as the non Pentecostal position would have us believe, then any statements concerning the non reception of the Spirit after conversion would be nonsensical. How could Luke conclude that *the Holy Spirit had not yet come upon any of* the believers in Samaria (Ac 8:16)? How could Paul ask the Ephesian disciples, "*Did you receive the Holy Spirit when you believed* (Ac 19:2)*?*" If the Pauline doctrine of the reception of the Spirit at conversion (Rom 8:9) were assumed in Luke-Acts, these statements would not have occurred. Another explanation must be given, one which is consistent with the context of Luke-Acts.

Interpreting passages in context

How do we discern the meaning of expressions such as "baptized with the Spirit" and "filled with the Spirit"? As we can see from the discussion above, interpretations differ considerably. All of the authors cited above have a healthy respect for the inspiration and authority of the Word of God. All are determining the meaning of these expressions by examining biblical passages. They are simply giving priority to different details. How do we assign priorities to the various biblical and historical details which determine the meaning of a biblical expression? Which details are more important than others? There are no simple answers to these questions. But there are important principles to consider. Although perhaps he has not effectively implemented his own standard, Dunn does an excellent job of defining the correct priorities in the interpretation of biblical passages. He writes,

> The method ... is to take each author and book separately and to (attempt to) outline his or its particular theological emphases; only when he has set a text in the context of its author's thought and intention (as expressed in his writing), only then can the biblical-theologian feel free to let that text interact with other texts from other books.[37]

Two different levels of context can be discerned from Dunn's methodology. The first and most important is the literary context of the passage. We need to understand the thought patterns and logical flow of the book where the passage is found and attempt to understand why the passage is there. The second is its canonical context. Every book of the Bible is a part of a coherent body of Scripture. Every passage is inspired by God, who wishes to communicate his message to his people. Therefore we find that the various parts of Scripture contribute to a coherent whole.

Because the whole is inspired by God, we do not expect to find contradictions. When our study of individual passages and books produces contradictory interpretations, we must reexamine the texts to discover where our first reading may have led us astray. But we must not force a text to say what we want it to say. The balance between these two disciplines, studying the passage in its literary context and developing a theology from the whole of Scripture, is difficult to maintain. With Dunn, I am convinced of the necessity of understanding a passage in its literary context before comparing it to texts in other books.

Before we move on to the application of these priorities to our study of these Spirit expressions in Luke-Acts, I would like to elaborate a little on different aspects of context. It is important to understand that not all the information in a book is equally important for the interpretation of a particular expression. The immediate context, or the verses which immediately precede and follow the use of that expression, contains the most important information. Authors and speakers communicate in a logical manner. The task of the interpreter is to discern the logical flow of thought in a passage and determine the meaning of terms and expressions according to that thought flow. Of all the possible meanings for these expressions, which fits the immediate context best?

---

[37] Dunn, p. 39.

The next best place to look for pertinent information is the rest of the book, or the greater literary context. The author may use the same expressions more than once. The immediate literary context of the other uses of the same expression can help us to choose between possible meanings. However, we must be careful to give priority to the immediate literary context of the passage we are trying to interpret. An author can change how he or she uses a particular expression within the same book. I believe this to be the case for the expression "baptized with the Spirit" in Luke-Acts.

Other literary factors in the book should influence our interpretation. For example, Luke defines his purpose for writing at the beginning of his work (Lk 1:1-4). We need to discern Luke's theology of the Spirit and his use of Spirit expressions within the context of this stated purpose. What role does the Spirit play in accomplishing Luke's goal? How does Luke's description of Spirit experiences fit into this logic? Other aspects of his theology of the Spirit may be inferred by drawing logical conclusions from statements about the Spirit in Luke-Acts.

Finally, the interpreter should take into consideration the influence of related texts. These related texts are called the intertextual[38] context. (A distinction is made here between texts which influence the text and texts on the same subject.) New Testament authors draw many of their ideas and concepts from the Old Testament, or more specifically, from the Greek version of the Old Testament called the Septuagint (LXX), a body of literature including what Protestants call the Apocrypha. We find numerous allusions to concepts and passages from the Septuagint in addition to direct citations from the text. Some might want to consider this information under the category of historical context. It is considered a sub-category of literary context in this study because bits and pieces of this intertext are found in the text and because New Testament authors clearly rely on this intertext for their ideas and vocabulary. Sometimes the use of such vocabulary even makes them sound antiquated like some preachers who speak using 'King James' English. For example, when we read about Zachariah and Elizabeth having no children "because Elizabeth was barren, and they were both advanced in years," it feels like we are reading a story in Genesis (Lk 1:7, NASB,[39] cf. Gen 18:11).

Another important level of context, not mentioned in the quote by

---

[38] According to Green, "*Intertext* refers to the location of a text within the larger linguistic frame of reference on which it consciously or unconsciously draws for meaning." Green is also interested in "how Luke's narrative draws and/or builds on the LXX," p. 13.

[39] New American Standard Bible, © Copyright The Lockman Foundation 1960,1962, 1963, 1968, 1971, 1972, 1973, 1975, 1977, 1988, 1995. Used by permission.

Dunn, is historical context. How does our knowledge of the New Testament historical era inform our interpretation of the text? This knowledge is derived from the Scriptures, from other writings of that time period and from archeological discoveries. It is from these studies that we discover the possible meanings for expressions in our text and underlying concepts which color the interpretation of these expressions. We can also sometimes determine which meanings or concepts were more commonly used or accepted at that time. For example, there were varied messianic expectations at the time the New Testament was written, but one set of expectations was much more popular than all the others. It is this popular set of expectations which seems to provide the background for understanding Luke's strategy in writing.

Chart 1: Levels of context

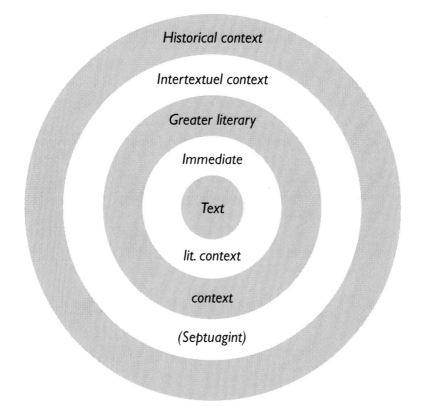

Historical context

Intertextuel context

Greater literary

Immediate

Text

lit. context

context

(Septuagint)

These levels of context which help us determine the meaning of biblical terms, expressions, and passages can be illustrated by a series of concentric circles. If you toss a stone into a pond, it will create ripples in concentric circles, which are greatest at the point of impact. Every circle is related to the original impact, but those closest to this point are more important. In the same way information which is closest logically to any passage we are examining is more important than information which is further removed. Any of that information may be important. But we need to give priority to what is closest. However, we should also understand that the intertextuel context is sometimes logically closer to the passage than the greater literary context. We should look for clues in the passage which indicate the importance of other related passages.

In the following chapters, we will discover how the various levels of context help to define the expressions "baptized in the Holy Spirit," "filled with the Spirit," and other Spirit expressions in Luke-Acts. In chapter 3, the meaning of the expression "baptized in the Spirit" will be interpreted in its immediate context in John the Baptist's message. Intertextual, historical and literary contexts lend supporting evidence to this interpretation. In chapter 4, I will examine the literary context of Luc-Acts in greater detail, paying particular attention to Luke's stated purpose for writing, his strategy for accomplishing that purpose and how Spirit experiences fit into that strategy. In chapters 5 through 7, we will see how Luke's literary context helps define the various expressions he uses for describing Spirit experiences. We will also take a look at how Paul uses some of this vocabulary differently. In chapter 8, we will look at a coherent solution for apparent contradictions between Luke and Paul. In chapter 9, I will discuss principles and ideas for applying these discoveries in the church today.

Chapter 3

Blown away by the Spirit

John the Baptist's saying in Context

○ t is often assumed that Luke gives the meaning of John the Baptist's prophetic words, *He will baptize you with the Holy Spirit* (Lk 3:16), in the events at Pentecost.[1] This is undoubtedly correct. Luke certainly brings the reader to this conclusion. However, it seems apparent that Luke's narrative does not start with this conclusion. Neither John the Baptist nor his audience would have understood this conclusion. Any interpretation which attributes a meaning derived from the disciples' Pentecostal experience to John the Baptist's words in Luke's gospel is in danger of ignoring the immediate context. If we follow the priorities outlined in the previous chapter, we must first understand John's prophetic words in their immediate literary context.

The logical flow of thought in Luke 3 *(Immediate literary context)*

In the fifteenth year of the reign of Tiberius Caesar— when Pontius Pilate was governor of Judea, Herod tetrarch of Galilee, his brother Philip

---

[1] See, for ex., Marshall, p. 146 and Evans, p. 243.

tetrarch of Iturea and Traconitis, and Lysanias tetrarch of Abilene— ² *during the high priesthood of Annas and Caiaphas, the word of God came to John son of Zechariah in the desert.* ³ *He went into all the country around the Jordan, preaching a baptism of repentance for the forgiveness of sins.* ⁴ *As is written in the book of the words of Isaiah the prophet: "A voice of one calling in the desert, 'Prepare the way for the Lord, make straight paths for him.* ⁵ *Every valley shall be filled in, every mountain and hill made low. The crooked roads shall become straight, the rough ways smooth.* ⁶ *And all mankind will see God's salvation.'"* ⁷ *John said to the crowds coming out to be baptized by him, "You brood of vipers! Who warned you to flee from the coming wrath?* ⁸ *Produce fruit in keeping with repentance. And do not begin to say to yourselves, 'We have Abraham as our father.' For I tell you that out of these stones God can raise up children for Abraham.* ⁹ *The ax is already at the root of the trees, and every tree that does not produce good fruit will be cut down and thrown into the fire."* ¹⁰ *"What should we do then?" the crowd asked.* ¹¹ *John answered, "The man with two tunics should share with him who has none, and the one who has food should do the same."* ¹² *Tax collectors also came to be baptized. "Teacher," they asked, "what should we do?"* ¹³ *"Don't collect any more than you are required to," he told them.* ¹⁴ *Then some soldiers asked him, "And what should we do?" He replied, "Don't extort money and don't accuse people falsely— be content with your pay."* ¹⁵ *The people were waiting expectantly and were all wondering in their hearts if John might possibly be the Christ.* ¹⁶ *John answered them all, "I baptize you with water. But one more powerful than I will come, the thongs of whose sandals I am not worthy to untie. He will baptize you with the Holy Spirit and with fire.* ¹⁷ *His winnowing fork is in his hand to clear his threshing floor and to gather the wheat into his barn, but he will burn up the chaff with unquenchable fire."* ¹⁸ *And with many other words John exhorted the people and preached the good news to them.* ¹⁹ *But when John rebuked Herod the tetrarch because of Herodias, his brother's wife, and all the other evil things he had done,* ²⁰ *Herod added this to them all: He locked John up in prison.*

In the opening verses of chapter 3, Luke introduces John the Baptist in a manner reminiscent of Old Testament prophetic books naming John's father, as well as several political and religious rulers at the time of the beginning of his ministry. Especially important is the phrase, *the word of God came to John.*[2] The reader is expected to understand that John the Baptist is another prophet in Israel, whose word is reliable because it comes from God. The introduction continues with a summary statement of John's ministry. He preached a *baptism of repentance for the forgiveness of sins* (Lk 3:3). Finally, Luke finishes his introduction with a statement that Jean's ministry fulfills a prophecy from Isaiah. John's message of repentance is

> *A voice of one calling in the desert, 'Prepare the way for the Lord, make straight paths for him. Every valley shall be filled in, every mountain and hill made low. The crooked roads shall become straight, the rough ways smooth. And all mankind will see God's salvation.'* (Lk 3:4-6)

John is preaching *in the desert* to *prepare the way for the* Lord (Lk 3:4) and *God's salvation* (Lk 3:6). How does he prepare the way? He must *make paths straight, fill in* valleys, level off mountains and hills and *make crooked roads straight* and *rough ways smooth* (3:4-5).

My own experience in the jungles of the Congo might help us understand these images. When important political figures used to visit our area in the Congo, all the inhabitants would be summoned to work on the dirt roads. Tropical rains and heavy trucks would create enormous potholes and gullies during the rainy season, rendering travel on the roads long and bumpy. The six-mile trip between Ibambi, where we first lived, and the Nebobongo mission hospital could easily take 30 minutes in the rainy season. The 300-miles from Isiro, our second home, to Kisangani, our third home, took two days in the dry season. The road was often impassable in the rainy season. In the Congo it would be disgraceful to make important people travel on such roads. On the rare occasions when political leaders needed to travel on these roads, the local inhabitants would be asked to get out their hoes and level the way.

Isaiah is talking about the arrival of a king. The sort of preparation he describes would make the king's arrival easier and more pleasant. These images of leveling and straightening are compared to (*as it is written*) John's preaching the message of repentance. The preaching of repentance prepares the way for the Lord's coming and the salvation he brings.

These introductory statements are followed by several specific examples of John's preaching (3:7-14). John emphasizes two things in his preaching. On the one hand he warns his audience about God's coming judgment us-

---

[2] See the opening lines of Jeremiah, Hosea, Micah, Joel, Jonah, Zephaniah, Haggai and Zechariah.

ing vivid imagery. Vipers must *flee the coming wrath* (3:7). Trees that do not produce fruit will be *cut down and thrown into the fire* (3:9). On the other hand he tells the crowds what fruit they must produce in preparation for this coming judgment: *fruit in keeping with repentance* (3:8). They must not simply rely on their ancestral heritage in Abraham (3:8); they must change their behavior. They must share their possessions with the poor (3:11). Those in powerful positions, such as tax collectors and soldiers, should act justly, not extorting gain or abusing their power (3:12-14). All of these subjects – coming judgment, calls for repentance, concern for the poor, and instructions for the powerful – are typical of Old Testament prophetic preaching. Luke ends this section on John the Baptist with a typical prophetic event. John is imprisoned for rebuking an ungodly and evil political ruler, Herod the tetrarch (3:19-20). The reader should have no doubts about John. Like the prophets of old, he does not pull his punches. He warns the crowds of coming destruction and appeals to them to change their behavior in order to avoid suffering the consequences of God's wrath.

The specific examples of John's preaching are followed by a paragraph pertaining to messianic expectations. Luke writes, *The people were waiting expectantly and were wondering in their hearts if John might possibly be the Christ* (3:15). This subject does not appear here coincidentally. The quotation from Isaiah about God's coming salvation (3:4-6; Is 40:3-5) would have evoked messianic expectations. The coming of the Messiah, or anointed one (Is 61:1-2), who will usher in God's salvation is an integral part of the message of judgment and hope which begins with this passage in Isaiah chapter 40.[3] The fact that chapter 61 is quoted in Luke's next chapter (4:18-19) is further evidence for this connection.

John answers the people's question with a series of comparisons. Each comparison is intended to underline the superiority of the Messiah in relation to John. The coming Messiah will be *more powerful* than John. He is also more worthy; John is not even worthy to untie his sandals. John uses the image of baptism, the image used to summarize his ministry, to show that the Messiah's ministry will be greater and more significant than his. John baptizes with water, but the Messiah will *baptize* the people *with the Holy Spirit and with fire* (3:16). It is important to note that the Greek preposition

---

[3] Is 61 is not the first appearance of messianic hope in Isaiah. We see a glimpse of the Spirit anointed ruler in 11:1-4. The message from chapter 40 to the end of the book is particularly related to future judgment and salvation.

en, translated in English by the word "with," is not repeated in the Greek phrase as it is in English. We should understand by this that John is talking about one baptism with Holy Spirit and fire.[4]

Before we attempt to define this enigmatic expression, *he will baptize you with the Holy Spirit and fire*, we need to make a few observations. These prophetic words are addressed to the group of people listening to John and *waiting expectantly* for the Messiah (3:15) and not specifically to a select group of disciples. These people are apparently those he has just warned of coming destruction, those he also called to repentance (3:7-14).[5] He warned the same listeners not to count on their ancestral ties to Abraham. John's Jewish listeners were waiting expectantly for deliverance and salvation. John's message to them up to this point is that judgment awaits them unless they repent. Should we at this point understand that John is now changing the tone of his message and promising the gift of the Holy Spirit to those who believe, like Peter did on the day of Pentecost (Ac 2:38-39)?

The image of winnowing the wheat, immediately following this expression of being baptized with Holy Spirit and fire, clarifies the meaning. Verse 17 is the beginning of a new sentence in the English translation but not in the Greek. (Starting a new sentence makes the text more readable in English.) The concepts in verses 16 and 17 are inescapably and grammatically connected. A more literal translation would read, *He will baptize you with Holy Spirit and fire, whose winnowing fork is in his hand...*[6] The thought of the expression *baptized with Holy Spirit and fire* is continued and clarified in the analogy of winnowing.

To comprehend this analogy, one needs to understand that the Greek word for Spirit (*pneuma*) is also translated with the words "wind" or "breath" and that the Scriptures often use this play on words to express God's activity by his Spirit. Some examples will help demonstrate this. Jesus *breathed on* his disciples *and said, Receive the Holy Spirit* (Jn 20:22). This event brings to mind the creation account in which God breathed into man's nostrils the breath of life (Gn 2:7). In both cases the play on words seems to communicate that God breathes his Spirit/breath into the recipients. In another example, *The Spirit (pneuma) of the Lord will rest on him* (Is 11:2a), that is on the messianic

---

[4] Dunn, p. 11.

[5] The definite article used in Lc 3:15 (*the* people, τοῦ λαοῦ) must refer to a specific group of people. The most likely group is the one John addresses in the preceding verses.

[6] See The English Young's Literal Translation of the Holy Bible 1862/1887/1898, by J. N. Young.

king. The ensuing verses describe the attributes of the Spirit (11:2b) and what this Spirit anointing will enable him to do. He will rule righteously in favor of the poor and needy (11:3-4a), and *with the breath (pneuma) of his lips he will slay the wicked* (Is 11:2-4). In this passage it is the messianic (Spirit/ *pneuma* anointed) figure who breaths the *pneuma* of destruction.

John the Baptist's winnowing image (Lk 3:17) utilizes a similar play on words. The wind of the Spirit blows, separating the chaff from the wheat. The unrepentant chaff is blown away by the Spirit and burned up *with unquenchable fire* (end-time judgment). The wheat is *gathered…into his barn* (end-time salvation). The meaning is clear. *He will baptize you with Holy Spirit and fire* is another way of saying the Messiah will judge the world, saving those who repent and destroying those who do not.

This interpretation falls right into line with the other images in John's preaching. Trees which do not produce the fruit of repentance *will be cut down and thrown into the fire* (Lk 3:9). Vipers that *flee the coming wrath* probably evoke an image of snakes fleeing a brush fire (Lk 3:7; see Ac 28:3). The Messiah will *baptize …with Holy Spirit and fire* (Lk 3:16). The chaff will be burned up with *unquenchable fire* (Lk 3:17). All four images have in common end-time judgment and the element of fire eliminating the unrepentant.

The immediate context surrounding John's expression clearly points to an end-time judgment interpretation. The images, before and after the expression, are images of end-time destruction. If we are to understand John's expression any other way, we must believe that he changes the tone and the gist of his message in the middle of a sentence just long enough to introduce this baptismal saying before changing back to his original tone and message. Such a break in John's prophetic warnings seems highly unlikely, especially since the final image, which is grammatically connected to John's expression in the same sentence, seems tailor-made for explaining it. The two elements in Jesus' baptism, Spirit/wind and fire are the two elements used in the winnowing process.

Other supporting evidence

Before adopting an end-time judgment interpretation for John's prophecy that Jesus *will baptize you with the Holy Spirit and fire*, we should examine some additional supporting evidence and some of the arguments against this interpretation. Supporting evidence includes allusions to Old Testament end-time prophecies (especially in the book of Isaiah) popular messianic expectations in John's day, possible meanings for the term "baptize" and the use of similar expressions in Luke-Acts. Notice that the various categories for supporting evidence correspond to the different levels of context presented in chapter 2.

Allusions to Old Testament end-time prophecies
(Intertextual context)

Possible allusions to Old Testament end-time prophecies are copious, making it difficult to discern which ones legitimately served as background material for Luke. However, the book of the prophet Isaiah is clearly an important background text for Luke-Acts. Remember that Luke introduced John's ministry with a quote from Isaiah 40:3-5 (Lk 3:4-6). The importance of this prophetic description is underlined by the repetition of certain key terms throughout the work. Jesus and his disciples proclaim the same message of repentance for the forgiveness of sins (Lk 3:3; 5:32; 24:47; Ac 2:38; 5:31; 13:38). *The way* or *the way of the Lord* becomes a technical term for indicating the essential message of the disciples (Ac 13:10; 16:17; 18:25; 19:9, 23; 22:4; 24:14, 22). The contrasting images of *crooked* and *straight* are repeated in the disciples' preaching (Ac 2:40; 8:21; 13:10). The universal proclamation *to all people* is repeated in Peter's preaching (Ac 2:17) and illustrated in the rest of Acts. *God's salvation* summarizes the message which *has been sent to the Gentiles* in the conclusion of Luke-Acts (Ac 28:28).

Luke cites another passage from Isaiah in the following chapter to introduce the ministry of Jesus (Lk 4:17-19; Is 61:1-2). He quotes Jesus saying, *The Spirit of the Lord is on me, because he has anointed me to preach good news to the poor. He has sent me to proclaim freedom for the prisoners and recovery of sight for the blind, to release the oppressed…* The importance of this passage in Luke-Acts is seen particularly in two allusions to this passage. In the first allusion, Jesus mentions several sections of this passage to describe his ministry to the envoys sent by John the Baptist to ask if he is the Messiah (Lk 7:18-22). In the second allusion, Peter summarizes Jesus' ministry in terms which are clearly parallel to this passage. He talks about *how God anointed Jesus of Nazareth with the Holy Spirit and power, and how he went around doing good and healing all who were under the power of the devil* (Ac 10:38).

The significance of these two quotes and other phrases taken from Isaiah[7] justifies a search for other parallels in the book of Isaiah which might shed some light on the interpretation of John's preaching. Luke obviously considers Isaiah's end-time prophecies to be a source for describing what is happening in the New Testament era. We need to be careful here not to go beyond Luke's use of Isaiah.[8] Luke is not trying to interpret Isaiah for his readers. He sees prophecies in Isaiah which correspond to what is happening in the life of Jesus and his disciples and which underline the points he is trying to make.

On the other hand, if our goal is to understand John the Baptist's prophetic words in their historical and literary context, we must not read Isaiah with New Testament eyes. Most of us have a tendency to look for familiar concepts from the New Testament as we read the prophecies in the Old Testament. A favorite is the suffering servant passage in Isaiah chapter 53 which reminds us of Christ's sacrifice on the cross for our sins. We tend to linger longer on the various verses quoted in the New Testament, like the ones from chapters 40 and 61 I mentioned above. Our knowledge of their interpretation in the New Testament tends to color how we look at the passage in the Old Testament, and we tend to assume that John the Baptist or his listeners or other characters in the New Testament also had this knowledge. This is usually not the case.

As we read the book of Isaiah looking for clues to the interpretation of John the Baptist's preaching, we need to assume the mindset of sincere Jewish believers living before the fulfillment of these passages in Jesus. We must try to understand how they would read these passages. In Isaiah's day the imminent concern was the invasion of Assyria and the exile which followed. Isaiah's message is filled with judgment proclamations against Israel for her sins, but also against Assyria and the nations who are oppressing Israel. His message is also filled with hope that God will one day deliver Israel from her oppressors and usher in an era of kingdom blessings for his people. Jewish

---

[7] James A. Sanders refers to 3 passages which Luke cites mentioning Isaiah as the author (Lk 3:4-6/Is 40:3-5; Lk 4:18-19/Is 61.1-2 and 58.6; Lk 22.37/Is 53:12) and the following explicit phrases Lk 2:30-32/Is 52:10; 42:6; 49:6; Lk 7.22/Is 26:19; 29:18; 35:5-6; 61:1; Lk 8:10/Is 6:9-10; Lk 19:46/Is 56:7 and Lk 20:9/Is 5:1-2, "Isaiah in Luke," *Luke and Scripture: The Function of Sacred Tradition in Luke-Acts*, ed. Craig A. Evans and James A. Sanders, Minneapolis MN, Fortress Press, 1993, p. 19-20.

[8] David W. Pao, for example, uses themes in the book of Isaiah as the hermeneutical key for understanding Luke's entire 2-volume work, *Acts and the Isaianic New Exodus*, Grand Rapids, Baker Academic, 2000, p. 38-39. Some of these themes are found in Luke-Acts, but others are forced upon Luke's text. Pao sees these themes as "controlling motifs of the narrative of Acts," p. 249. Isaiah does not "control" Luke. Luke uses Isaiah to develop and validate his ideas.

believers during New Testament times could easily relate to such a message of hope. They were also oppressed under the regime of the Roman Empire. How did they understand these passages?

The following is a list of concepts and images used in Isaiah which correspond to the different elements in John's preaching:

1. The concept of coming wrath (*orgê*) (Is 13:9; Lk 3:7),

2. The concept of preaching *good news* (Is 40:9; 52:7; 60:6; 61:1; Lk 3:18; 4.18; etc.),

3. The image of stones becoming descendants of Abraham (Is 51:1-2; Lk 3:8),

4. The image of judgment by fire (Is 1:31; 4:5; 5:24; 9:17-18; 10:16-17; 26:11; 29:6; 30:27-33; 33:11, 14; 47:14; 66:15-16) and specifically with *unquenchable* fire (Is 66:24; Lk 3:9, 16; 12:49; 17:29-30),

5. The image of judgment by the breath of God (*ruach*, translated in the Septuagint by the term *pneuma*, Is 4:4; 11:4; 30:28; 33:11; Lk 3:16; translated by the term *anemos*, Is 17:13; 41:16),

6. The image of unfruitful trees being cut down and burned in judgment (Is 6:13; 10:33-34; 32:19; Lk 3:9; 13:6-9),

7. The image of judgment by winnowing as a means of separating the good from the bad (Is 17:13; 29:5; 40:24; 41:2, 15-16; 47:14; Lk 3:17).[9]

A few observations from these allusions are worth mentioning. First of all, there is considerable accumulation of judgment images. Both the vocabulary and the images used by John are also used in the book of Isaiah to describe end-time judgment carried out by an anointed royal figure. These acts of judgment are good news for those who are being delivered from their oppressors, but bad news for their enemies. Secondly, these images are juxtaposed in a similar manner in both books. For example, in the book of Isaiah, the breath (*ruach, pneuma*) of God is compared to a torrent of water (38:28) or of burning sulfur (30:33) or to a consuming fire (33:11). The wind

---

[9] For a discussion of some of these allusions see Fitzmyer, 1981, p. 468-69, 474; Green, p. 177-78; Marshall, p. 141, 147-48; John Nolland, *Luke 1-9.20*, Word Biblical Commentary, vol 35a, Dallas, Word, 1989, p. 148 and Léopold Sabourin, *L'Évangile de Luc : Introduction et commentaire*, Rome, Editrice Pontificia Università Gregoriana, 1985, p. 117.

(*ruach/anemos*) is also associated with judgment by winnowing (41:15-16). The enemies of God's people will be like chaff which is blown away. God will destroy them with earthquakes, windstorms, tempests and flames of devouring fire (29:5-6). In John's preaching, images of judgment by fire are followed by a baptism with the *pneuma* of God, which is in turn followed by an image of winnowing judgment with fire. The parallels are too close to ignore. John the Baptist must have been inspired by these and other images from the prophet Isaiah.

Several of Isaiah's passages are worth examining in greater detail because they so closely parallel John's message. Isaiah's Spirit-empowered judge and ruler is introduced in chapter 11 as a *shoot* from *the stump of Jesse*, indicating a Davidic messianic ruler. About this ruler Isaiah says,

> *The Spirit of the LORD will rest on him— the Spirit of wisdom and of understanding, the Spirit of counsel and of power, the Spirit of knowledge and of the fear of the LORD— and he will delight in the fear of the LORD. He will not judge by what he sees with his eyes, or decide by what he hears with his ears; but with righteousness he will judge the needy, with justice he will give decisions for the poor of the earth. He will strike the earth with the rod of his mouth; with the breath of his lips he will slay the wicked* (Is 11:2-4).

Those of us who live in countries where elected officials and law enforcement officers are expected to uphold the law have difficulty appreciating the magnitude or even the goodness of these promises. We might find the promise to slay the wick a bit morbid. We may want to read a more positive New Testament message into the passage. Max Turner, for instance, underlines the fact that the Spirit anointing the Messiah is *the Spirit of knowledge and of the fear of the Lord* (Is 11:2). He concludes that the Spirit is a means of ethical purification for the Messiah.[10] He has failed to interpret this phrase in context. The Spirit is not a means for enabling the Messiah to live ethically, but for enabling him to govern ethically (Is 11.3-4).[11] Turner's interpretation also fails to take into account the repetition of Spirit (*pneuma*) in verse 4, where its function is to *slay the wicked*, and not to purify the righteous. We must allow Isaiah's message to speak from its own context and then determine how that message

---

[10] Turner, p. 132-33, 183.

[11] William W. and Robert P. Menzies, *Spirit and Power: Foundations of Pentecostal Experience*, Grand Rapids, Zondervan Publishing House, 2000, p. 92.

sets the stage for a New Testament interpretation. Isaiah promises a messianic deliverer and king who will slay Israel's wicked oppressors and rule with righteousness, allowing the righteous remnant to live in peace and prosperity.

An example from the Congo may help us to understand the original context. On the morning after Christmas one year, we woke up to discover that the Congolese government had decided to change their currency. New bills had been printed. All the old bills had no value. The entire country had three days to take their old bills to the bank and exchange them. There was chaos everywhere. The largest offerings of the year are given during Christmas celebrations, and the church depended on those funds to pay its pastors in the coming months. Most of the pastors, like the vast majority of the population, lived too far away and had no transportation to get their money to the banks in time. The missionaries mobilized and facilitated transporting thousands of dollars from hundreds of churches in our area. We transported the money to Isiro, on the horrible roads described earlier, to the only bank in our area, only to discover that the banks had closed shortly after the announcement was made. Thousands waited patiently and unsuccessfully outside the bank. Occasionally, someone would drive up to the bank in a luxury vehicle, carrying trunk loads of cash. Armed guards would escort them into the bank. Some time later the same guards would escort them back to their cars with the loaded trunks of money. The poor of the country lost all their cash reserves overnight. The rich and powerful got richer and more powerful.

The poor and needy, who endure such injustices day after day, can only hope for a deliverer such as the messianic king described by Isaiah. Bribery, corruption, and injustice are the norm rather than the exception in most of the world, both in Isaiah's day and in our own. The rich wins his or her case against the poor as the judge gets a little richer. The rulers tax the poor to increase their power and luxury. This happens all the time in most of the world. The promise that the Messiah would rule the earth with righteousness was incredibly good news. The promise that this Messiah would also slay their wicked oppressors with the breath of his lips was also extremely good news. In Jesus' day those oppressors were the Romans and their local puppets. The people were ready to hear such a message against these oppressors. The novelty of John's message is that it is addressed, not only to Israel's oppressors, but to all his listeners.

Isaiah's prophecy is clearly messianic and a clear parallel to John's. The Spirit comes upon a descendant of David, as on the Lord Jesus in Luke's gospel (Lk 3:22). The Spirit enables the Messiah to rule with justice, delivering the righteous and the poor and destroying the wicked. This destruction occurs through the *rod of his mouth* and the *breath (pneuma) of his lips*. As in John's message, the *pneuma* (breath/Spirit) of the Messiah is the means of destruction.

A second close parallel to John's message requires a look at the wider context in Isaiah to understand the message. In the first few chapters of Isaiah he introduces images of judgment: redemption and justice for the righteous (1:27) and destruction for the proud and haughty of Jerusalem. *The mighty man will become tinder and his work a spark; both will burn together, with no one to quench the fire* (1:31). In the next chapter, the *proud and lofty* are compared to the cedars of Lebanon and the oaks of Bashan (2:12-13), an image which reminds us of the trees ready to be cut down for burning in John's message. Chapter 3 describes the downfall of Jerusalem's leaders, warriors and elite. In chapter 4, Isaiah describes the condition of Jerusalem after this Day of Judgment. The remnant which remains alive will be few in number (4:1). "Those …who remain…will be called holy (4:3). When the Lord has washed away the filth…and purged the bloodshed of Jerusalem from her midst, by the spirit (Spirit, *ruach*) of judgment and the spirit (Spirit, *ruach*) of burning" (4:4, NASB).[12] Isaiah's point is not, as some have proposed,[13] that the Spirit will render holy those who remain, but that those who remain in Jerusalem will be holy because the Lord will have eliminated those who are not holy by a Spirit and fire judgment, as in John the Baptist's message. The *Branch of the Lord* in 4:2 is often considered to be a reference to the Messiah, like its synonym *shoot* in 11.1.[14] If this is the case, then we have another instance in Isaiah in which Spirit and fire end-time judgment is connected to the work of the Messiah.

Another important parallel passage in Isaiah is the one used by Luke to introduce John's ministry. John is *a voice (phônê) of one crying* (form of the verb *boaô) in the desert* (Is 40:3-5; Lk 3:4-6). In the next verse *a voice (phônê) cries (boaô), All men are like grass, and all their glory is like the flowers of the field. The grass withers and the flowers fall, because the breath* (Spirit/*ruach*) *of*

---

[12] NIV translates the verb "wash" in the future, "*will wash away.*" The *qal* or completed Hebrew verb form is more easily translated with a past tense. Here it is probably in past tense with reference to the future condition described in the preceding verses and could be translated "when the Lord shall have washed away" (RSV).

[13] Fitzmyer, p. 474. Turner, p. 344; M. L. Strauss, *The Davidic Messiah in Luke-Acts: The Promise and its Fulfillment in Lukan Christology*, JSNTSS 110, Sheffield, JSOT Press, 1995, p. 201.

[14] J. A. Motyer, *The Prophecy of Isaiah: An Introduction and Commentary*, Downers Grove, IL, InterVarsity Press, 1993, p. 65, E. J. Young, *the Book of Isaiah*, vol. 1, NICOT, Grand Rapids, Eerdmans, 1964, p. 173-75.

the LORD blows on them (Is 40:6-7)[15]. The repetition of "a voice crying" connects these two messages together. Again we see, as in John's message, that the Spirit/breath of God is the agent of destruction. If our understanding is correct, John's initial message of repentance (Lk 3:6-14) corresponds to the first instance of a voice crying in Isaiah's prophecy (Is 40 :3-5). The next part of John's message, where the Messiah breathes destruction on the unrepentant (Lk 3:16-17), corresponds to Isaiah's second instance of a voice crying (Is 40:6-7). Luke's logic is clear. His entire description of John the Baptist's ministry parallels the entire passage in Isaiah. Any reader familiar with this passage in Isaiah could not miss this connection, especially since Luke quotes from the beginning of the passage in Isaiah before giving the details of John's ministry. Luke tells the story so that his readers will understand that the entire passage from Isaiah is being fulfilled.

Two other important passages in Isaiah describe the Spirit as being *on* the Messiah (Is 42:1; 61:1; cf. 11:1). Isaiah does not use the same play on words in these passages, but judgment is still an integral part of the immediate context in both. The first passage speaks of God's chosen servant. Concerning this chosen one God says,

> *I have put my Spirit upon him; he shall bring forth judgment to the Gentiles...he will not falter or be discouraged till he establishes justice on earth...I, the LORD, have called you in righteousness; I will take hold of your hand. I will keep you and will make you to be a covenant for the people and a light for the Gentiles, to open eyes that are blind, to free captives from prison... The LORD will march out like a mighty man, like a warrior he will stir up his zeal; with a shout he will raise the battle cry and will triumph over his enemies* (Is 42:1, 4, 6-7, 13).

The second passage, quoted by Jesus in Luke's gospel (4:18-19), places words in the mouth of God's anointed one,

> *The Spirit of the Sovereign LORD is on me, because the LORD has anointed me to preach good news to the poor. He has sent me to bind up the brokenhearted, to proclaim freedom for the captives [and recovery of sight for the blind][16] and release from darkness for the prisoners, to proclaim the year of the LORD's favor and the day of vengeance of our God* (Is 61:1-2).

---

[15] The Septuagint leaves out the phrase, "because the breath/Spirit of the Lord blows on them."

[16] This phrase, quoted by Jesus in Lk 4:19, comes from the Septuagint translation.

Several repeated themes tie these two passages together. In both passages an individual is anointed with God's Spirit giving them the ability to announce good news. He announces both justice and deliverance for captives and the blind and judgment for his enemies. The message of deliverance and salvation for the oppressed is tied to a message of judgment for their oppressors, not only in these two passages but throughout the book of Isaiah.

It is true that Jesus ended his quote before repeating the last phrase of the passage concerning a day of vengeance (Lk 4:18-19), with the result that he only announced the fulfillment of God' deliverance. Luke-Acts and the rest of the New Testament teach that this day of vengeance will take place when Jesus returns. But John the Baptist and his audience did not know this! They undoubtedly expected the Messiah to fulfill both aspects of Isaiah's prophecy.

The images and concepts from the Old Testament alluded to by Luke can be found in other Old Testament books besides Isaiah. I have chosen to examine the book of Isaiah more closely because of its obvious ties to John the Baptist's preaching in Luke chapter 3 and to the rest of Luke-Acts. But the same images and vocabulary are used in other end-time prophecies in the Old Testament. For example, according to Joseph Fitzmyer's commentary on Luke, the *coming wrath* (*orgē*) of God is an Old Testament expression for "God's judgment by which evil is to be wiped out." He states that "it is associated with the Day of the Lord" not only in Is 13:9, but also in Zeph 1:14-18; 2:2; and Ez 7:19.[17] Notice that wrath is also associated with fiery destruction (Zeph 1:18) and chaff being swept away (Zeph 2:2) in these passages. The image of winnowing (Jer 15:7) and of felling trees (Ez 31:12; Dn 4:14) are also used elsewhere to represent judgment. Fiery judgment is a frequent prophetic theme (Ez 38:22; Am 7.4; Zeph 1.18; 3.8; Mal 4.1). A quick perusal of these passages and those in Isaiah reveals that, though John the Baptist may be using stock prophetic images for end-time judgment, the clearest parallels are found in the book of Isaiah.

Popular messianic expectations in John's day
(Historical context)

Any interpretation of John the Baptist's message must take into consideration how his original hearers would have understood it. John is not speak-

---

[17] Fitzmyer, p. 468.

ing in a vacuum. He and his hearers share knowledge which influences his choice of vocabulary and images in communicating with his audience. We have already looked at some of this knowledge by examining possible allusions to the Old Testament and especially to the book of Isaiah. We should also consider how readers in John's day understood these prophecies in Isaiah and elsewhere. The interpretation of messianic passages in Isaiah is not entirely straightforward. For instance, it is uncertain whether the reference to the *Branch* of the Lord in Isaiah 4:2 refers to the Messiah. The capital letter at the beginning of the word "branch" means that the translators of the NIV considered the term to be messianic. However, neither the Greek nor the Hebrew versions use capital letters, making it impossible to discern this meaning from the word itself. A messianic meaning is determined from context. The interpretation of such passages is not uniform among scholars today, and neither was it uniform among scholars in John's day. We have access to some of these interpretations through a study of the Jewish literature of that time. A few general observations accepted by the majority of scholars and a couple of illustrations from this literature will help provide a general knowledge of popular messianic expectations in John's day.[18]

John's message that Jesus *will baptize … with Holy Spirit and fire* is found in a paragraph pertaining to messianic expectations. Luke tells us, *the people were waiting expectantly and were all wondering in their hearts if John might possibly be the Christ* (Lk 3:15). What kinds of expectations did John's hearers hold concerning this coming Messiah? First of all, we need to understand that the giving of the Spirit is not connected with the work of the Messiah in pre-Christian literature. Max Turner points out that such an association would imply the Messiah's lordship over the Spirit, an idea which would be very troubling to the Jewish concept of monotheism.[19] It is the Lord, Yahweh, who promised to send the Spirit. Any thought of the deity of the Messiah (Christ) before the incarnation, life, death and resurrection of Jesus would have been considered a form of polytheism.[20] We must rule out, therefore, any idea that John intends to communicate what Peter communicated on the day of Pentecost, i.e., that the Messiah will pour out the Spirit on repentant believers.[21]

---

[18] For a more detailed treatment of this literature see Turner, p. 82-138, Menzies, p. 48-102 and the evaluation of these two authors by Harrison, p. 17-31.

[19] Turner, p. 178, 277-79.

[20] John N. Oswalt, *Isaiah: The NIV Application Commentary*, Grand Rapids, Zondervan, 2003, p. 431.

[21] John could have received special revelation concerning a task not previously assigned to the Messiah, but nothing in the context supports such a revelation. John would need to specify very

Messianic expectations at the time of the New Testament were very diverse.[22] Craig Blomberg distinguishes at least "six different strands of messianic expectations." However, he affirms that "a substantial portion of mainstream Judaism looked for a *warrior* king who would help the Jews shake off the shackles of Rome."[23] This hope was built on Nathan's prophecy to David that God would *establish the throne of his kingdom forever* (2 Sam 7:12-13). Edward Lohse writes about this most popular messianic expectation, developed among the Pharisees, in which God would raise up a Davidic king to liberate Israel and lead her into a glorious future, in accordance with Nathan's prophecy. The clearest expression of this hope is found in the Psalms of Solomon:[24]

> *You, O Lord, chose David to be king over Israel, and swore to him about his descendents forever, that his kingdom should not fail before you…See, Lord, and raise up for them their king, the son of David, to rule over your servant Israel in the time known to you, O God. Undergird him with strength to destroy the unrighteous rulers, to purge Jerusalem from gentiles who trample her to destruction; in wisdom and in righteousness to drive out the sinners from the inheritance; to smash the arrogance of sinners like a potter's jar; to shatter all their substance with a rod of iron; to destroy the unlawful nations with the word of his mouth* (PssSol 17:4, 21-24).[25]

Clearly, the main task of the Messiah in popular expectations at the time of the New Testament was to set up a righteous kingdom by destroying the unrighteous oppressors. The writer of the Psalms of Solomon probably draws his images from Psalms 2:9, where both the rod of iron and the potter's vessel are mentioned, rather than Isaiah 11:4, where the rod of his mouth is mentioned in conjunction with the breath of his lips, but the emphasis is the same in Psalm 2, Isaiah 11 and in John the Baptist's warning.

We find another example of end-time judgment in the intertestamental book of Fourth Ezra, written around 100 AD,[26] which uses images similar

---

clearly what he intended to say, if he wanted his hearers to understand such a message.

[22] See James H. Charlesworths, ed., *The Messiah: Developments in Earliest Judaism and Christianity*, Minneapolis, Fortress Press, 1992 and I. Howard Marshall, "The Messiah in the First Century: A Review Article," *Criswell Theological Review* 7, 1993, p. 67-83.

[23] *Jesus and the Gospels: An Introduction and Survey*, Nashville, Broadman and Holman Publishers, 1997, p. 410.

[24] Edward Lohse, *The New Testament Environment*, trans. John E. Steely, Nashville, Abingdon Press, 1976, p. 188-89. He quotes PssSol 17:4, 21, 27, 32, 45-46.

[25] PssSol, p. 665, 667.

[26] B. M. Metzger, "The Fourth Book of Ezra," *The Old Testament Pseudepigrapha Vol 1*, Doubleday, 1983, p. 520.

to John's, probably also based on images in Isaiah 4:4 and 11:4.[27] In chapter 13, we read about "the man who came up out of the sea" (13:5), an end-time apocalyptic figure, who executes God's judgment on the unrighteous.

> ...he sent forth from his mouth as it were a stream of fire, and from his lips a flaming breath (*pneuma*), and from his tongue he shot forth a storm of sparks. All these were mingled together; the stream of fire and the flaming breath (*pneuma*) and the great storm; and fell on the onrushing multitude which was prepared to fight, and burned them all up, so that suddenly nothing was seen of the innumerable multitude but only the dust of ashes and the smell of smoke (4 Ezra 13:10-11).[28]

My interpretation of John's prophecy is clearly consistent with Jewish thought at that time. It fits with the predominant role ascribed to the Messiah in the Jewish literature of the time. We even find in this literature an almost identical interpretation of the same passages in Isaiah. In both passages (4 Ezra and Luke) fire and *pneuma* work in conjunction to deliver the righteous through the annihilation of the wicked.

Possible meanings for the term "baptize"
(Historical and intertextual context)

In our discussions thus far, I have avoided defining the term "baptize." This is because the term has several possible meanings, but is much more closely tied to one of those meanings in modern Christian thinking. Its constant use as an initiation rite might tend to influence interpreters toward such an understanding here, hindering serious consideration of other possibilities. Thus, I wanted to look at the context and other background texts before determining a meaning for this term here.

None of the Old Testament passages we have examined thus far use the term "baptize." This term is not a part of prophetic stock expressions used in messianic passages. In fact, the term is only used twice in the Old Testament (2 Kgs 5:14; Is 21:4) and two other times in the Septuagint (Jdt 12:7; Sir 34:30), but never in a messianic or end-time prophecy. A baptism of repentance with water for the forgiveness of sins is a New Testament innovation, probably de-

---

[27] Turner, p. 174.
[28] Metzger, p. 551-52.

rived from Jewish proselyte baptism.[29] The expression "baptized in the Spirit" is only used in the New Testament. All six occurrences refer to John the Baptist's use of the expression, once in each Gospel (Mt 3:11; Mk 1:8; Lk 3:16; Jn 1:33) and twice in Acts referring back to John's preaching (Ac 1:5; 11:16).[30]

Four different meanings for the term "baptize" have been discerned from the various contexts in which it is used.[31] The basic or root meaning appears to be spatial: to dip, to submerge or to plunge. For example, it is used to describe "sunken vessels" (Polybius 1, 51, 6; 8, 8, 4). Elijah told Naaman to "dip" himself seven times in the Jordan (2 Kgs 5:14). Secondly, the verb can be used to describe certain results of this action; to cleanse or wash by dipping or submerging. Judith "'washed' herself at the spring of the camp" (Jdt 12:7). In a metaphorical sense the results may involve ritual cleansing or purification. Sirach asks, "If a man again touches a corpse after he has 'bathed,' what did he gain by the purification?" (Sir 34:30). Finally, the results may be more intense and require a stronger word to describe them. The Greek version of Isaiah 21:4 reads, "My heart wanders, and transgression 'overwhelms me.'" Other Greek literature widely used the term in a similar manner.[32] Galba talks about being "overwhelmed by debts" (Plutarch, Galba 21:3). Josephus talks about a city being "overwhelmed ... with misery" (*Jewish Wars* 4:137).

While it is possible to understand John's baptism in terms of ritual cleansing or purification, Jesus' baptism in Holy Spirit and fire is much more likely an 'overwhelming' experience. John plunges the repentant believers into water to signify their repentance and prepare them to face the coming judgment. Jesus' baptism is far more significant. He will plunge us all into 'overwhelming' Holy Spirit and fire. This baptism is not intended to prepare us for the coming judgment; it is the coming judgment, separating the wheat from the chaff. The repentant (wheat) is delivered from their oppressors and gathered into the kingdom (his barn), and the unrepentant (chaff) is destroyed with *unquenchable fire* (Lk 3:17).

James Dunn and Max Turner both see some sort of purification of the believer in John's baptismal metaphor derived from an allusion to the refiner's

[29] Craig S. Keener, *A Commentary on the Gospel of Matthew*, Grand Rapids, Eerdmans, 1999, p.120-21.
[30] For contextual and syntactical reasons, the repetition of the terms *pneuma* and *baptizō* in 1 Corinthians should not be considered as a repetition of the same expression. See chapter 6 for a discussion of this passage.
[31] The following is a combined summary of definitions given in BAGD, "βαπτίζω", p. 131-32, and Joseph Henry Thayer, *A Greek-English Lexicon of the New Testament*, New York, American Book Company, 1886, p. 94.
[32] Dunn, p. 12, Turner, p. 182. See his examples in note 41, p. 182-83.

fire in the third chapter of Malachi (3:2-3).[33] While an allusion to Malachi cannot be ruled out,[34] none of the "fire" images used in John's preaching would connect his prophetic words to this passage in Malachi. Both of the other images of "fire" used by John refer to the total destruction of the element thrown into the fire, not to a removal of dross. I might also point out that the refiner's fire in Malachi is not associated with the Spirit of God. In fact, the Spirit of God is not even mentioned in Malachi. The supposed link between John's words and the passage in Malachi must be derived from the possible meaning of "washing" or "cleansing" for the term baptism. In this case there might be some sort of parallel with the combined images of "washing" with launderer's soap and purifying with fire (Mal 3:2). I hold to the position that the only clear picture of "cleansing" or "purification" in John's imagery of the coming messianic upheaval is the removal of the wicked, not the removal of wicked practices committed by the righteous.

The use of similar expressions in Luke-Acts
(Greater literary context)

Luke uses similar vocabulary and expressions in the progression of his work. How do these repetitions shed light on the interpretation of John's imagery? Three repetitions are significant. Jesus speaks of baptism and fire in Luke 12. He also speaks of baptism and Spirit in Acts 1. Peter refers back to this saying of Jesus in Acts 11. The repetition of these terms in their respective contexts needs to be considered. Another passage in Acts 19 referring to the experience of some of John's disciples is also relevant to this discussion.

Jesus uses similar images in Luke chapter 12. He says, I *came to bring fire on the earth*, and *I have a baptism to undergo* (12:49, 50). We know that the fire which Jesus came to bring most likely refers to end-time judgment, since this passage is found in the middle of a series of warnings about end-time judgment (Lk 12:35-13:9). The previous mention of fire in Luke's account is an allusion to fiery judgment by the prophet Elijah (9:54; 2 Kgs 1:10, 12). In fact, if our interpretation of John's prophecy is correct, every mention of fire up to this point in Luke's story is a reference to judgment. The repetition of

---

[33] Dunn, p. 10, Turner, p. 183-84.
[34] Luke alludes to Mal 3:1 in a prophecy concerning John the Baptist in 1:17. But this allusion and Zechariah's prophecy refer to the ministry of John the Baptist and not specifically the work of the Spirit.

this judgment image would make it difficult for the reader to attribute any other meaning to the metaphor. The author would need to clearly indicate another meaning. He has not done this, undoubtedly because this is the meaning he intends to convey. If the "fire" which Jesus brings on the earth is indeed a reference to judgment, then Jesus ascribes the task of "fiery" end-time judgment to himself in the same manner that John the Baptist ascribed this task to the coming Messiah.

While the term "baptize" is not used in Luke 12 to refer to messianic judgment, context requires a meaning similar to that which we gave the term in John's prophetic words. All the other possible translations for the term do not work in this context. When Jesus says, *I have a baptism to undergo*, he cannot possibly refer to a water baptism. He has already been baptized (Lk 3:21). He cannot refer to a reception of the Spirit. He has already received the Spirit (Lk 3:22). It is theologically and contextually impossible that he is referring to ethical purification. The only remaining possibility is that he is referring to some sort of 'overwhelming' experience.[35] Undoubtedly he is referring to his own persecution and death. This would explain his distress and the following explanation of the persecution to be endured by his disciples (Lk 12:50-53). Like their master, they would also experience rejection and persecution.

The whole passage makes sense if we assume a background of prophetic end-time judgment similar to what I have proposed for John's message.[36] Like the prophets of old, Jesus proclaims a divisive message. It has a "winnowing" effect, separating faithful servants (grain) from those who do not repent (chaff, cf. Lk 3:17). Those who adopt the message are estranged and persecuted in society, even by their own families (Lk 12:51-53), but they will be rewarded for their faithfulness at the final judgment (Lk 12:43-44). Jesus himself will be 'overwhelmingly' rejected and persecuted (Lk 12:50). Those who find themselves on the wrong side and who do not repent will be held accountable (Lk 12:48). They will all perish (Lk 13:5). Two of the same images John used for the end-time destruction to be ushered in by the Messiah (Lk 3:9, 17) are also used in this section. Jesus will judge the earth with fire (Lk 12:49), and unfruitful trees will be cut down and eliminated (Lk 13:6-9). Even though Jesus does not use the same expressions as John, he uses similar

---

[35] Ajith Fernando, *Acts: The NIV Application Commentary*, Grand Rapids, Zondervan, 1998, p. 51, Larry W. Hurtado, *Mark: New International Biblical Commentary*, Peobody, MA, Hendrickson, 1989, p. 176.

[36] See Marshall, *Luke*, p. 546-47.

vocabulary and images to describe end-time judgment in a similar manner.

Even though the two repetitions in the Acts of the Apostles of the expression "baptized with the Holy Spirit" appear to emphasize a much more positive side of things than what I have proposed for John's audience (Ac 1:5; 11:16), there is some evidence in these repetitions to support the idea that John's saying was understood in terms of end-time judgment. In a discreet manner, Luke dissociates these repetitions from John's original words. First, the key term most associated with destructive end-time judgment, "fire," drops out of the expression. It is no longer a baptism with the Holy Spirit and fire, but a baptism with the Holy Spirit. Secondly, Luke is careful in both repetitions to inform his readers that the prophetic saying now belongs to Jesus. Jesus does not quote John. He announces the prophecy in his own words, adding and subtracting elements to make it fit the events of Pentecost. He does this, apparently in order to give John's prophecy a new and unexpected meaning (See chapter 6).

Although there is no repetition of John's expression in Acts chapter 19, the interpretation proposed earlier for this expression helps to explain the dialogue in this passage. Paul asks some of John's disciples in Ephesus if they had received the Holy Spirit since their conversion.[37] They respond by saying that they had not heard of the Holy Spirit (Ac 19:2). It is difficult to understand how these disciples could be in complete ignorance of the existence of the Holy Spirit, since the Spirit was known in both the Old Testament and pre-Christian Judaism.[38] It is more likely that their response is abbreviated and that we should understand that they had not heard anything about receiving the Holy Spirit. Some early interpreters must have understood it in this way, since several Greek manuscripts add the words "some are receiving" (*lambanousin tines*).[39] Even this response is difficult to swallow if John taught that the Messiah would give the Spirit to repentant believers. How could they be disciples of John and not hear about receiving the Holy Spirit? However, if John's teaching about the Spirit is actually a reference to end-time judgment, the Ephesian ignorance concerning the reception of the

---

[37] The aorist participle *pisteusantes* can refer to simultaneous action and be translated "when you believed." In this case the question would be whether or not they received the Holy Spirit at conversion. More commonly the aorist participle refers to antecedent action. I have adopted this more common use in the translation of this question. In either case the possibility of conversion without receiving the Spirit is assumed by the question.

[38] Gonzalo Haya-Prats, *L'Esprit force de L'église: Sa nature et son activité d'après les Actes des Apôtres*, Lectio Divina 81, trans. José J. Romero and Hubert Faes, Paris, Cerf, 1975, p. 35.

[39] P[38] P[41] D* sy[hmg] sa, see Barrett, p. 894.

Spirit is perfectly understandable. The idea that the Messiah would give the Holy Spirit to repentant believers became clear at Pentecost (Ac 2:33, 38). Disciples, like those described in Ephesus, who did not participate in the Pentecost experience, would not be aware of this.

Overwhelming evidence

In conclusion, there is overwhelming evidence that John's prophetic promise that the Messiah would *baptize with the Holy Spirit and fire* refers to end-time judgment, whereby the repentant are delivered from their oppressors in order to enjoy the blessings of the kingdom, and the unrepentant are destroyed by the fiery breath of the Messiah. Many others have also proposed such an interpretation.[40] If the evidence is so overwhelming, why is there no consensus on this question? There are at least two very good reasons.

I have already alluded to the first reason above. Commentators assume that the interpretation of this expression must be the same in the gospel of Luke and the book of Acts. Clearly, the expression emphasizes a more positive interpretation in the book of Acts than what I have proposed for John's saying in Luke. I am forced to concede that the repetitions of the same expression by the same author in the same literary work are extremely important in determining the meaning of this expression. According to the graph on levels of context in chapter 2, the importance of this information is only superseded by the immediate literary context of the passage. This is surely the most important reason many commentators are unwilling to adopt an end-time judgment interpretation for this saying. This interpretation does not adequately fit the two repetitions in the book of Acts. If the book of Acts were out of the picture, commentators would probably have very little trouble coming to a consensus. We definitely need to examine these repetitions more closely and propose a solution to this problem, if we wish to maintain an end-time judgment interpretation for John's saying in Luke. The answer lies in discovering how Luke uses the interpretation of this saying and other end-time prophecies to accomplish his stated goals. We will examine this more closely in chapter 6.

The second reason some interpreters are unwilling to adopt an end-time

---

[40] See, for example, C. K. Barrett, *The Holy Spirit and the Gospel Tradition*, London, SPCK, 1954, p.125-26.

judgment interpretation for this expression is experiential. Interpreters already have an idea of what the expression means, either from church background, previous experience, or other interpreters, and they look for the assumed meaning in the context of John's preaching.

This scenario brings to mind a story of a little boy in Sunday school. The teacher asked, "What is a little animal with a furry tail which likes to jump from tree to tree and eat nuts." A little boy raised his hand and replied, "Teacher, I know the answer is supposed to be 'Jesus,' but it sure sounds like a squirrel." In Sunday school, the answer is so often 'Jesus' that the little boy assumed the answer was always 'Jesus,' even when all the evidence pointed to a squirrel.

This often happens in the interpretation of Scripture. We have heard an interpretation so many times that it is difficult to consider any contradictory evidence. Hopefully with regard to John the Baptist's words, *He will baptize you with the Holy Spirit and fire,* I have described the "squirrel" in sufficient detail so as to entice interpreters to consider the possibility that we might really be looking at a "squirrel."

Chapter 4

Validated by the Spirit

The role of the Spirit in Luke-Acts

n the previous chapter, we discovered that John the Baptist's prophetic description of the Messiah's future work, *he will baptize you with Holy Spirit and fire*, appears to have a different meaning for John than it does for Jesus and his disciples in the book of Acts. How should we understand this discrepancy of meaning? The answer lies in how Luke uses John's prophecy to accomplish his purposes. In this chapter we will examine Luke's purpose for writing and demonstrate how apparent inconsistencies are purposefully used by Luke in a well-developed strategy to communicate *certainty* to his readers. We will also discover the role played by the Holy Spirit in Luke's strategy. In chapters 5 to 7, this information regarding Luke's strategy will help us to understand the various expressions used for the Spirit's activity in the life of the Christian community in Acts.

How to write a book

When I decided to write this book, it was for a particular purpose. Several years ago I finished a doctoral dissertation entitled, "The Holy Spirit in Luke's Story: A Search for Coherence in the Pneumatology of the Implied

Author of Luke-Acts."[1] I tried to use parts of my dissertation in course work for my students in Africa. These were very bright and enthusiastic students, hungry for knowledge, but also under great pressure from heavy course loads. Although I had written the dissertation in a readable style, it was too long and too detailed for my students. They would get lost in the details. This is the nature of a doctoral dissertation. I had written the dissertation with a certain audience in mind, the members of my jury. They were looking to see if I had covered all my bases. However, because I wanted others to appreciate my research, I needed to write for a new audience. Some of the detailed arguments had to go. A more personal twist needed to be added. More illustrations were needed. Some of my readers may still feel that there are too many details. Others may feel that I have left out some important arguments. I am writing for students of the Bible, whether formal or informal, whether in a biblical seminary or in a church, who want logical biblical answers to their questions but do not have the time or the inclination to read a doctoral dissertation.

My point is this; as an author, I have to determine who will read my book, and then I must write the book for that reader. It is difficult to ask this reader what kinds of things to include or not to include. Instead, I have to imagine what vocabulary this reader understands, what interests this reader has, what questions they want answered, how much detail they want, etc. In literary studies, this reader is usually called the implied reader.[2] It is the reader an author imagines as he or she writes.

I also needed to decide what I want to accomplish. What effect do I want my book to have on my imagined reader? These two things, for whom I am writing and what I want to accomplish, determine not only what I put in the book but also how I put it together. I must constantly imagine what my reader will understand or not understand and what effect my text will have on him or her and write accordingly.

Biblical writers had to do the same thing. The fact that they were inspired by God does not change the fact that they were human authors writing to human readers, using human communication. Inspiration simply means that God enabled them to communicate the message God intended them to communicate. God did not bypass human communication; he used it for

---

[1] This is an English translation of the French title, *Le Saint-Esprit dans le récit de Luc: Une recherche de cohérence dans la pneumatologie de l'auteur implicite de Luc-Actes.*
[2] Seymour Chatman, *Story and Discourse: Narrative Structure in Fiction and Film*, Ithaca and London, Cornell University Press, 1978, p. 149.

his glory. Thus, the more we can do to discern the biblical author's purpose in writing and the readers he had in mind, the better we will be able to understand what he has written. In some ways, this task is more difficult for biblical texts, because the writers wrote such a long time ago and we do not have a very precise knowledge of their world. In other ways it is easier, because ancient writers followed literary convention more closely. That is, they did not try, like some modern authors, to break the mold and write something totally new. They were usually content to follow the well-trodden paths of what was considered 'good literature' at that time.

Luke appears to be an author who followed literary convention. Some of the well-trodden paths are easily discernible in his work. He begins his work with a preface which resembles closely other works of his time.[3] His first few chapters read like portions of the Old Testament, using similar vocabulary, phrases and idioms.[4] He uses literary parallels and repetitions like many other works.[5] Like other historians of his day, Luke begins his 2-volume work with a preface describing the entirety of the work (Lk 1:1-4) and his second volume with a summary of the content of the first volume (Ac 1:1-3) before continuing the story.[6] He appears to write history in conventional ways.[7] I believe that Luke's conventional style makes it easier to discern his purpose in writing and the strategy he used to accomplish this purpose.

The purpose of Luke-Acts

Discerning the purpose of any literary work, if we do not have the option of simply asking the author, is a difficult and somewhat subjective task. The great number of theories regarding Luke's purpose for writing attests to this fact.[8] Luke provides an explicit description of his purpose in the preface of his work (Lk 1:1-4), but some interpreters believe that this specific purpose

---

[3] Aune, p. 120-21.

[4] John Drury, *Tradition and Design in Luke's Gospel: A Study in Early Christian Historiography*, London, Darton, Longman & Todd, 1976, p. 185-86, Brown, p. 256-499.

[5] Clark, p. 185.

[6] Aune, p. 117, 120. The literary technique is technically called *recapitulation* and *resumption*. Aune extends the recapitulation to Ac 1.5. I believe resumption begins with verse 4, where Luke resumes his story with the last two elements of his first volume, instructions for kingdom proclamation (Lk 24:47-49; Ac 1:4-8) and the ascension (Lk 24:50-51; Ac 1:9-11).

[7] Lucian, "How to Write History," Loeb Classical Library, ed. by G. P. Goold, Lucian VI, trans. by K. Kilburn, Cambridge/London, Harvard University Press, 1990, p.1-73.

[8] See Harrison, p. 78-79, for a discussion of some of the possibilities.

should "not be applied too seriously to the work as a whole," since "subjects discussed in prefaces were limited both naturally and by tradition."[9] However, the traditional style of Luke's preface does not rule out the possibility that his expressed purpose genuinely reveals his intent. As we shall see, evidence in Luke-Acts supports this assumption.

According to the preface, Luke writes his account *so that you* [the reader] *may know the certainty of the things you have been taught* (Lk 1:4). Three very important questions about this purpose will guide our investigation. First, who is the reader? Secondly, for what things does this reader need certainty? Lastly, how does Luke intend to give his reader certainty?

Who is the reader?

Even though the reader is given a name, *Theophilus*, and a title, *most excellent*, his identity is ambiguous. According to the literary practice of the time, the work was probably addressed to the public rather than just to one person.[10] Theophilus was probably a wealthy patron who subsidized the extensive research for this work (Lk 1:3). Regardless of the ambiguity of the name, the preface still gives us some important information about Luke's readers. Luke talks about events *that have been fulfilled among us* (Lk 1:1). This most likely implies that the readers are aware of most of the events. The traditions concerning these events were *handed down* to Luke and his readers (Lk 1:2). Knowledge about these events is probably not as important as the *orderly* manner in which they are written. The term *orderly* (*katheksês*) refers to the logical sequence of events.[11] The logical sequence of events recorded in Luke-Acts is intended to communicate certainty about the things the readers have been taught (Lk 1:4).

For what things does the reader need certainty?

How can we determine for which "things" the reader needs certainty? The preface does not specify this information. We must look for clues in

---

[9] Cadbury, *Preface*, p. 490.
[10] Cadbury, *Preface*, p. 490.
[11] BAGD, , "καθεξῆς," p. 388.

the body of Luke-Acts. The first question we might ask is, "What 'things' in Luke-Acts are associated with the terms 'know' and 'certainty'?" One "thing" in particular stands out. The term "certainty" (*asphaleia/asphalôs*) is repeated three other times in the entire work. Twice it is used to refer to prison security (Ac 5:23; 16:23). Only once is it used to refer to something which must be "known" with "certainty." At the end of Peter's Pentecost sermon, Peter states emphatically, "Therefore let all the house of Israel know for certain (*asphalôs*) that God has made Him both Lord and Christ— this Jesus whom you crucified" (Ac 2:36, New American Standard Bible[12]). Another repetition of the verb to know seems significant even if the term "certainty" is not repeated. A very similar phrase at the end of the book indicates a second "thing" for which the readers need certainty. Paul states emphatically three verses before the end of Luke-Acts, *Therefore I want you to know that God's salvation has been sent to the Gentiles, and they will listen* (Ac 28:28)!

In both cases the intended hearers of the message of assurance extend beyond the immediate context. Peter wants all Israel to know that Jesus is both "Lord and Christ." The intended hearers at the end of the book are more ambiguous. The text simply states *I want you to know.*" The antecedent of the pronoun "you" is a "larger number," a very ambiguous term which serves Luke's purpose (Ac 28:23). He has chosen to place these words from Paul at the end of the book for a reason. This sentence is the climax of a long series of episodes and sayings leading up to this conclusion (Lk 2:32; 24:47; Ac 1:8; 9:15; 11:18; 13:46-47; 14:27; 15:12-19; etc.). As in the case of Peter's conclusion in Acts 2:36, Luke allows Paul, another important character in his story to draw the conclusion he wants his readers to adopt.

These two "things," the messianic identity of Jesus and the salvation of the Gentiles, are very important themes in Luke-Acts. From a study of Jewish literature of that time, we can discern why early Christians needed certainty for these two issues. In the previous chapter, we looked at popular messianic expectations in John's day. One of the "central motifs" in these popular hopes was that God would raise up a Davidic king to liberate Israel from her enemies.[13] This hope involved the destruction of the Gentiles, not

---

[12] Scripture taken from the NEW AMERICAN STANDARD BIBLE, © Copyright The Lockman Foundation 1960, 1962, 1963, 1968, 1971, 1972, 1973, 1975, 1977, 1988, 1995. Used by permission.

[13] Ladd, p. 150.

their salvation. It was hoped that the Messiah would "destroy the unlawful nations with the word of his mouth" (PssSol 17:24). Jesus did not meet these prophetic expectations. How could he be the messianic Davidic king without sitting on the throne in Israel and establishing his kingdom? How could this new Christian "way" be the fulfillment of end-time prophecy when, not only are the Gentiles not destroyed, but they are the major recipients of the promised salvation? Luke answers these questions for his readers by allowing them to draw these conclusions as they encounter the evidence along with the characters in his story.

How does Luke intend to give his reader certainty?

Four different elements in Luke's preface concern the means he uses to give his readers certainty. Two of these require little or no comment. First, Luke underlines the reliability of the "eyewitnesses" who "handed down" the traditions (Lk 1:2). His account does not rely on hearsay evidence. Eyewitnesses are harder to disregard. Secondly, He underlines his own "careful investigation" (Lk 1:3). The two other means we will need to examine more closely are the logical sequence of events mentioned above (Lk 1:3) and the fulfillment of prophecy (Lk 1:1).

The logical sequence of events

David P. Moessner has demonstrated how Luke's composition resembles the logic of another ancient Greek author, Dionysius of Halicarnassus in *On Thucidide*. Dionysius also uses the logical sequence of events to create an intended effect among his hearers.[14] Such a comparison helps us to know that we are not reading modern literary devices into Luke's account. Since these conventions were used by other authors of the same time period, it is plausible, if the context suggests such a strategy, to think that Luke followed a similar logic. For Dionysius, the important elements of composition were the logical divisions of the work, the sequence of events and the beginning and the end of the work.[15] We have already seen the importance of the end of Luke-Acts. We will need to examine the other elements.

---

[14] Moessner, p. 156-62.
[15] Moessner, p. 159-62.

Robert Tannehill explains how the logical sequence of events can lead the reader to certainty concerning the related events.[16] He uses the example of Peter, who also tells his story in an *orderly sequence* (Ac 11:4, *katheksés*) of events to convince his accusers of the legitimacy of his actions. Peter is criticized for eating with the uncircumcised (Ac 11:3). In isolation this act could be seen as a violation of God's law. Peter repeats the story already told in chronological order by Luke, the narrator (Ac 10). Peter's version, however, is told from his perspective in the order in which he lived the experience, allowing his hearers to draw the same conclusions he did as they happened (Ac 11.1-18). Luke's version begins with Cornelius' encounter with an angel. Peter's version begins with his own vision, which God used to prepare him for adopting the seemingly illegitimate conclusion of God's salvation extended to the Gentiles.

First, Peter describes how, in the beginning, he resisted the heavenly voice on this issue because of its apparent discrepancy with God's law, and then how God miraculously confirmed his leading step by step. Peter first explains how he received a vision in which a voice from heaven told him to eat animals prohibited for consumption in Old Testament law (Ac 11:5-7; see Lv 11:1-47). Peter replied, *Surely not, Lord! Nothing impure or unclean has ever entered my mouth* (Ac 11:8). The voice from heaven replied, *Do not call anything impure that God has made clean* (Ac 11:9). *Right then three men* from the household of Cornelius arrived (Ac 11:11; 10:7). They were Gentiles sent by a Gentile, but Peter does not mention this. He only mentions the fact that the Holy Spirit instructed him to go with them (Ac 11:12).

The significance of this *orderly sequence* of events is that Gentiles were also considered to be unclean, partly because they ate unclean food.[17] Remember the reason Peter is telling this story: he is being criticized for eating with Gentiles. Peter is showing his accusers that, like them, he had been reluctant to associate with Gentiles, but revelation from God convinced him to cooperate with God's plan. An angel had given this Gentile who was sent to Peter supernatural knowledge about Peter (Ac 11:13). When Peter began to speak, the Holy Spirit descended on the Gentiles, just as he had on the disciples at Pentecost (Ac 11:15). His conclusion, and that which he convinces his hearers to adopt through this *orderly sequence* of events, is that to

---

[16] Robert C. Tannehill, *The Narrative Unity of Luke-Acts: A Literary Interpretation, Volume one: The Gospel according to Luke*, Philadelphia, Fortress Press, 1991, p. 11.
[17] Barrett, vol. 1, p. 494.

do other than what he did would be to *oppose God* (Ac 11:17). His accusers are convinced and come to the same conclusion (Ac 11:18).

Suppose for a moment that Peter had not answered his accusers in this manner. Suppose he had simply answered, "It is alright to eat with these uncircumcised men now, because they have also repented of their sins." The circumcised believers might well have answered, "How can you know if they really repented? Shouldn't we wait and see if their faith is genuine? And even if their faith is genuine, how does that change the law of God?" Peter would then need to answer each of their objections. Instead, Peter gained his audience's hearing by showing that, in the beginning, he had the same reservations they did. Through relating the events as they had happened to him, he showed his audience how God transformed his opinion. He brought his audience along with him to the right conclusion.

In telling this story through Peter's eyes, Luke is also relating to his readers. The inclusion of the Gentiles is also a problem for Luke's readers. Luke actually tells the story twice, once from an omniscient narrator's perspective and once from Peter's perspective. In this way, he drives the point home. God is validating his decision to include Gentiles in the end-time kingdom. Like Peter's accusers, Luke's readers should have *no further objections.* They are also convinced that *God has granted even the Gentiles repentance unto life* (Ac 11:18).

This is just one example of how Luke uses the sequence of events to communicate certainty to his readers. We will want to explore how he uses Spirit experiences for the same purpose and see how this strategy helps determine the definition to be given to the terms and expressions Luke uses to describe these experiences.

The fulfillment of prophecy

The fourth means Luke uses to give certainty to his readers is fulfilled prophecy. Luke begins his work by referring to those who *have undertaken to draw up an account of the things that have been fulfilled*[18] *among us* (Lk 1:1). Even if it is not clearly stated in the preface as a means of generating certainty, fulfilled prophecy was a recognized means of validation at

---

[18] *Plêrophoreô* used only here in Luke-Acts, is a synonym for *plêroô*, see Joel B. Green, *The Theology of the Gospel of Luke*, Cambridge University Press, 1995, p. 29. *Plêroô* is used frequently in Luke-Acts to refer to the fulfillment of prophecy (Lk 1:20; 4:21; 9:31, 51; 21:24; 22:16; 24:44; Ac 1:16; 3:18; 13:27, 33).

that time,[19] and a standard element in Christian apologetics.[20] Luke's use of the term in his first sentence demonstrates that this theme is central in his thinking. The importance of this theme becomes immediately clear in Luke's account of these *things* or events. In fact, the fulfillment of prophecy provides a framework which Luke uses to organize events into an *orderly sequence*. This organizing framework has been recognized by a large number of interpreters.[21]

The prophetic introduction to Luke-Acts

Dionysius suggested that there are four important elements of composition: the logical divisions of the work, the sequence of events, and the beginning and the end of the work. We have already looked at an important prophetic prediction at the end. We now want to examine the beginning of Luke's work, where he sets the stage for what follows. Many interpreters have suggested that the organizing framework and a major theme of the work is the fulfill-ment of prophecy. Luke does not disappoint us in the opening chapters. They are filled with this theme.

Before we examine some of the details, it would be helpful to consider what Luke includes in this theme. Fulfilled prophecy is also a major theme in the Gospel of Matthew, but not in the same way. Matthew relates an event and then affirms that the event occurred to fulfill what was spoken by an Old Testament prophet (Mt 1:22; 4:14; 8:17; 12:17; 21:4). Luke is not limited to this way of describing fulfilled prophecy. In addition to the explicit ful-fillment of certain Old Testament prophecies (Lk 3:4-6; 4:17-21; Ac 2:16-21), Luke highlights the theme of fulfilled prophecy in four other important ways, according to Luke Timothy Johnson.

[19] See Charles H. Talbert, *Reading Luke: A Literary and Theological Commentary on the Third Gospel*, New York, Crossroad Publishing Company, 1982, p. 2-4; Robert L. Brawley, *Luke-Acts and the Jews: Conflict, Apology, and Conciliation*, SBL Monograph Series 33, ed. Adela Yarbro Collins, Atlanta, Scholars Press, 1987, p. 49-63; and Philip Francis Esler, *Community and Gospel in Luke-Acts: The Social and Political Motivations of Lucan Theology*, Cambridge/New York/Melbourne, Cambridge University Press, 1987, p. 16-20.
[20] Johnson, *Luke-Acts*, p. 221.
[21] See, for example, Robert Minear, *To Heal and to Reveal: The Prophetic Vocation according to Luke*, New York, Seabury Press, 1976, p. 85; Paul Schubert, "The Structure and Significance of Luke 24," *Neutestamentliche Studien für Rudolf Bultmann su seinem siebzigsten Geburtstag am 20. August 1954*, 2nd ed. corrected, Berlin, Alfred Tömelmann, 1957, p. 176, 178; Nils A. Dahl, "The Story of Abraham in Luke-Acts," *Studies in Luke-Acts*, ed. Leander E. Keck and J. Louis Martyn, Philadelphia, Fortress Press, 1980, p. 139-158; Johnson, *Function*, p. 15-19. Shepherd, p. 245.

1. The term 'it is necessary' (*dei*) is used to show that certain events were "determined by prophecies: the suffering and glorification of the Messiah (Luke 9.22; 17.25; 24.7; Acts 3.21; 17.3), the apostasy of Judas and the election of Matthias (Acts 1.16-22), the sufferings of Paul (Acts 9.16) and those of all Christians (Acts 14.22)...

2. Literary prophecy. Things predicted by characters within the story are later shown to be fulfilled explicitly in the narrative...

3. Programmatic prophecies. These are spoken by characters at critical junctures within the narrative and provide an interpretation of the narrative that follows...

4. Luke arranges speech and narrative so that a story immediately following upon a saying fulfills the saying.[22]

The opening pages of Luke's gospel are filled with 'literary prophecy.' However, we are forced to modify Johnson's definitions. Things are predicted by characters in the story, but not all of the details are "shown to be fulfilled explicitly in the narrative." However, both what is fulfilled within the narrative and what is not fulfilled are presented as prophetic speech. The following is a summary of literary prophetic predictions in the introduction to Luke-Acts (Lk 1:5–2:52).

1. The angel of the Lord predicts that Zechariah's wife Elizabeth will bear a son (Lk 1:13). In this prophecy, John's future ministry is predicted in terms reminiscent of Malachi's prophecy concerning a future "Elijah" who will prepare for the coming day of the Lord (Lk 1:17; Mal 3:1; 4:5-6). Because of Zachariah's doubt, the angel also predicts that he will not be able to speak until this prophecy is fulfilled (Lk 1:20). All of these predictive elements are fulfilled within the narrative (Lk 1:57, 64; 3:4; 7:1).

2. The angel Gabriel predicts the birth of Jesus to the virgin Mary and the establishment of an everlasting kingdom in terms reminiscent of Nathan's prophecy to David (Lk 1:31-33; 2 Sam 7:16). The birth occurs within the narrative (Lk 2:7), but Jesus does not inherit the throne of his father David or establish an everlasting kingdom in a political sense.[23]

---

[22] Johnson, *Luke-Acts*, p. 221-22.

[23] Mary's praise song (Lk 1:46-55) is also a form of prophetic speech. I have not included it in this list because it describes God's character more than it predicts future events. However, some of the

3. Zechariah prophecies at the birth of John the Baptist concerning the future ministries of John and Jesus (Lk 1:67-79). His words do not recall any one specific prophecy, but common prophetic themes and vocabulary from Old Testament prophetic literature. John will prepare the way for the coming Savior. Jesus, the Davidic ruler, will save his people and rescue them from their enemies. John's predicted ministry occurs within the narrative (Lk 3:1-18). While it is true that Jesus brings salvation and deliverance from sin within the narrative, he does not save the people *from* their *enemies* or *from the hand of all who hate* them (Lk 1:71).

4. An angel of the Lord tells some shepherds that the Davidic Savior, Messiah, and Lord has been born, and that they will find him in a manger (Lk 2:11-12). The shepherds find him in the next few verses (Lk 2:15-16).

5. Simeon receives a prophetic word that he will see the Lord's Christ before he dies (Lk 2:26). Simeon recognizes him in the temple and prophetically rejoices over the salvation he will bring in terms reminiscent of Isaiah's prophecy concerning a light to the Gentiles and Israel's glorious future (Lk 2:28-32; Is 42:6; 49:6). The promise concerning light to the Gentiles is definitely fulfilled in Acts (Ac 13:47; 26:23), but probably in an unexpected manner. Israel's glorious future does not seem to be realized within the narrative.

6. Simeon then prophecies over the child in enigmatic terms predicting his destiny and the contrasting results of his ministry in Israel. He announces, that the *child is destined to cause the falling and rising of many in Israel, and to be a sign that will be spoken against* (Lk 2:34). The contrasting results are probably also inspired by a passage in Isaiah (8:14-15) and considered to be fulfilled in Luke-Acts by the contrasting responses to Jesus' ministry and by examples of those in Israel who speak against Jesus (Lk 21:15; Ac 13:45; 28:19, 22).

7. The prophetess Anna *spoke about the child to all who were looking forward to the redemption of Jerusalem* (Lk 2:38). This hope is also not fulfilled within the narrative.

What can we discern from these literary prophecies and their fulfillment or

statements anticipate themes in Luke-Acts. God has done and will continue to do mighty deeds. He brings down the proud and lifts up the humble. He fills the hungry and sends the rich away empty.

non fulfillment in Luke-Acts? Again, we need to be careful not to read these prophecies with New Testament eyes. The characters pronouncing these prophetic words were devout Jews, inspired by the Spirit, but also by Old Testament prophecies. They did not prophesy in the light of the incarnation, life, teaching, death and resurrection of Jesus the Messiah. God revealed to these individuals that the time for the fulfillment of Old Testament prophetic promises had come to pass.

Luke, like other New Testament authors, will infuse new meaning into much of the vocabulary used in this section. Jesus will not sit on a throne in Jerusalem and establish his political kingdom in the narrative of Luke-Acts; rather, he will be *exalted to the right hand of God* (Ac 2:30-33; 7:49, 55-56). His kingdom is not political, nor is it limited to a political domain. Wherever he exercises authority in healing (Lk 10:9) or in casting out demons (Lk 11:20), his kingdom is present. This is why he can say, "The kingdom of God is in your midst" (Lk 17:21, NASB). Jesus' immediate task is not to save the nation of Israel from her enemies. Rather, he *came to seek and to save what was lost* (Lk 19:10) and to heal "all who were oppressed by devil" (Ac 10:38, NASB).

Although Luke gives new meaning to these expressions, several details demonstrate that the prophetic voices in this first section of Luke's gospel mostly reflect an Old Testament perspective. Gabriel announces that God will give the Christ child *the throne of his father David* (Lk 1:32). These very concrete elements, a throne and Davidic ancestry, create an expectation for a king like David and an earthly kingdom like David's. In his prophecy, Zechariah even tells us that what is taking place is according to what God *said to his holy prophets long ago* (Lk 1:70). The salvation which he prophetically proclaims is personalized. He will save us *from **our** enemies and from the hand of all who hate **us*** (Lk 1:71). Surely these personal pronouns are understood to refer to personal human enemies familiar to Zachariah and his audience. The people to whom the prophetess Anna spoke about the child Jesus were not hoping to be rescued from sin by the blood of the lamb, but rather they were anticipating the rescue of *Jerusalem,* a physical place, from her political enemies (Lk 2:38). In fact, the term *redemption* is only used with this meaning in Luke-Acts (Lk 1:68; 2:38; 24:21). Unlike Matthew (20:28) and Mark (10:45), Luke does not introduce the idea of a ransom for sinners.

We must not read New Testament concepts into these 'pre-Christian' prophetic pronouncements. We must allow Luke to introduce these new concepts in the course of his narrative when and where he desires. But first, we need to understand what these inspired speakers and their audiences understood by these words and why Luke introduces them here at the beginning of his work. None of the other gospels give an account of these prophecies. Luke must have a good reason for including them.

Most of the expectations awakened in these opening chapters are very much like the popular messianic expectations described earlier. Devout and faithful Israel is awaiting a messianic king who will deliver her from her oppressors and establish his righteous, glorious, and everlasting kingdom from his throne in Jerusalem. This is further evidence that we have correctly interpreted John the Baptist's prophetic messianic saying. John is the last in a series of divinely inspired messengers announcing the arrival of the messianic age in terms which bring to mind popular expectations.

The question which begs asking is, why does Luke stir up these popular expectations if Jesus did not fulfill them? The answer lies with Luke's strategy. Through an *orderly sequence* of events, he wants to assure his readers that Jesus is the Messiah, even if he did not fulfill popular expectations. He must address these expectations because they are legitimately rooted in the messianic prophecy of the Old Testament. Like Peter, he must guide his readers from their old and popular understanding of the Scriptures to new understandings. He must demonstrate that these new understandings are, in fact, divinely inspired. Peter did this by showing his hearers that he, himself, shared their understanding. According to their common understanding of the Scriptures, Peter should not have eaten unclean food or associated with Gentiles who did. Peter took his listeners back to his own pre-understanding and then carried them along on his own journey to new understanding, describing how God convinced him through miraculous interventions that he had indeed brought salvation to the Gentiles.

Unlike Peter, Luke is unable to take his readers along with him on a personal journey from pre-understanding to new understanding. According to his use of the first-person pronoun, Luke enters the story on Paul's second missionary journey as they are leaving Troas in Asia Minor and heading for Macedonia on the Aegean peninsula (Ac 16:11-12). By this time, the new understandings concerning the messianic identity of Jesus and the inclusion of the Gentiles among the people of God were already firmly established in this rapidly expanding church. Instead of using his own experiences to give his readers certainty, Luke uses the experiences of divinely inspired characters in his story. Peter is one of these characters. We have already seen how Luke used Peter's experience to convince his readers of a new understanding concerning the Gentiles.

Luke used the experiences of other inspired prophetic characters in his story to give his readers certainty concerning a new understanding of the fulfillment of messianic prophecy. We have just examined the inspired messages of some of these characters in Luke's introductory chapters. In Luke's strategy, they play the same role that Peter played in his orderly account. These inspired messengers mirror the starting point for Luke's readers. They represent their pre-understanding of messianic expectations. The experiences of John the Baptist and of Jesus' disciples will help his readers to adopt a new understanding. Before we look at these examples, we need to examine more closely Luke's logical sequence of events.

Divisions and sequence organized around prophetic proclamations

We have already taken a look at two very important elements of literary composition, the beginning and end of the book. We discovered that the end does not look very much like the beginning. In the beginning chapters, the characters are anticipating an anointed David-like king who will deliver them from their oppressive enemies and restore the kingdom to Israel. At the end of Luke-Acts, the characters are preaching the good news of the kingdom with a very different twist, and Israel's enemies are not the recipients of God's judgment, but the recipients of kingdom salvation. A change in perspective like this is not unusual for narrative accounts. It shows that the author has purpose and that his narrative is intended to take the readers in the direction of that purpose.

We get into trouble when we try to homogenize the elements in the story. This is the main reason why we have trouble defining the expression, "Baptized in the Holy Spirit." Interpreters have tried to homogenize the three references to this expression at various points in the story, but the expression is not used in the same way each time. The elements in Luke's story were not meant to be homogenized; they were meant to be understood in sequence as the story develops.

According to Dionysius, the other two important elements of literary composition are its divisions and sequence. How is the book organized to communicate its message? What narrative strategy does Luke use to communicate certainty to his readers? Luke uses prophecy and its fulfillment to organize his narrative and communicate certainty. Luke divides his story into four main sections, not including the preface (Lk 1:1-4): a prophetic introduction (Lk 1:5-2:52) followed by three sections devoted to the prophetic ministry of the main characters in each section, John the Baptist (Lk 3:1-20), Jesus (Lk 3:21-Ac 1:11) and the disciples of Jesus (Ac 1:12-28:31). These sections are organized and logically glued together around the theme of fulfilled prophecy.

The prophetic introduction

The first two chapters of Luke are almost universally considered to be a unified and separate section in Luke's work. This is so for several reasons. First, the material in these two chapters is not found in Matthew or Mark. It appears that Luke has done his research and added this material to the already accepted traditions (Lk 1:2-3). Secondly, chapter three is set off from the first two chapters by the use of a clearly recognized literary introduction called a synchronism.[24] In this type of introduction, the events which follow are set in their historical context by relating them to the various political leaders of that time (Lk 3:1-2). Finally, the material in these two chapters is clearly organized into a tight pattern of comparison and contrast.[25] The narrator compares and contrasts John the Baptist and Jesus, switching back and forth between the two. The following chart shows the parallels in this comparison and interchange.

Chart 2: Parallel structure in Luke 1-2

John the Baptist	Jesus
Birth of John predicted (Lk 1:5-25)	Birth of Jesus predicted (Lk 1:26-38)
Mother of Jesus visits mother of John the Baptist (Lk 1:39-56)	
Birth of John the Baptist (Lk 1:57-66)	Birth of Jesus (Lk 2:1-20)
Prophecy concerning John and a summary of his childhood (Lk 1:67-80)	Prophecies concerning Jesus and a summary of his childhood (Lk 2:21-52)

The comparison and contrast does not stop with the first two chapters. In fact, there is explicit contrast between John and Jesus 10 more times in

[24] Aune, p. 133.
[25] Brown, p. 248-53, 292-98, 408-12, R. Laurentin, *Structure et Theologie de Luc 1-2*, Paris, Lecoffre, 1964, p. 23-33, Augustin George, "Le parallèle entre Jean-Baptiste et Jésus en Luc 1-2," *Études sur l'œuvre de Luc*, Paris, Gabalda, 1978, p. 43-65.

Luke-Acts (Lk 5:33-39; 7:28; 9:7-9, 18-20; 11:1; Ac 1:5; 11:16; 13:23-25; 18:25; 19:1-6). In some ways, the following two sections are anticipated by the comparison and contrast in this first section. A section on John's prophetic ministry (Lk 3:1-20) is followed by a section on Jesus' prophetic ministry (Lk 3:21-Ac 1:11).

More importantly, these first two introductory chapters prepare the reader for the following chapters through predictive prophecy. Prophecy is given in the first section which awaits fulfillment in the following sections. Zechariah prophesies that John the Baptist will be *a prophet of the Most High* who *will go before the Lord to prepare the way for him, to give his people the knowledge of salvation through the forgiveness of their sins* (Lk 1:76-77). This anticipates what happens in the next section of the book. In chapter 3, Zechariah's prophecy is fulfilled. The same vocabulary is used to link John's prophetic ministry with Zechariah's prophecy. (Note: in the following sentences, words in bold print are repetitions from Zechariah's prophecy.) John preaches a *baptism of repentance for the **forgiveness of sins*** (Lk 3:3). This is understood as a fulfillment of prophecy in Isaiah about ***preparing the way for the Lord*** so that *all mankind will see God's **salvation*** (Lk 3:4-6). The rest of this section describes some of the details concerning John's preaching and teaching.

The angel Gabriel, Zechariah, Simeon, and Anna all pronounce prophetic words anticipating the ministry of Jesus the Messiah. These prophecies await their fulfillment in the third section of Luke's work (Lk 3:21-Ac 1:11). The Messiah comes and commences his prophetic ministry of preaching and deliverance. The link between prophecy and fulfillment is less clear here than with John the Baptist, because the prophecies anticipate an anointed warrior-king and Jesus is presented as an anointed prophet. Jesus preaches, teaches, heals the sick, casts out demons, and opposes religious hypocrisy, but he does not do battle with Israel's enemies and restore the kingdom to Israel. This dissonance is deliberate. Luke has established a pattern up to this point of prophecy and fulfillment. The reader, like the characters in the story, expects the Messiah to fulfill all the messianic prophecies in the introductory chapters. However, unlike the characters in the story, the reader knows that Jesus did not fulfill all these prophecies as expected. Luke informs us clearly that Jesus is the Messiah, but he fulfills messianic prophecy in an unexpected manner.

It is essential to understand why Luke chose to destabilize the reader in this way. It is part of his strategy. He wants to assure his readers that Jesus is the Messiah. In order to do this he must demonstrate that God has given messianic prophecies 'new' meaning. This is not to say that the old meanings were wrong or that the new meanings were not inherent in the prophecies. The 'new' meanings are new to popular Jewish thought because they were not easily discernible in the prophecies of the Old Testament. An important concept for Luke's strategy is that predictive prophecy becomes clear only as the prophecy is fulfilled. Therefore, we must not allow pre-understanding of these predictive prophecies to hinder us from discovering how God wants to fulfill them. Luke Timothy Johnson suggests that prophecies in Luke-Acts are intended "to provide an interpretation of what follows."[26] In other words, the prophecies and subsequent fulfillments guide the reader to an understanding of the events as fulfillment of prophecy. In addition, the events following the prophecy often help define what is meant by the prophecy.

Prophetic predictions concerning the salvation of the Gentiles provide a good example for understanding this process. In the beginning of Luke-Acts, we are introduced to the idea of salvation for the Gentiles. Simeon talks about the salvation which God *has prepared for all people, a light for revelation to the Gentiles and glory to* his *people Israel* (Lk 2:31-32). The theme is reiterated in the description of John's ministry of preparation. The phrase quoted from the Greek version of Isaiah proclaims that *all mankind will see God's salvation* (Lk 3:6). The theme is repeated again in the Joel prophecy quoted in Peter's Pentecost message. Joel prophesies that *everyone who calls on the name of the Lord will be saved* (Ac 2:21). This idea appears to be reinforced by Peter's declaration to repentant inquirers at the end of his message. He declares that God's promise is *for you and your children and for all who are far off—for all whom the Lord our God will call* (Ac 2:39).

If Peter had already adopted the idea of salvation for the Gentiles at Pentecost, we have to ask why he has to be convinced of this through miraculous events in the Cornelius episode (Ac 10.1-11.18). The obvious answer is that he did not understand this 'new' meaning of Joel's prophecy until it was fulfilled in the household of Cornelius. Before that episode, Peter did not understand that the phrase *everyone who calls on the name of the Lord* (Ac 2:21) included Gentiles. It should be noted that Peter did not hear Simeon's prophecy about salvation for the Gentiles (Lk 2:30-32). He probably shared

---

[26] Johnson, *Luke-Acts*, p. 221.

the Jewish belief that "the Kingdom of God would bring salvation to Israel and judgment to her enemies." References to salvation for the Gentiles are rare in Jewish literature.[27] He most likely understood the term *everyone* to mean 'all levels of society,' *sons and daughters, young men* and *old men, my servants, both men and women* (Ac 2:17-18). He probably understood that God had now poured out his Spirit in end-time salvation on 'all classes of people,' (Ac 2:17) not just on a few prophets, kings, and leaders of the people, as he did in the Old Testament, but also on lowly people such as a fisherman like himself, and on any other Jew who repents.

The prophetic ministries of John, Jesus, and Jesus' disciples

The three major sections of Luke-Acts are organized in a careful pattern of prophecy fulfillment. Near the beginning of each of the three sections, Luke includes a programmatic prophetic quote from the Old Testament. They are considered programmatic because key terms and ideas in these prophecies determine much of the events and ideas reported in the succeeding narrative. The prophecy is intended to introduce and explain the prophetic ministry of the main character in that section. Luke 3:4-6 (Is 40:3-5) introduces John the Baptist's prophetic ministry. Luke 4:18-19 (Is 61:1-2) introduces the prophetic ministry of Jesus the Messiah. Acts 2:17-21 (Jl 2:28-32) introduces the prophetic ministry of Jesus' disciples. In each case the narrative explicitly states that these prophetic quotes are being fulfilled (Lk 3:4; 4:21; Ac 2:16).

Near the end of each of these three main sections, we find a literary prophecy pronounced by the main character in that section and fulfilled by the main characters in the following sections. John the Baptist declares that one more powerful than he will come and baptize his hearers with the Holy Spirit and fire (Lk 3:16). At the end of Luke's gospel and at the beginning of Acts, Jesus informs his disciples that they will receive the promised Holy Spirit and be his witnesses to the ends of the earth (Lk 24:47-49; Ac 1:8). Jesus' prophetic words are repeated not only because of their importance, but also because of the literary convention for a two-volume work of resuming the story where it left off. Paul declares close to the end of the book that *God's salvation has been sent to the Gentiles, and*

---

[27] Ladd, p. 109. He writes, "In a few places (En.50.1-3; 90.30; 91.14) salvation is extended to Gentiles who repent, but this is rare."

they will listen (Ac 28:28). These literary patterns are illustrated in chart 3 on the following page.

Other important details lend support to this description of Luke's organizational pattern. For instance, the main character in each section is removed from the narrative at the end of the section. John the Baptist is imprisoned by Herod (Lk 3:20). Luke reports this fact out of chronological order. Reading Luke's gospel, unlike the other gospels, one might get the impression that John was not even present at Jesus' baptism. Luke writes, *Jesus was baptized* without mentioning who baptized him (Lk 3.21). According to Luke's literary sequence, John is in prison when Jesus is baptized. Jesus is also removed from the narrative at the end of the section devoted to his ministry. He is taken up into heaven (Ac 1:9-11)! Paul also finds himself in prison at the end of the final section (Ac 28:20, 30). We cannot say that Paul is removed from the ensuing section because it is not written; only anticipated in Paul's prophetic words, *Gods salvation has been sent to the Gentiles, and they will listen* (Ac 28:28)! However, it may be implied, as Paul's movements were limited by his imprisonment and he was not in a position to carry the message of God's salvation to other Gentile nations.

The divisions proposed for the composition of Luke-Acts are also substantiated by geographical patterns. John the Baptist's ministry takes place in the area of the Jordan River (Lk 3:3). Jesus ministry begins after he *returned from the Jordan* (Lk 4:1). There is a geographical movement from Galilee to Jerusalem in the section devoted to Jesus' ministry (Lk 9:51, etc). The geographical movement in the final section is from Jerusalem to the ends of the earth (Ac 1:8).

The characters in Luke's story also lend credence to the proposed divisions. They explicitly mention beginnings and ends which coincide with these divisions. Peter describes the time of Jesus' ministry *beginning from John's baptism to the time when he was taken up* (Ac 1:22). The chief priests said that Jesus stirred up trouble with his teaching beginning *in Galilee* and coming all the way to Jerusalem (Lk 23:5). Peter specifies that Jesus began in Galilee after John's baptism (Ac 10:37). *All Jesus began to do and to teach until the day he was taken up to heaven* is Luke's own summary of his first volume (Ac 1:1-2).

Chart 3: Prophetic structural parallels in Luke-Acts

Explanatory OT prophecy   **Literary prophecy**

Lk 3:4-6 *A voice of one calling*   **John the Baptist's**   **Lk 3:16** *one more powerful than*
in the desert, 'Prepare the way for   **Prophetic ministry**   *I will come, the thongs of whose*
the Lord, make straight paths for   around the Jordan   *sandals I am not worthy to*
him. Every valley shall be filled   **Lk 3:1-20**   *untie. He will baptize you with*
in, every mountain and hill made   *the Holy Spirit and with fire.*
low. The crooked roads shall become
straight, the rough ways smooth.
And all mankind will see God's
salvation.' (Is 40:3-5)   **FULFILLMENT**

Explanatory OT prophecy   **Literary prophecy**

Lk 4:18-19 *The Spirit of the Lord*   **Lk 24:47-49** *repentance and*
is on me, because he has anointed   **Jesus'**   *forgiveness of sins will be*
me to preach good news to the poor.   **Prophetic ministry**   *preached in his name to all*
He has sent me to proclaim freedom   Galilee to Jerusalem   *nations, beginning at Jerusalem.*
for the prisoners and recovery of   **Lk 3:21-Ac 1:11**   *You are witnesses of these things.*
sight for the blind, to release the   *I am going to send you what my*
oppressed, to proclaim the year of   *Father has promised; but stay*
the Lord's favor. (Is 61:1-2)   *in the city until you have been*
                                                                            clothed with power from on high.
                                               FULFILLMENT   **Acts 1:8** *you will receive power*
                                                                            when the Holy Spirit comes on
                                                                            you; and you will be my witnesses
                                                                            in Jerusalem, and in all Judea
                                                                            and Samaria, and to the ends of
                                                                            the earth.

Explanatory OT prophecy   **Literary prophecy**

Acts 2:17-21 *In the last days, God*   **Acts 28:28** *God's salvation has*
says, I will pour out my Spirit on   **The disciples'**   *been sent to the Gentiles, and*
all people. Your sons and daughters   **Prophetic ministry**   *they will listen!*
will prophesy, your young men will   from Jerusalem to
see visions, your old men will dream   the ends of the earth
dreams. Even on my servants,   **Acts 1:12-28:31**
both men and women, I will pour out
my Spirit in those days, and
they will prophesy. I will show
wonders in the heaven above and
signs on the earth below, blood and   **FULFILLMENT**
fire and billows of smoke. The sun will
be turned to darkness and the moon
to blood before the coming of the great
and glorious day of the Lord. And
everyone who calls on the name of the
Lord will be saved. (Jl 2:28-32)

John the Baptist's perspective

John the Baptist announced the coming of one more powerful than he, who would baptize with the Holy Spirit and fire. A short time later he sends emissaries to ask Jesus, *Are you the one who was to come, or should we expect someone else* (Lk 7:18)? Why would John begin to have doubts about the messianic identity of Jesus? He is the one who prophesied his arrival saying, *But one more powerful than I will come* (Lk 3:16). He can have no doubts concerning the fact that Jesus is *more powerful*. John asks his question immediately after hearing about Jesus raising a person from the dead (Lk 7:11-18) in a manner reminiscent of a similar miracle in Elijah's ministry (1 Kgs 17:17-24). Some might want to attribute John's doubts to psychological factors stemming from the fact that he is persecuted and in prison. This might be enough to discourage John, maybe even send him into a depression. But it is highly unlikely that it would make him doubt the word of the Lord. John is presented as a great prophet and *more than a prophet* (Lk 7:26). Jesus says of John, *among those born of women there is not one greater than John* (Lk 7:28). Persecution and imprisonment are regular fare for true biblical prophets. According to Jesus, that is how prophets were treated (Lk 6:23). Persecution might even serve to confirm John's calling and strengthen his convictions.

John's doubts must be theological. Jesus has not done what John expects the Messiah to do. George Eldon Ladd describes John's problem like this: "the eschatological salvation and judgment he has proclaimed were not being fulfilled in Jesus. Jesus' answer ... assured John's disciples that the messianic salvation was present and in process of fulfillment, but in unexpected terms."[28] He has not fulfilled John's prophecy concerning a baptism in the Holy Spirit and fire. John's question is whether Jesus is going to fulfill this expectation, or if John needs to wait for someone else to fulfill it. That John is waiting for end-time judgment is the interpretation which fits the situation. John can clearly see that God's people, including him, are still being oppressed by their enemies. They have not been delivered by Jesus. Jesus has not restored the kingdom to Israel. If Jesus is the Messiah, why has he not yet done what he came to do?

How does Jesus answer John's question? Jesus tells John's emissaries, *Go back and report to John what you have seen and heard: The blind receive sight, the lame walk, those who have leprosy are cured, the deaf hear, the dead are raised, and*

---

[28] Ladd, p. 201.

the good news is preached to the poor (Lk 7:22). His response is a close parallel to the messianic prophecy from Isaiah which Jesus quoted to describe his upcoming ministry (Lk 4:18-19; Is 61:1-2). Jesus' answer is intended to assure John that he is, in fact, fulfilling messianic prophecy, although not in the way John expected.

If we look back at how Jesus quoted this passage from Isaiah, we can already discern a deliberate attempt to modify popular messianic expectations. Jesus stops in the middle of a sentence to avoid saying the last phrases of Isaiah 61:2. Isaiah prophesies that the Messiah is anointed *to proclaim the year of the Lord's favor and the day of vengeance.* Jesus stops with the year of the Lord's favor. *The day of vengeance* would bring to mind popular messianic expectations. Jesus leaves it out because the judgment of the nations is not his current task. Luke-Acts relocates this task to a future time (Lk 12:35-13:5; 17:22-37; 19:11-27; 20:9-18; 21:5-36; Ac 3:21; 10:42; 17:30-31; 24:25).[29] Such a division of time for messianic tasks was not anticipated in Old Testament prophecy. The Messiah's current task is to proclaim the good news, heal the blind and the sick, and deliver those who are oppressed by the devil (Ac 10:38). And this is what we find Jesus doing in Luke's gospel. Luke does not focus on the political enemies of Israel, but on the spiritual enemy of all peoples, the devil. This is probably one reason the devil is introduced at the beginning of Luke 4. Jesus' task is to deliver those who are oppressed by the devil. To do this, he must first conquer the devil (Lk 11:22).

The reader can easily empathize with John. John did everything right and was suffering unjustly for it. If we continue on in the book of Acts, we have every reason to believe that God's people, Luke's readers, continued to suffer unjustly. John the Baptist mirrors doubts for which the readers also need assurance. As in the case of Peter's orderly account, the readers will receive answers to their questions along with the characters in the story. The narrative does not tell us if Jesus' reply was sufficient to eliminate John's doubts. This may be purposeful. Notice that Jesus' answer to John concludes with a more universal encouragement toward persevering faith. He says to John's envoys, *Blessed is the man who does not fall away on account of me* (Lk 7:23). These words are intended to encourage not only John, but anyone listening to his reply to persevere in faith. By leaving out John's response, Luke encourages the reader to respond in John's place.

---

[29] For a discussion on the changes in eschatology in Luke-Acts see A. J. Mattill, Jr., *Luke and the Last Things: A Perspective for the Understanding of Lukan Thought*, Dillsboro NC, Western North Carolina Press, 1979, p. 113-55.

The disciples' perspective

The disciples are convinced that Jesus is the Messiah early in the story. But this belief is not an unshakeable conviction and it is based on a popular conception of the coming Messiah. After witnessing the powerful acts of Jesus, Peter, speaking for all the disciples, declares him to be *the Christ of God*, that is "God's anointed" (Lk 9:20). Peter uses the title to refer to the promised anointed warrior-king. This fact becomes clear in the following passages of Luke's narrative. Shortly after Peter's declaration, we find the disciples arguing about *which of them would be the greatest* (Lk 9:46). That this argument concerns their relative positions in the coming kingdom is clear from the repetition of this theme later on (Lk 22:24-30). They expect to be top administrators in the new kingdom, eating and drinking at the king's table and sitting on thrones, *judging the twelve tribes of Israel* (Lk 22:30). They also expect to have supernatural power at their disposal to destroy their enemies. In the next passage in chapter 9, when Jesus is not welcomed by a group of Samaritans, James and John ask, *Lord, do you want us to call fire down from heaven to destroy them* (Lk 9:53-54)? Later on, when the crowd came to take Jesus away, his followers are ready to draw swords and go to battle with Jesus, their anointed king, and inaugurate his kingdom (Lk 22:49-50). They are confident of victory because they are convinced that Jesus is the promised warrior-king Messiah. Yet when Jesus is crucified, all hope is lost. Jesus was dead, and he had not ushered in the promised kingdom. Some disciples who were departing Jerusalem after this crushing defeat express the painful realization with these words: *We had hoped that he was the one who was going to redeem Israel* (Lk 24:21).

With the resurrection, hope for the kingdom is renewed, but it is still anchored to popular conceptions of this coming kingdom. Luke's account in Acts informs us that Jesus appeared to the disciples *over a period of forty days and spoke about the kingdom of God* (Ac 1:3). One might think that forty days of instruction would be enough time to clear up all their misconceptions about the kingdom, but pre-understandings die hard. So, when Jesus mentions that in a few days they will be *baptized with the Holy Spirit*, the disciples assume he is talking about inaugurating the Messiah's political kingdom. They ask, *Lord, are you at this time going to restore the kingdom to Israel* (Ac 1:6)? This is another indication that we have correctly interpreted John the Baptist's understanding of his baptism metaphor in terms of end-time judgment. Of the possible meanings for this metaphor, overwhelming end-time judgment is the only one which explains the disciples' assumed connection between John's expression, *baptized with the Holy Spirit,* and the restoration of the kingdom to Israel.

Jesus immediately endeavors to correct this misunderstanding. The misunderstanding is not so much the expectation, but the timing of it. John did predict end-time judgment, but that judgment will come later. And the disciples do not need to know *the times or dates the Father has set by his own authority* for this end-time judgment (Ac 1:7). Jesus wants them to know what they need to do now to build the kingdom, and he gives new meaning to John's expression. The baptism with the Holy Spirit, from Jesus' perspective at the beginning of Acts, is not concerned with eliminating the wicked in fiery judgment. This is probably why Jesus omitted the final words of John's expression *and with fire* (Lk 3:16). Jesus uses John's metaphor to describe another overwhelmingly powerful experience with the Spirit, one in which the disciples will be endued with power for witnessing to their world (Ac 1:8).

Although Jesus is not speaking of the end-time destruction of God's enemies, he may still have some of John's emphasis in mind. The baptism with the Holy Spirit still has a winnowing effect in the book of Acts; however, the emphasis is not on burning up the chaff (the Spirit's effect on the wicked), but rather, on gathering the grain into the barn (the Spirit's effect on the righteous). The wind of the Spirit still separates the grain (repentant believers in Christ) from the chaff (those who reject Christ) with two demonstrated effects. First, when the wind of the Spirit blows upon the repentant in the book of Acts, it confirms or validates their entrance into God's kingdom (into his barn) by endowing them with visible prophetic gifts. Secondly, these Spirit-endowed believers are enabled to boldly proclaim the message of the kingdom, causing further separation of the grain and the chaff as their listeners respond to the message.

The role of the Holy Spirit in accomplishing Luke's goal of certainty

The preceding paragraph naturally leads into a discussion on the role of the Holy Spirit in Luke's strategy for giving certainty to his readers. John A. Darr sees the Spirit in Luke-Acts as the source of accrediting or legitimating that something reflects the divine point of view. He notes that even the

Scriptures are accredited by the Holy Spirit.[30] William Shepherd feels that Darr does not go far enough in his evaluation of the Spirit's function, because "he does not connect this function of the Spirit with Luke's intent to provide 'certainty' (Luke 1:4)."[31] For Shepherd, what is at issue in Luke's stated goal is "reliability." Are "the traditions which have been passed down" reliable? The Spirit's primary function in the narrative is to ensure this reliability.[32] Shepherd's conclusion also does not go far enough, because he does not specify clearly how the Spirit ensures reliability in the narrative. As a result, he is unable to find a consistent picture of the reception of the Spirit in Luke's theology.[33] A clear understanding of the Spirit's function in the context of Luke's strategy will demonstrate that Luke's theology of Spirit reception is entirely consistent and coherent.

The mere mention of the Spirit in a narrative does not ensure reliability. Because the Spirit is invisible, the reader needs proof that the Spirit is actually present and that he does validate what is being said and done. Prophets who claim a connection to the Spirit are not always right. Four hundred prophets told Ahab that the Lord would give Ramoth Gilead into his hand. Only Micaiah predicted otherwise. Zedekiah and the other prophets also claimed to have the approval of the Spirit. It was not the claim of divine inspiration which validated the prophet, but the fulfillment of his prophecy (1 Kgs 22:5-38).

The need for validating proof of the Holy Spirit's influence is also important today. Where we serve in Ivory Coast, West Africa, there are many "prophets" who claim to be led by the Spirit of God, but lead many astray. Self-proclaimed prophets have always been a problem. Hopefully, most Christians are not gullible enough to believe everyone who claims to have the Spirit's approval.

Luke was also aware of the need for proof. He did not ask his readers to rely on his word that his characters were validated by the Spirit. Instead, he carefully recorded the tangible and visible evidence of the Spirit's activity in the life and ministry of his Spirit-anointed witnesses. The most common

---

[30] Darr, p. 52-53.

[31] Shepherd, p. 40.

[32] Shepherd, p. 112. Shepherd cites the following passages as examples where the Spirit "assures the reliability of human characters" Luke 1:35, 41-44, 67; 2:25-27, 36; 3:16; 10:21; Acts 2:1-4; 4:8, 31; 5:32; 6:3, 5; 7:55; 8:29, 39; 9:17; 10:20, 44-46; 11:15, 24, 28; 13:1-3, 9, 52; 15:8, 28, 16:6-7; 19:6, 21; 20:22-23, 28; 21:4.

[33] Shepherd, p. 183.

proof of the Spirit's activity in the Old Testament and in Jewish literature during Luke's time was fulfilled prophecy (Dt 18:15-22; Is 38:7; 44:26; 55:11). This is why fulfilled prophecy is so important in Luke-Acts. It is the essence of Luke's argumentation.

Two key prophecies are particularly important for Luke's strategy: one which validates Jesus as Messiah (Lk 4:18-19) and one which validates his disciples as God's end-time community of prophets (Ac 2:17-21). There is near consensus among scholars on the programmatic value of these prophetic passages.[34] A key factor in both of these prophecies is the anointing of the Spirit. Jesus quotes Isaiah's messianic prophecy, *The Spirit of the Lord is on me, because he has anointed me...* (Lk 4:18; Is 61:1). Peter quotes Joel's end-time prophecy, *In the last days, God says, I will pour out my Spirit on all people* (Ac 2:17; Jl 2:28). The verb *pour out* is used for anointing in the Old Testament, because oil was poured out on the person being anointed (1 Sam 10:1; 2 Kgs 9:3).[35] Joel uses this anointing imagery to describe the Spirit's descent on the end-time community. Both speakers claim that these prophecies are being fulfilled at that moment (Lk 4:21; Ac 2:16). How do we know their word is reliable?

To be convincing, Luke must give tangible proof. He does this in two ways. First of all, the descent of the Spirit on these two occasions is accompanied by tangible signs. The Spirit descended on Jesus *in bodily form like a dove* and a voice from heaven gives approval (Lk 3:22). On the day of Pentecost, the descent of the Spirit was accompanied by *a sound like the blowing of a violent wind* and visible *tongues of fire* which *came to rest on each of them* (Ac 2:2-3). On another occasion, *the place where they were meeting was shaken* (Ac 4:31).

Secondly, the anointing with the Spirit is attested by the phenomenal and perceptible effects he produces. In Luke-Acts, visible or perceptible phenomena are mentioned in every account in which the presence of the Spirit is indicated. The most common phenomenon is prophecy. Joel predicted that, in the last days, those who are anointed with the Spirit will prophesy. Numerous individuals or groups who receive the Spirit or who are filled with the Spirit in Luke-Acts do prophesy (Lk 1:41, 67; 9:21, 44; 18:31-33; 21:5-36; Ac 1:5, 8; 2:17-18, 38-39; 5:9; 11:28; 21:10-11). Each time a Spirit-filled

---

[34] See Craig S. Keener, *The Spirit and the Gospels in Acts: Divine Purity and Power*, Peabody, MA, Hendrickson , 1997, p. 190, 200, 205; Shepherd, p. 163, Robert B. Sloan, "'Signs and Wonders': A Rhetorical Clue to the Pentecost Discourse," *Evangelical Quarterly* 63, 1991, p. 225; Huub van de Sandt, "The Fate of the Gentiles in Acts: An Intertextual Study," *Ephemerides Theologicae Lovanienses* 66, 1990, p. 56-77; Johnson, *Literary Function*, p. 41.

[35] The Septuagint uses the compound verb *epicheô* with the preposition "upon" (*epi*) added. Luke uses the simple form of the verb "pour out" (*ekcheô*), but uses the same preposition in the sentence.

character in Luke's story predicts future events and at least some of those events are fulfilled within the narrative, proof is accumulated for the fulfillment of Joel's prophecy. Several groups speak in tongues (Ac 2:4; 10:46; 19:6), a phenomenon which Peter equates with prophesy (Ac 2:16).[36] On the day of Pentecost, this phenomenon certainly served as tangible proof of the Spirit's outpouring as the disciples were supernaturally enabled to speak the native languages of those in the crowd (Ac 2:5-12).

Luke is not limited to prophetic words to prove that Joel's prophecy is being fulfilled in the early church. Prophetic acts and qualities also demonstrate that Luke's characters have received Joel's promised prophetic anointing. In other words, Luke's Spirit-filled characters act like the great prophets of the Old Testament. They speak the word of God boldly (Ac 4:31; 9:27-28; 13:46; 28:31), heal the sick and cast out demons (Lk 7:21-22; Ac 5:12-16; 10:38; 19:11-12), do signs and wonders (Ac 2:22, 43; 5:12; 6:8; 8:13; 14:3; 15:12), and curse those who oppose the proclamation of God's word (Ac 13:9-11). They have visions (Ac 7:55; 10:11-16; 16:9) and revelations (Ac 21:1), they are led by the Spirit (Lk 2:26-27; 4:1; Ac 10:19; 11:2; 13:2; 16:6-7; 20:23), they have extraordinary wisdom (Ac 6:3), faith (Ac 6:5; 11:24) and joy (Ac 13:52). By these phenomena, the disciples demonstrate that they have received a prophet's anointing, fulfilling Joel's end-time prophecy.

The Spirit's role in validating the fulfillment of these end-time prophecies is not limited to Jesus and his initial disciples. Luke intentionally writes his account to show that other groups have also been validated by the Spirit. Echoes of Pentecost are intended to demonstrate the legitimate incorporation of other groups into God's end-time kingdom community by showing that they also have experienced the fulfillment of Joel's prophecy. Samaritans and Gentiles were both traditionally excluded from Jewish worship, but when believers from both groups received the promised Holy Spirit with visible signs, their incorporation into the messianic kingdom community was an inescapable conclusion (Ac 8:14-18; 10:44-46; 11:15-18).

Validating Samaritan believers

The specific visible signs are not identified in the case of the Samaritan believers, but something perceptible indicated that the Samaritan believers

---

[36] Peter tells his audience that the phenomenon they just witnessed *is* what was spoken by the prophet Joel. According to Paul, speaking in tongues which is interpreted has a similar function and value to prophecy (1 Cor 14:2-5). At Pentecost speaking in tongues is interpreted by their hearers.

did, in fact, receive the Spirit (Ac 8:17), something which was not perceptible previously (Ac 8:16). The text also states that *Simeon saw that the Spirit was given at the laying on of the apostles' hands* (Ac 8:18). The logical conclusion is that the Samaritan believers manifested some visible prophetic gift associated with Spirit anointing elsewhere in Luke-Acts, when the Apostles laid their hands on them and prayed, such as speaking in tongues and prophecy.[37] Before such a visible manifestation of the Spirit, it was assumed that they had not received the Holy Spirit (Ac 8:16). This is a logical conclusion from Joel's prophecy and from the apostles' own experience. Joel promised that God would pour out his Spirit on all people and that they would prophesy (Ac 2:17-18). The Apostles' own experience confirmed this prophecy. When God poured out his Spirit on them, they spoke in other tongues, which they considered to be equivalent to prophecy (Ac 2:4, 16). When the Samaritan believers did not manifest any type of prophetic gift, the Apostles concluded that they had not yet received the Spirit anointing promised by Joel. When they did manifest such visible gifts, their entrance into God's end-time community was validated. They had received the Spirit.

Validating Gentile believers

The events do not fall into the same chronological order, but the logic is the same in the validation of Gentile believers. *While Peter was still speaking… the Holy Spirit came on all who heard the message* (Ac 10:44). The circumcised believers knew that these Gentile believers had received the promised gift of Spirit anointing (notice the verb "to pour out"), because *they heard them speaking in tongues* (Ac 10:45-46). The Spirit had validated the incorporation of Gentiles into the end-time kingdom community through the visible manifestation of prophetic gifts. Peter and the other Jewish believers drew the logical conclusion that there was nothing preventing them from receiving water baptism as a sign of this incorporation (Ac 10:47-48).

Validating John's disciples

Two more validating episodes need to be considered. They are written back-to-back in Luke's orderly account. They are obviously written to underline both the parallels and the differences between the two accounts. They both concern

---

[37] Turner, p. 373.

believers with closer ties to John the Baptist than to the disciples who accompanied Jesus. Apollos, who taught in Ephesus, *knew only the baptism of John* (Ac 18:25), and some disciples in Ephesus had received John's baptism but had not been *baptized into the name of the Lord Jesus* (Ac 19:3-5). In both episodes the believers are deficient in something and need a remedy to follow the way of God correctly. The two remedies are strikingly different and therefore significant.[38] Apollos only needs the *way of God* explained to him *more adequately* (Ac 18:26). The Ephesian disciples need the identity of the Messiah explained. They must be re baptized *into the name of the Lord Jesus*. Paul then lays hands on them for them to receive the Holy Spirit (Ac 19:4-6). Why are these remedies so different? Even though the details are not as clear in these episodes, the same logic which explains the validation of the disciples at Pentecost, the Samaritan believers, and the Gentile believers provides the best explanation here.

The interpretation of these two episodes is more complex than the other validating episodes. There are two major reasons for this complexity. First, we simply do not have enough historical information regarding John's disciples. Luke's intended readers must have had an understanding we do not have. We are forced to speculate on why these believers needed to be validated. Secondly, there are difficulties with the translation of three important phrases, most likely due to theological bias.

What can we know about these disciples of John the Baptist? It is clear that their understanding of the *way of God* was deficient. Priscilla and Aquila needed to explain to Apollos *the way of God more adequately* (Ac 18:26). The disciples in Ephesus either had not heard about the Holy Spirit or, more likely, about receiving the Holy Spirit (Ac 19:2). Paul felt the need to explain to them some of the implications of John's teaching. John *told the people to believe in the one coming after him* (Ac 19.4). Paul explained that the coming one is Jesus. We know from the gospels that John exercised his ministry in the area around the Jordan (Lk 3:3). We know that Jesus came to the Jordan to be baptized by him and then returned to Galilee from there a short time later (Mt 3:13; Lk 3:21; 4:1). We also know that John identified Jesus as the Messiah and later had doubts about his identity (Lk 7:19). Finally, we know that John had his own disciples who followed him. John's disciples are compared to, Jesus' disciples in Luke's gospel (Lk 11:1).

Given the existence of a separate group of disciples and the relatively

---

[38] Joseph A. Fitzmyer, *The Acts of the Apostles: A New Translation with Introduction and Commentary*, The Anchor Bible 31, New York, Doubleday, 1998, p. 637.

short period of John's ministry after his encounter with Jesus, we might sur-
mise that John had some disciples who followed him in his ministry before
Jesus came along but who did not witness Jesus' baptism and identification as
Messiah. If so, these disciples would have expected the Messiah to come but
not known his identity. Such a scenario would explain some of the details in
the Ephesian episode. Others might have overheard some of John's doubts
about Jesus' messianic identity and not heard Jesus' reply to these doubts.
Still others may have been convinced of Jesus' messianic identity but not
have had the opportunity to physically follow Jesus and hear his teachings.
Many would not have heard of the subsequent experiences and teachings of
his disciples. This may have been the case with Apollos.

The point of these observations and hypotheses is that we cannot lump
John the Baptist's disciples into one category. They represent different levels
of understanding and commitment to the way of God and require varying
responses in accordance with that knowledge and commitment.[39] We cannot
simplistically assume that, just because Apollos and the Ephesian disciples
only knew John's baptism, they were not real 'Christians.' This is the error
committed by some interpreters when they try to make a distinction between
John's disciples and Jesus' disciples, claiming John's disciples are not 'Christian' while Jesus' disciples are. This type of labeling assumes that Luke is
addressing the problem of distinguishing between true believers and nomi-
nal believers. It is unlikely and probably anachronistic to think that Luke is
addressing such a problem. Luke presents the picture of a marginalized and
persecuted church. Those who believed were added to their number, but others were afraid to join them (Ac 5:12-16). It is difficult to imagine that some
'disciples' would pretend to be 'Christian.' The key to salvation in Luke-Acts
is not baptism in the name of the Lord Jesus but repentance. Both John's
baptism and baptism in the name of the Lord Jesus involve repentance (Lk
3:3; 13:3; Ac 2:38; 11:18; 17:30).[40] In light of this, both John's disciples and
Jesus' disciples are adherents to the 'way of God' and thus candidates for receiving all the benefits of salvation (Ac 9:2; 18:25-26; 19:9).

---

[39] Barrett, p. 885.

[40] In fact, parallels in the accounts would indicate that Peter's call to repentance at Pentecost is
purposely modeled after John the Baptist's preaching. Both hearers ask, "What shall we do (Lk
3:12; Ac 2:37)?" Both Peter and John link baptism with repentance and the forgiveness of sins (Lk
3:3; Ac 2:38). Both messages are for all peoples (Lk 3:6; Ac 2:17). Both talk about crooked ways
(Lk 3:5; Ac 2:40) and God's salvation (Lk 3:6; Ac 2:21). Both exhort their hearers with many other
words (Lk 3:18; Ac 2:40). Tannehill, p. 40-41 and David Ravens, *Luke and the Restoration of Israel*,
JSNT 119, Sheffield, Sheffield Academic Press, 1995, p. 151.

Validating Apollos

To fully understand this example of Spirit validation, attention needs to be given to the translation of certain terms. Apollos is described as *an eloquent man... **with a thorough knowledge of** the Scriptures, who spoke **with great fervor** and taught about Jesus accurately* (Ac 18:24-25). The translations given in bold type are the result of assumptions based on a particular theological bias. It is assumed by many interpreters that disciples of John must first become disciples of Jesus, symbolized by baptism in the name of the Lord Jesus, before they can receive the Holy Spirit. This interpretation may seem legitimate because it appears to match some of the details in the next episode about some other disciples of John in Ephesus (Ac 19:1-6). Interpreters also assume that this sort of remedy must have also been necessary for Apollos. It has even been suggested that the reader would be expected to read this remedy back into the Apollos episode.[41] Assuming this theological presupposition to be true, translators needed to find a way to translate expressions in the Apollos episode so as not to imply any influence of the Spirit in the ministry of Apollos.

Let's take a quick look at the terms behind the translation in bold type above. The first term, *dunatos*, translated here with the expression *with a thorough knowledge of*, literally means "powerful" and is used to describe the powerful prophetic ministries of both Jesus and Moses. They were both *powerful in word and deed* (Lk 24:19; Ac 7:22). The noun form, *dunamis*, is also used constantly for the power of the Holy Spirit in Luke-Acts (Lk 1:35; 4:14; 24:49; Ac 1:8; etc.). Luke uses the same term and the same grammatical structure to describe Apollos, Jesus and Moses. The only difference is that he has substituted the term *Scriptures* for the term "word". However, the term "word" is also used in the description of Apollos. What is translated above as *an eloquent man* literally means "a man of the word". Given the literary context of Luke-Acts, a better translation of this phrase would be "a man of the word...powerful in the Scriptures,"[42] indicating a prophetic enabling of the Spirit in the teaching ministry of Apollos.

The NIV translates the second expression, *zeòn tô pneumati*, with the words *with great fervor* and gives the following footnote, "or with fervor *in the Spirit*." The footnote means that a significant minority of translators in

---

[41] Shepherd, p. 226.
[42] New American Standard has the translation "mighty" in the Scriptures.

the NIV translation committee disagreed with the way the text was translated. The Greek literally means "boiling in the Spirit" or "boiling in spirit," depending on whether the term is referring to the divine Spirit or to the human spirit. The term can mean either. Context must determine which translation is correct. Undoubtedly for theological reasons, the majority of the NIV translation committee has decided that Luke is referring here to the human spirit. Considering Luke's emphasis on the powerful influence of the Spirit and the use of this expression to refer to the influence of the Holy Spirit elsewhere in Luke-Acts (Lk 2:27; 4:1; 10:21; Ac 6:10), Luke's intended reader would naturally assume that he is talking about the Holy Spirit here as well.[43] Apollos spoke "with fervor in the Spirit."

The above conclusions concerning the translation of a few key terms change the description of Apollos considerably. If our translations are correct, Apollos is "a man of the word...powerful in the Scriptures" who "spoke fervently in the Spirit and taught about Jesus accurately." With this description, there is no need for further validation. The Spirit has already validated Apollos' entry into the messianic kingdom community. He is clearly prophetically endowed with the Spirit. Like Jesus, Moses and other great prophets, Apollos is "powerful in word." This Spirit-endowed capacity is highlighted and confirmed by his ability *to speak boldly in the synagogue* (Ac 18:26). Speaking boldly (*parrêsiazomai*) is a common characteristic of Spirit-filled characters in Luke-Acts (Ac 2:29; 4:13, 29, 31; 9:27-28; 13:46; 14:3; 19:8; 26:26; 28:31). Apollos is also "fervent in the Spirit." There is therefore no further need for validation. Like Jesus' disciples on the day of Pentecost, he does not need to be rebaptized. He does not need to be filled with the Holy Spirit, because he is already filled.[44]

Validating the Ephesian disciples

In the very next episode, Paul finds a group of "believers" in Ephesus and asks them, *Did you receive the Holy Spirit when you believed* (Ac 19:1-2). Again,

---

[43] The term Spirit/spirit (*pneuma*) is used 106 times in Luke-Acts. 20 times, a textual clue is provided to indicate clearly that Luke is referring to an evil or impure spirit. 4 other times, the context makes it clear that the text refers to a spirit as opposed to a living person. 5 times, a personal pronoun indicates clearly that the term refers to the human spirit. The other 77 occurrences of the term probably all refer to the Holy Spirit. Only 3 occurrences are seriously debated (Lk 1:17, 80 and Ac 18:25). Since Luke mostly uses the term to refer to the Holy Spirit and he makes it a habit of giving some sort of textual clue when he does not refer to the Holy Spirit, it seems logical to understand the term to refer to the Holy Spirit when there are no textual clues to indicate otherwise.

[44] See I. Howard Marshall, *The Acts of the Apostles: An Introduction and Commentary*, Grand Rapids, Eerdmans, 1980, p. 304.

we must question the translation. The NIV places the alternative translation "after" in a footnote. "When you believe" is the choice of the majority. A significant minority of translators on the committee prefer the translation "after you believed." This decision was made in spite of the fact that Greek aorist participles, such as the one translated here, are much more commonly used to refer to antecedent action (action occurring before the main verb). The majority of translators on the committee chose to understand coincident action in this case (action occurring at the same time as the main verb).[45] The aorist participle can be used to refer to events which are coincident in time if it "denotes the same action that is expressed by the verb."[46] This means that, for this participle to be translated "*when* you believed," the translator must conclude that receiving the Spirit denotes the same action that is expressed by the verb believing. Obviously, the theology of the interpreter, not Greek grammar, is the deciding factor in this translation.[47] But the decision to use the translation *when you believed* does not solve the problem of the underlying assumption for Paul's question. The question implies that Paul entertains the possibility of "believers" not receiving the Holy Spirit at conversion. Regardless of which translation we adopt, the problem still remains. How can Paul even ask such a question, if it is assumed that the reception of the Spirit takes place at conversion?

No explanation is given as to why Paul would ask this question. According to Romans 8:9, those who believe have received the Holy Spirit. If Paul had already developed this theology of the reception of the Spirit at conversion, and if he is referring to the same experience in Acts 19, it is nonsensical for him to ask such a question. If we lay aside the presupposition of Paul's theology in the book of Romans long enough to consider this text in the context of Luke-Acts, the same logic which gave coherence to the Samaritan episode and to the Gentile episode also works well here. Paul probably asked the question because there was no evidence of Spirit anointing. In other words, he did not see prophetic gifts manifested among the Ephesian believers demonstrating the Spirit's presence and influence.[48] He asked the ques-

---

[45] Wallace, p. 555.

[46] Ernest de Witt Burton, *Syntax of the Moods and Tenses in New Testament Greek*, Edinburgh, T. & T. Clark, 1898, p. 59, 64.

[47] Ervin, *Conversion*, 1984, p. 61-63. Dunn clearly states his theological reasons. He writes, "As most commentators recognize, πιστεύσαντες in 19.2 is a coincident aorist; it is Paul's doctrine that a man receives the Spirit when he believes," p. 87.

[48] Barrett, p. 894.

tion presumably because he had not been there long enough to determine whether or not these proofs were evident among them. Later, when Paul *placed his hands on them, the Holy Spirit came on them, and they spoke in tongues and prophesied* (Ac 19:6). Again we see that the reception of the Holy Spirit is closely connected with the manifestation of prophetic gifts. Given the parallels with the Pentecost, Samaritan and Gentile episodes, it is reasonable to assume that the non-reception of the Spirit was perceived because of a lack of prophetic gifts, and the reception of the Spirit was perceived when these gifts were manifested. The Spirit anointing with the evidence of prophetic gifts serves to validate the inclusion of these disciples of John in the end-time kingdom community. The only problem with this interpretation is that it appears to be in contradiction with Paul's theology as expressed in Romans 8. We will deal with this issue in chapter 8.

The Spirit's indispensable role in Luke's strategy

Luke's goal is to give his readers certainty (Lk 1:4) on two major troublesome issues: the messianic identity of Jesus (Ac 2:36) and the growing Gentile membership of the church (Ac 28:28). He does this by demonstrating how the Spirit of God has tangibly and visibly validated Jesus as Messiah and confirmed the incorporation of the Gentiles into the church. There are at least two major components to this strategy. First, Luke shows how end-time prophecies concerning these issues have been fulfilled. Secondly, Luke recounts how the characters in the story became convinced of the fulfillment of these prophecies. We are mainly concerned with the first component: how Luke demonstrates the fulfillment of end-time prophecies.

Jesus is validated as the Messiah (the anointed one) when the Spirit visibly descends upon him (Lk 3:22) and anoints him for ministry in accordance with Isaiah's end-time messianic prophecy (Is 61:1-2; Lk 4:17-21). Jesus' miraculous ministry demonstrates this prophetic anointing (Lk 7:21-22). Jesus' disciples are validated as end-time anointed prophets when the Spirit visibly descends on them (Ac 2:2-3) and anoints them for ministry in accordance with Joel's end-time prophecy (Jl 2:28-32; Ac 2:16-21). The disciples' miraculous ministry then demonstrates their prophetic anointing (Ac 2-28). Each new group, Samaritans, Gentiles and followers of John the Baptist, experiences a similar prophetic anointing with similar miraculous and tangible proof (Ac 8, 10-11, 18-19). These anointed prophets are then miraculously and tangibly led by the Spirit to share the Good News with the Gentile nations (Ac 2-28). The Spirit of God validates each step of the process with tangible signs. It is difficult to overestimate the importance of this tangible evidence in understanding both Luke's strategy and his view of the Spirit.

Chapter 5

Anointed with the Spirit

*Understanding the vocabulary of Spirit
experiences in Luke-Acts*

In the previous chapter, we discovered the importance of fulfilled prophecy in Luke's strategy for giving his readers assurance concerning the messianic identity of Jesus and the surprising predominantly Gentile membership of the early church. Two of those prophecies are of particular importance for his strategy: a prophecy from Isaiah quoted by Jesus to describe his anointing and ministry (Is 61:1-2/Lk 4:17-21) and a prophecy from Joel quoted by Peter to describe the disciples' anointing and ministry (Jl 2:28-32/Ac 2:16-21). In this chapter, we will see how these structural elements help to define the vocabulary Luke uses to describe Spirit experiences in Luke-Acts. First, we will look at some similarities between Luke's Spirit-anointed characters and some of the great Old Testament prophets, and we will see how these similarities further substantiate the fulfillment of these two prophecies concerning end-time prophetic anointing. Secondly, we will examine the similarities between the prophetic anointing of Jesus and that of his disciples, and we will examine how these parallels help in determining the meaning of Luke's terminology. Thirdly, we will discover how the vast majority of Luke's expressions describing experiences with the Spirit fit into two related series of metaphors which reflect the ideas and vocabulary used in these two prophetic passages. In other words, we will learn how Luke uses Spirit-experience vocabulary to demonstrate the fulfillment of these prophecies. Finally, all of these observations lead to the almost inevitable conclusion that Luke uses a variety of metaphors and allusions to the Old Testament to demonstrate that Jesus and his disciples have been anointed with the Spirit to function as end-time prophets.

Parallels with Old Testament prophets in Luke-Acts

Luke's penchant for literary parallels is well known among biblical scholars.[1] Two types of parallels are easily discernible in Luke-Acts: parallels within Luke's narrative between different characters and events, and parallels between the characters and events of Luke-Acts and characters and events in the Old Testament. The first two chapters of Luke's gospel contain a clear example of parallel descriptions of John the Baptist and Jesus. In this instance the parallels are used to show contrast, demonstrating the superiority of Jesus. For example, John *will be great in the sight of the Lord* (Lk 1:15) and *will be called a prophet of the Most High* (Lk 1:76), but Jesus *will be great and will be called the Son of the Most High* (Lk 1:32). This contrast between John and Jesus is maintained throughout Luke-Acts.

Many of the parallels employed by Luke underline the similarities between the various prophetic figures in Luke-Acts and prophets of the Old Testament. Luke describes the life and ministry of Jesus and his disciples in a manner which recalls events in the lives of some of the major Old Testament prophets. He uses these parallels to draw attention to the continuity between Spirit-anointed characters in Luke-Acts and Spirit-anointed prophets in the Old Testament. Such parallels contribute to the credibility of his claim that Isaiah's and Joel's end-time prophecies are being fulfilled through the prophetic ministry of Jesus and his disciples.

---

[1] Clark, p. 102. Marguerat and Bourquin affirm that, among New Testament authors, Luke is the "champion" for this technique, p. 161. Darr affirms that this conclusion is "firmly established" among Lukan scholars, p. 158. He writes, "The literature on this subject is voluminous. We can cite only a sample: Hastings (1958:50-75); Swaeles (1964); Hinnebusch (1967); Wink (1968:42-44); Hammer (1970); Brown (1971 [77]); Dubois (1973); Franklin (1975:67-69); Hausman (1976); Minear (1976); Johnson (1977:58-59); Büchele (1978:91-92); George (1978); Tiede (1980); Moessner (1983; 1989)," note 11, p. 193-94.

Jesus – the prophet like Elijah and Elisha

Luke begins his account of the ministry of Jesus with an unusual story from Jesus' hometown of Nazareth. None of the other gospel writers tell of this event, but it is extremely important in Luke's account. After astonishing the inhabitants of his hometown by declaring Isaiah's messianic prophecy to be fulfilled in their hearing (Lk 4:17-21), Jesus appears to purposefully alienate them. Luke tells us that *all spoke well of* Jesus *and were amazed at the gracious words that came from his lips* (Lk 4:22a). Recognizing that Jesus was one of their own, the people of Nazareth hoped to benefit from Jesus' Spirit-endowed power (Lk 4:22b-23).[2] If Jesus is the promised Messiah, then they should be the first to benefit from his powerful position. Jesus' reply not only appears to eliminate them as beneficiaries, but hints at the idea that their enemies will be the new beneficiaries.

For those who live in countries in which political nepotism is highly discouraged, the undertones of this episode may be less apparent. But even in countries such as the United States, inhabitants of the hometown or home state of an elected official hope to gain some benefit from their compatriot's newly acquired power. In much of the biblical world as well as in many countries today, such expectations are considered completely normal. The president's hometown receives enormous governmental subsidies. His family and friends get the best jobs. People are not offended by this; it is expected. What did the inhabitants of Nazareth hope to receive from their new and powerful David-like king? They had already heard about some of the things he did in Capernaum (Lk 4:23). Expectations were undoubtedly very high.

Why did Jesus respond the way he did? It is very likely that he wanted to clarify his current earthly mission, which he had just described using a messianic prophecy in Isaiah. Anticipating his own rejection, Jesus pronounces the maxim that *no prophet is accepted in his hometown* (Lk 4:24), and then gives two examples to emphasize his point. Elijah gave aid to the Sidonian widow of Zarephath and not to any widows in Israel. Elisha cleansed Naaman, the Syrian, and not any of the lepers in Israel (Lk 4:25-27). In giving these two illustrations, Jesus soundly rejects any idea of 'hometown advantage' for his Spirit-anointed mission. The mission of Jesus is universal. The two examples from the ministries of Elijah and Elisha foreshadow the wit-

---

[2] See Green, p. 214-15 and Robert Tannehill, " 'Cornelius' and 'Tabitha' Encounter Luke's Jesus," *Gospel Interpretation: Narrative-Critical & Social-Scientific Approaches*, Jack Dean Kingsbury ed., Harrisburg, PA.: Trinity Press International, 1997, p. 139.

ness of the church to the ends of the earth in the book of Acts. The prophecy
from Isaiah, the maxim concerning the unpopularity of prophets and the two
illustrations from the lives of Old Testament prophets introduce a paradigm
shift for the mission of the Messiah. Jesus does not compare himself to King
David, as we would expect from the jubilant revelations of deliverance expressed in Luke's introductory chapters, but to Elijah and Elisha. Jesus did
not quote the messianic prophecy in Isaiah chapter 11, which clearly points
to a messianic warrior-king, who *will give decisions for the poor of the earth...
strike the earth with the rod of his mouth* and *slay the wicked with the breath of his
lips* (Is 11:4). Instead, he quotes the messianic prophecy from Isaiah 61:1-2,[3]

> *The Spirit of the Lord is on me,*
> *because he has anointed me*
> *to preach good news to the poor.*
> *He has sent me to proclaim freedom for prisoners*
> *and recovery of sight for the blind,*
> *to release the oppressed,*
> *to proclaim the year of the Lord's favor* (Lk 4:18-19).

Even so, Jesus' compatriots in Nazareth probably understood Isaiah's
prophecy (Is 61:1-2/Lk 4:18-19) as another reference to the promised
warrior-king, who would deliver Israel from her enemies. The verb used for
proclaiming good news (*euangelizō/bassar*) is most often used in the Old
Testament for announcing good news from the battle field (1 Sam 31:9;
2 Sam 1:20; 4:10; 18:19-20; 26:31; 1 Kgs 1:42; 1 Chr 10:9). The 'poor' in
Isaiah's day, who initially received this good news, could easily be identified
as the oppressed exiles. By analogy, the 'poor' in Jesus' day could easily be
applied to oppressed Israel under Roman domination. The parallel phrase of
proclaiming freedom for the prisoners would support such an understanding.
Freedom for the oppressed is also specifically mentioned. *Recovery of sight for
the blind* was probably understood in a metaphoric sense.

In the following chapters, Luke reveals how Jesus understood the fulfillment of this messianic prophecy. Jesus preaches the good news of the
kingdom (Lk 4:43). This good news includes casting out evil spirits with
authority and healing the sick (Lk 4:31-41). He frees or releases those held

---

[3] The quote in Luke leaves out "to heal the brokenhearted" from Is 61 and adds "to release the
oppressed" from Is 58:6.

captive by the devil (Lk 4:36, 41; 13:16; Ac 10:38). He also forgives or releases those held captive by sin (Lk 5:17-26). He literally gives sight to the blind (Lk 7:21). These are definitely not the activities of a warrior-king! Jesus is presented as a healing prophet. Two healing episodes in chapter 7 are particularly interesting because of the parallels with the two illustrations from the Old Testament already mentioned in chapter 4. Joel Green lists the following parallels between the healing of Naaman the Syrian and the healing of the Roman centurion's servant:

Chart 4: Parallels between Naaman and Luke's centurion

Luke 7	*2 Kings 5*
The centurion: a well-respected Gentile officer (v. 2, 4-5).	Naaman: a well-respected Gentile officer (v.1).
Intercession of Jewish elders in the healing (v. 3-5).	Intercession of a Jewish girl in the healing (v. 2-3).
The centurion does not meet Jesus (v. 6-9).	Naaman does not meet Elisha (v. 5-10).
The healing takes place at a distance (v. 10).	The healing takes place at a distance (v. 14).[4]

As David Ravens points out, the probability that these parallels are not the result of pure coincidence is increased by the fact that the first three parallels are not included in Matthew's version of this same event.[5] Luke appears to have purposely chosen these details to bring to mind similar details in Old Testament accounts of prophetic events. David Ravens also mentions three parallels between the raising of the widow's son at Zarephath (1 Kgs 17:10-24) and at Nain (Lk 7:11-15). In both stories, the dead man is the son of a widow, there is a meeting at the city gate, and the son is given back to his mother by the prophet.[6]

It is significant that immediately following these two episodes the crowds conclude that *a great prophet has appeared among us* (Lk 7:16) and John the Baptist sends envoys to question Jesus concerning his messianic identity (Lk

---

[4] Green, p. 284.
[5] Ravens, p. 130.
[6] Ravens, p. 132.

7:18-20). The crowds conclude that Jesus is *a great prophet* because he performs miracles like the great prophets Elijah and Elisha. When John's envoys ask Jesus if he is the promised Messiah, Jesus describes his own Elijah/ Elisha-like prophetic ministry in a manner which recalls Isaiah's messianic prophecy (Lk 7:21-23; Is 61.1-2). The implied answer is that Jesus is the promised Messiah or Anointed One. His prophetic ministry proves that he has been anointed by the Spirit and that he is fulfilling Isaiah's prophecy. In fact, the entire section from Luke chapter 4 to chapter 7 is recounted in such a way as to demonstrate that Jesus is the messianic prophet described in Isaiah 61. This does not contradict the jubilant declarations of Jesus as messianic king in the first three chapters of Luke. He will be *exalted to the right hand of God* (Ac 2:33; 7:56) and will one day return as king (Lk 19:12) to *judge the world with justice* (Ac 17:31). But for now, he is anointed and empowered to carry out a prophetic healing and deliverance ministry (Ac 10:38). God has *accredited* him through the tangible proofs of *miracles, wonders and signs* (Ac 2:22).

These proofs are tied to Luke's goal to give assurance to his readers that Jesus is the promised Messiah. Like the characters in Luke's account, his readers probably held the predominant expectation of a coming warrior-king. They probably would have understood Isaiah's prophecy in those terms. By choosing to recount these events in the life of Jesus in this order (Lk 1:3), Luke is assuring his readers that Jesus is God's Anointed even though he has not yet fulfilled the prophecies concerning the coming warrior-king.

Parallels with Elijah and Elisha do not stop with Luke chapter 7. In Luke chapter 9, the feeding of the five thousand recalls the event in which Elisha feeds a hundred men with twenty loaves (Lk 9:10-17; 2 Kgs 4:42-44). In both stories the anointed prophet tells his disciples to give the people something to eat. In both stories the disciples inform the prophet of their lack of adequate resources. The prophet's instructions are repeated in both stories. There is food *left over* in both stories. As in chapter 7, the Elijah/Elisha parallel is placed in sequence with questions concerning Jesus' messianic identity. Both before and after this story, speculations from the people are revealed that Jesus might be *Elijah* or *one of the prophets of long ago ... come back to life* (Lk 9:8, 19). Then, when Jesus asks his disciples concerning his identity, Peter replies, saying that Jesus is *the Christ* [Anointed] *of God* (Lk 9:20).

Two further allusions to Elijah and Elisha are recorded at the end of chapter 9. When the people of a Samaritan village did not welcome Jesus, his disciples asked him if they *should call fire down from heaven to destroy them* (Lk 9:54) as Elijah did in the Old Testament (2 Kgs 1:10, 12). The episode reveals not only the close association in the minds of Jesus' disciples between Elijah and Jesus but also the misunderstanding of his disciples concerning his mission. The disciples' response appears to be another example of expectations for a Messiah who would execute judgment upon his enemies. The second allusion has to do with excuses given for not following Jesus at the very end of the chapter. One person asks to first go and bury his father. Another asks to go back and say goodbye to his family (Lk 9:59, 61). Both recall the Old Testament story of Elisha's call. Elisha asked Elijah if he could first kiss his father and mother goodbye (1 Kgs 19:20). Jesus' reply shows that he was also thinking of this same Old Testament episode, because Elisha was plowing his field when Elijah called him (1 Kgs 19:19). Jesus replies to his reticent would-be disciples, *No one who puts his hand to the plow and looks back is fit for service in the kingdom of God* (Lk 9:62).

This particular parallel is significant because it establishes links not only between Jesus and an Old Testament prophet (Elijah) but also between his disciples and an Old Testament prophet (Elisha). The important factor is the relationship between the prophet and his disciples, not the specific link with an individual prophet. Jesus has already compared himself with Elijah and Elisha. He is not simply a prophet like Elijah. He is a prophet like all the miracle producing prophets of the Old Testament. But, just as Elijah needed to pass his prophetic ministry on to Elisha (1 Kgs 19:16), Jesus must also pass his prophetic ministry on to his disciples.

Luke exploits the possibilities for parallels between Elijah and his disciple, and Jesus and his disciples, on two other very important occasions: ascension and Pentecost. There are two clear verbal parallels between the beginning of the book of Acts and this passage in Luke 9, which is so closely associated with Elijah/Elisha stories. In the verses just before these allusions to Elijah's call of Elisha, Luke tells us that, *As the time approached for him to be taken up* (*analêmpsis*) *to heaven, Jesus resolutely set out for Jerusalem* (Lk 9:51). The word *taken up* is used 3 other times in Luke-Acts (Ac 1:2, 11, 22). Each is a reference to the ascension of Christ. It is also used in the Septuagint Greek version of 2 Kings 2:10-11 to refer to Elijah's ascension. A further verbal parallel exists between this sentence in Luke 9 and another event connected logically to the ascension in Acts. Both Luke 9:51, where the ascension is mentioned and followed by Elijah/Elisha parallels, and Acts 2:1 start with a rare and almost identical expression. The expression is never used elsewhere in the entire Bible. Since the English translation of these verses does not show a clear parallel, the following is a more wooden translation of the Greek:

In the fulfillment of the days of the ascension (Lk 9:51)
(*en tô sumplêrousthai tas hêmeras tês analêmpseôs*)

In the fulfillment of the day of Pentecost (Ac 2:1)
(*en tô sumplêrousthai tên hêmeran tês pentêkostês*)

What do these stories have in common? The common theme in all three stories, the Elijah ascension story, the ascension story in the book of Acts and the narrative in Luke chapter 9, is that of passing the baton from one prophet to another. Every episode in Luke chapter 9 contributes to the development of this theme. It begins with Jesus sending out the twelve to do the same things he did in the preceding chapters: preach the kingdom of God and heal the sick (Lk 9:1-9). In the feeding of the five thousand, it is the disciples who must carry on the work by giving the crowd something to eat (Lk 9:10-17). After Jesus explains how he must suffer, die and be raised to life, he instructs his disciples in how to follow him (Lk 9:18-27). A discussion of his *departure* on the mount of transfiguration follows these instructions (Lk 9:28-36). In the next episode, where the disciples' inability to cast out a demon is compared with the deliverance accomplished by Jesus, Jesus asks, *how long shall I stay with you?* (Lk 9:37-45), emphasizing the disciples' need for further equipping before his departure. Next, the disciples argue among themselves *as to which of them would be the greatest*, presumably in the coming kingdom. The chapter ends with a reference to Jesus' ascension followed by the Elijah parallels associated with the call of Elisha, Elijah's successor (Lk 9:51-62). Chapter 10 starts with Jesus sending out the seventy-two, an episode which parallels the beginning of chapter 9. All of these episodes are held together by the common theme of Jesus preparing his disciples to carry on his prophetic end-time ministry after his departure.

The greatest preparation for the disciples' continued ministry, highlighted by the comparison with the story of Elijah's ascension, is the reception of the Spirit. In both stories the reception of the Spirit is anticipated immediately before the ascension and occurs almost immediately after the ascension. In both stories there is an explicit connection between the ascension and the reception of the Spirit. In 2 Kings 2:1-15, Elisha must see Elijah *taken up* in order to inherit a double portion of his Spirit. Peter also explicitly connects the ascension of Jesus with the outpouring of the Spirit in his explanation of the events at Pentecost (Ac 2:33). The two stories also exhibit parallel results. Elisha picks up Elijah's mantle and begins to do the same things Elijah did (2 Kgs 2:13-14). This is seen as clear evidence that *the Spirit of Elijah is resting on Elisha* (2 Kgs 2:15). Just as Elisha received the Spirit of Elijah in order to carry on the prophetic work of Elijah, so Jesus' disciples must receive the Spirit of Jesus (cf. Ac 16.7) to carry on his prophetic work. In the light of these parallels with Elijah and Elisha, the reception of the Spirit at Pentecost should be understood as a prophetic anointing for ministry.

Jesus – the prophet like Moses

Luke does not limit his Old Testament prophetic images to Elijah and Elisha. Jesus is also a prophet like Moses. In Deuteronomy 18:15 Moses said, *The LORD your God will raise up for you a prophet like me from among your own brothers. You must listen to him.* Peter affirms that Jesus is that prophet (Ac 3:22), and Stephen implies the same (Ac 7:37). A third allusion to Moses' promise is probably contained in the story of the transfiguration. Both Moses and Elijah appear in glorious splendor and talk with Jesus. The episode ends with a voice from a cloud saying, *This is my Son, whom I have chosen; listen to him* (Lk 9:35). In light of all the other prophetic parallels in the passage, the command to *listen to him* is probably parallel to the same words in Deuteronomy.

Another parallel is probably present in the sending out of the 72 (Lk 10:1-12). God told Moses to consecrate 70 elders to help carry the burden of the people. God took of the Spirit that was on Moses and *put the Spirit on the seventy elders* and *they prophesied* (Nb 11:25). Two men, Eldad and Medad, had remained in the camp. The Spirit *also rested on them, and they prophesied* (Nb 11:26). Joshua wanted Moses to put a stop to this, but Moses replied, *I wish that all the LORD's people were prophets* (Nb 11:28-29). One interesting fact increasing the probability of an intended parallel here is that two variants exist for Luke 10:1. Some manuscripts say that the *Lord appointed 70 others* and some manuscripts say that he appointed 72. Both numbers are probably derived from the story in the book of Numbers, one considering the total number of consecrated elders, including Eldad and Medad, to be 70, the other thinking that Eldad and Medad are an addition to the 70. Besides the number of workers appointed, there are several other points of contact. In both stories, there is a lack of workers. The 70 elders are to help Moses *carry the burden* (Nb 11:17). Jesus says that *the workers are few* (Lk 10:2). If we include events in Luke chapter 9 in this comparison, close disciples of the anointed leader in both stories try to prevent someone from performing prophetic acts. Joshua wants to prevent Eldad and Medad from prophesying (Nb 11:28). Jesus' disciples want to prevent a man from driving out demons (Lk 9:49).

The transfer of the Spirit in Numbers chapter 11 has no parallel in Luke chapters 9 and 10. However, we learn from the parallel episode of the sending out of the 12 that Jesus gives his disciples *power and authority to drive out all demons and cure diseases* (Lk 9:1). Jesus himself was anointed with the Spirit to perform these functions (Lk 4:18ss; Ac 10:38). The logistics may be difficult to define, since the disciples are not endowed with the Spirit until Pentecost, but the ultimate source for the disciples' healing ministry in Luke chapters 9 and 10 must be the Spirit. The parallel with the elders in Numbers chapter 11 would tend to imply this conclusion as well.[7] The real points of contact for the transfer of the Spirit in Numbers chapter 11 happen on the day of Pentecost. The Spirit is transferred from an individual to a larger group in both episodes. The Spirit is on or upon (*epi*) the recipients in both episodes. Finally, the results are the same in both episodes. Those who receive the Spirit prophesy (Nb 11:25-26; Ac 2.4, 16-18).

Several other terms and phrases in Luke-Acts have verbal parallels in the life of Moses and thus contribute to the idea that Jesus is the prophet like Moses. On the mount of transfiguration Moses and Elijah discuss Jesus' *departure* (*exodus*), which brings to mind the exodus from Egypt (Lk 9:31; Ex 19:1). Jesus' reference to driving out demons *by the finger of God* (Lk 11:20) recalls the conclusion reached in Pharaoh's court concerning the signs and wonders which Moses performed (Ex 8:19). In his Pentecost speech Peter adds the word *signs* (Ac 2:19, *semeia*) to the prophecy from Joel and then describes Jesus as *a man accredited by God to you by miracles, wonders and signs* (Ac 2:22). *Signs and wonders* is a stock phrase used 11 times in the Old Testament[8] and once in Acts (7:36) to refer to the mighty deeds of God performed in Egypt through Moses. It is also used in Acts to describe the deeds performed by Jesus and his disciples (Ac 2:22, 43; 4:30; 5:12; 6:8; 14:3; 15:12). It is therefore no surprise to find both Jesus and Moses described in Luke-Acts as being *powerful in word and deed* (Lk 24:19; Ac 7:22).

No single Old Testament prophet provides a sufficient model for de-

---

[7] Turner writes that the analogy from Numbers 11 "would suggest Luke considered the disciples' power and authority to derive from some kind of 'extension' of the Spirit on Jesus, just as Jesus' own power and authority derived from the Spirit upon him (4.14; cf. 1.17, 35 and Acts 10.38)," p. 338.

[8] Ex 7:3; Dt 4:34; 6:22; 7:19; 26:8; 29:3; 34:11; Neh 9:10; Ps 135:9; Jer 32:20-21.

scribing the ministry of Jesus. Therefore, Luke uses a variety of prophetic images to paint his prophetic portrait of Jesus. He is a prophet like Moses in that he is powerful in word and deed and rejected by those to whom he is sent (Ac 7:35-36, 52). Like Moses, he appears in glory, participates in an exodus and we must listen to him (Lk 9:29-36). He is a prophet like Elijah and Elisha in that he heals the sick, raises the dead (Lk 7:1-17) and transfers the Spirit to his disciples at his ascension (Ac 2:33). He is like Isaiah's anointed servant in that he proclaims good news to the poor, delivers the captives and gives sight to the blind (Lk 4:18-19; 7:22).

Prophetic images are not limited in Luke-Acts to the ministry of Jesus. Luke seems intent on demonstrating that all of his Spirit-endowed characters look and act like the prophets of the Old Testament. Spirit-endowed characters in the first two chapters of Luke, Zechariah and Simeon, receive divine revelation and prophesy (Lk. 1:6; 2:25-32). It is John the Baptist and not Jesus who is presented as *the prophet Elijah* who must come to prepare the way before the Lord (Lk 1:17; 7:27; cf. Mal 3:1; 4:5-6). Luke uses the style and vocabulary from Old Testament prophetic introductions to introduce John the Baptist at the beginning of his ministry (Lk 3:1-2; Jer 1:1-2). Echoes from prophets of the Old Testament are also used to paint the prophetic portrait of the disciples in the book of Acts. In our next section we will discover some parallels with the prophet Jesus. But some of the parallels with Old Testament prophets have no equivalent parallel in the life and ministry of Jesus. For example, Philip is transported by the Spirit like the prophets Elijah and Ezekiel (Ac 8:39; 1 Kgs 18:12; 2 Kgs 2:16; Ez 11:24). Paul's call resembles that of Ezekiel (Ac 9:4; 26:16; Ez 1:28-2:1). God encourages Paul with words which recall the divine encouragement received by the prophet Jeremiah (Ac 18:9-10; Jer 1:5-8). All these parallels seem to lead to the conclusion that Luke-Acts fulfills Moses' wish that *all the Lord's people were prophets and that the Lord would put his Spirit on them* (Nb 11:29).

The disciples – prophets like Jesus

The numerous parallels between Jesus and his disciples are a well-known feature of Luke's style which interpreters have studied for centuries.[9] Of

---

[9] For a summary and evaluation of the history of the interpretation of these parallels see Clark, p. 63-72 and Susan Marie Praeder, "Jesus-Paul, Peter-Paul, and Jesus-Peter Parallelisms in Luke-Acts: A History of Reader Response," *SBL Seminar Papers* 23, ed. Kent Harold Richards, Chico CA, Scholars Press, 1984, p. 23-39.

particular importance for our study of Spirit experiences are the parallels between the inauguration of Jesus' ministry and the inauguration of the disciples' ministry. Both ministries are introduced with a scriptural quotation referring back to an experience with the Spirit in a preceding passage (Lk 3:21-22; 4:18-19; Ac 2:1-4, 16-21). A large number of interpreters agree that these passages are both parallel and programmatic for the following chapters.[10] In other words, Luke purposefully chose these quotations and included the various parallel details in these inaugural passages to draw attention to the similarities between the two events and to introduce the narrative which follows. The following is a list of some important parallels concerning these two inauguration passages:

1. A Spirit experience following a time of prayer precedes each passage. Jesus was praying when the Holy Spirit descended on him (Lk 3:21-22). The disciples were *constantly in prayer* in the days before they were all *filled with the Holy Spirit* (Ac 1:14; 2:4).

2. Each passage has an inaugural speech containing a long prophetic quotation from the Old Testament (Lk 4:17-19; Ac 2:16-21), describing the Spirit experience just mentioned as a prophetic anointing. Quoting from Isaiah 61:1 Jesus says, *The Spirit of the Lord is upon me because he has anointed me to preach good news* (Lk 4:18). Quoting from Joel, Peter says, *In the last days, God says, I will pour out my Spirit on all people … and they will prophesy* (Ac 2:17-18).

3. The speaker in each episode explicitly states that the prophecy is being fulfilled in that moment. Jesus says, *Today this scripture is fulfilled* (Lk 4:21). Peter says, *This* [the events which just occurred at Pentecost] *is what was spoken by the prophet Joel* (Ac 2:16).

4. Details in each quotation serve as an introduction to and as clues to the understanding of the prophetic ministry which follows. Details in the narrative then refer back to and explain the fulfillment of the prophetic quotation. In the first quotation, Jesus is *anointed* to *preach*

---

[10] For a list of a few of the authors, see the bibliographic notes in R. F. O'Toole, "Parallels between Jesus and His Disciples in Luke-Acts: A Further Study," *Biblische Zeitschrift* 27, 1983, p. 195 and Turner, p. 343.

good news to the poor, release (*aphesis*) to the prisoners and the oppressed and recovery of sight to the *blind* (Lk 4:18-19). After casting out demons and healing the sick in Capernaum, Jesus tells the people, *I must preach the good news of the kingdom of God to the other towns also, because that is why I was sent* (Lk 4:43). Jesus continues to cast out demons and heal the sick in the following chapters. He also forgives (*aphiēmi* the verbal form of *aphesis*) sins (Lk 5:20). This use of the term helps to explain how Jesus proclaimed *release* to the prisoners and the oppressed. Among other things, he released them from their sins. When John sends messengers to ask Jesus if he is *the one who was to come* (a reference to the Messiah or *Anointed* One, see Lk 3:15-16), Jesus replies, *Go back and report to John what you have seen and heard: The blind receive sight, the lame walk, those who have leprosy are cured, the deaf hear, the dead are raised, and the good news is preached to the poor* (Lk 7:20-22). Peter summarizes Jesus' ministry by telling *how God anointed Jesus of Nazareth with the Holy Spirit and power, and how he went around doing good and healing all who were under the power of the devil* (Ac 10:38). The sequence of events is intended to demonstrate how Jesus' prophetic ministry of casting out demons, healing the sick, forgiving sins and preaching the good news fulfills Isaiah's prophecy.

In the second prophetic quotation, Peter proclaims that *God will pour out* his *Spirit on all people … and they will prophesy* (Ac 2:17-18). The *Spirit* comes *on* the Samaritan believers (Ac 8:16-17), the believers in the house of Cornelius (Ac 10:44) and the Ephesian believers (Ac 19:6). Luke specifies that the Spirit was *poured out* on the Gentiles in the house of Cornelius (Ac 10:45) and that the Ephesian believers *prophesied* (Ac 19:6). The sequence of events and the repetition of key terms clearly show that Joel's prophecy is fulfilled among these various groups of believers.

5. Both passages speak of "release." Jesus is anointed to preach release (*aphesis*) for the prisoners and the oppressed (Lk 4:18). Peter instructs his listeners to repent and be baptized for the forgiveness (*aphesis*) of their sins (Ac 2:38).

6. In both passages, public amazement followed by a question concerning the identity of the person(s) receiving the Spirit is observed. After Jesus announces the fulfillment of Isaiah's prophecy, *all* the

people *were amazed* at his words and asked, *Isn't this Joseph's son* (Lk 4:22)? After hearing the disciples speaking in their own languages, the crowds were *utterly amazed* and asked, *Are not all these men who are speaking Galileans* (Ac 2:7)?[11]

All of these parallels are part of a very important larger structure of parallels. They are part of what Luke Timothy Johnson has called a "stereotyped pattern of description" for "Men of the Spirit" in Luke-Acts.[12] According to Johnson, all of these "Men of the Spirit ... speak the Word of God with boldness and power, certify that preaching by the performance of signs and wonders, and stimulate among their hearers a response of acceptance and rejection."[13] One can observe several other elements in Luke's stereotyped pattern of description not mentioned by Johnson. All of these "men of the Spirit" are commissioned for their service. Prayer plays a big role in the preparation of each one. All of them confront suffering and persecution. Many are arrested and must give testimony before religious and civil authorities. The chart on the following page summarizes this stereotyped description.

It should be pointed out that many, if not all, of these parallel acts fulfill prophetic statements made by Jesus. Jesus commissioned his disciples with a prophecy. (Ac 1:8). He promised to give the Holy Spirit to those who pray (Lk 11:13). He prophesied that the disciples would receive the power of the Holy Spirit to be his witnesses (Ac 1:8). He gave them the authority to cast out demons and heal the sick (Lk 9:1-2; 10:9). He predicted that they would be persecuted, arrested and brought before kings and governors (Lk 21:12). However, they should not worry about what to say, because Jesus would give them *words and wisdom that none ... will be able to resist or contradict* (Lk 21:14-15). The Holy Spirit will teach them what to say (Lk 12:11-12; cf. Ac 6:10). They were even taught to rejoice during times of persecution because that would show that they were like the prophets (Lk 6:22-23; cf. Ac 5:4).

---

[11] Tannehill, p. 29, "The Composition of Acts 3-5: Narrative Development and Echo Effect," SBL Seminar Papers 23, ed. Kent Harold Richards, Chico CA, Scholars Press, 1984, p. 230 and Etienne Samain, "Le discours programme de Jésus à la synagogue de Nazareth Luc 4.16-30," *Foi et vie*, 11, 1971, p. 41.

[12] Johnson, *Function*, p. 58.

[13] Johnson, *Function*, wrongfully limits this description to the major characters in Luke-Acts: the apostles, Stephen, Philip, Barnabas and Paul who are portrayed as prophets as opposed to other believers who are not, p. 41. Some of the other less important characters also exercise prophetic gifts and should also be considered as 'men of the Spirit.' Ananias of Damascus, for example, who is placed by Johnson in the category of other believers, receives instructions and a prophecy in a vision and performs a sign in an act of healing (Ac 9:10-18).

Chart 5: Stereotyped prophetic descriptions of "men of the Spirit" in Luke-Acts

	Jesus	Moses	Peter and the apostles	Stephen	Philip	Paul and Barnabas
Commission	Lk 4:18-19	Ac 7:34-35	Ac 1:8	Ac 6:3-6	Ac 6:3-6	Ac 13:1-3
Prayer	Lk 3:21		Ac 1:14	Ac 6:6	Ac 6:6	Ac 13:3
Filled with the Spirit[14]	Ac 10:38		Ac 2:4; 4:8, 31	Ac 6:3, 5; 7:55	Ac 6:3	Ac 9:17; 11:24
Bold speech *parrêsia parrêsiazômai*	Lk 24:19; Ac 10:36	Ac 7:22	**Ac 2:29;**[15] **4:13, 29, 31**	Ac 6:10	Ac 8:4	**Ac 9:27, 28; 13:46; 14:3; 19:8; 26:26; 28:31**
Signs and wonders *terata sêmeia dunameis*	Lk 24:19; **Ac 2:22**; 10:38	**Ac 7:22, 36**	**Ac 2:43; 5:12**	**Ac 6:8**	**Ac 8:6, 13**	**Ac 14:3; 15:12; 19:11**
Acceptance or rejection	Ac 2:23, 36; 10:39	Ac 7:27, 35, 39	Ac 2:41; 4:2, 4, 21	Ac 6:11-14; 7:54, 57-59	Ac 8:12	Ac 14:4; 28:24
Arrest	Lk 22:54		Ac 4:3, etc.	Ac 6:12		Ac 16:19; 21:27, etc.
Testimony	Lk 22:66-23:3		Ac 4:8s, etc.	Ac 7:1s	[Ac 8:26-39]	Ac ch. 23-26
Suffering and persecution	Lk 24:46; Ac 2:23	[Ac 7:52][16]	Lk 21:12-17; Ac 5:40-41	Ac 7:58	[Ac 8:1][17]	Ac 16:22-23; 21:30-33

This entire prophetic description could be summarized in one statement made by Jesus, *everyone who is fully trained will be like his teacher* (Lk 6:40). Jesus is the model and his disciples continue to do what *Jesus began to do and teach* (Ac 1:1). Just as Jesus was *powerful in word and deed* (Lk 24:19), so his disciples preach the word of God boldly (Ac 4:31) and perform signs and wonders (Ac 2:43; 5:12; cf. Ac 2:22). They heal the sick and the lame, give sight to the blind, cast out demons and raise the dead (Ac 3:1-10; 5:16; 9:9, 17-18; 32-42; cf. Lk 7:21-22). And all of this is accomplished through the

---

[14] The section framed with bold lines corresponds with Luke Timothy Johnson's observations.

[15] The references in bold font show where there are verbal parallels with the Greek terms in the left-hand column.

[16] This text infers that all the prophets were persecuted. Therefore, by association Moses was also persecuted.

[17] This verse directly precedes the episode about Philip and speaks of a general persecution which caused the dispersion of the disciples. Philip was one of those dispersed disciples.

power of the Holy Spirit in both the ministries of Jesus and his disciples (Lk 4:14, 18; Ac 2:17-18; 4:31).

The significance of prophetic parallels in Luke-Acts

What is the significance of all these prophetic parallels for understanding Luke's descriptions of Spirit experiences? Luke understands the descent of the Spirit on Jesus at his baptism (Lk 3:22) to be the beginning of the fulfillment of the messianic prophecy in Isaiah 61:1-2. The Spirit descended *on* Jesus and *anointed* him for his ministry. Luke understands the ministry of Jesus, his powerful words and deeds, to be the fulfillment of some of the other details in this passage. He *preached the good news* of the Kingdom of God, good news which included casting out demons, healing the sick and forgiveness for sin. He gave sight to the blind and delivered those held captive by the devil.

The parallels with the life and events of Old Testament prophets demonstrate clearly that these acts in the life and ministry of Jesus are prophetic acts. This is an easy conclusion. Even the crowds understand that Jesus is a *great prophet* (Lk 7:16). But, according to the crowds, he could be John the Baptist raised from the dead, or Elijah, who was predicted to prepare the way for the coming Messiah, or one of the prophets of long ago come back to life (Lk 9:7-8, 19).

The more difficult conclusion is to determine that this prophet is the promised Messiah. How could he be the Messiah when he has neither delivered Israel from her enemies nor established his righteous kingdom on earth like the prophets predicted? This is why John sends envoys to ask if Jesus really is the Messiah (Lk 7:18-20). In his response, Jesus emphasizes the fact that his prophetic acts match Isaiah's messianic prophecy (Lk 7:22-23). Jesus' disciples are convinced that he is the Messiah (Lk 9:20), but they obviously do not understand his mission. They argue about who will be the greatest in this coming kingdom (Lk 9:46). They also want to call fire down from heaven on any opposition (Lk 9:54).

What is the significance of these events for our study of Spirit experiences in Luke-Acts? For Luke, they serve to give assurance to his readers (Lk 1:4) that Jesus is the Messiah and that the church led by his disciples has God's approval. Jesus' prophetic acts demonstrate that he is the Messiah anticipated in Isaiah 61, and the disciples' prophetic acts demonstrate that they have received the prophetic Spirit promised in Joel 3. What is even more significant for our purposes is the understanding we gain from Luke's strategic presentation of these events concerning his use of vocabulary for describing Spirit experiences. Jesus' anointing in Luke chapters 3 and 4 is a prophetic anointing. He is anointed to function as a prophet. The disciples in Acts are also anointed to function as prophets. The logic of the fulfillment of the two programmatic prophecies and the multitude of parallels between Old Testament prophets, Jesus and his disciples all point to this obvious conclusion.

The dual function of the Spirit in Luke-Acts

This interpretation, which sees Spirit experiences in Luke-Acts primarily as prophetic anointings enabling them to function as prophets, creates problems for some interpreters. It is clear from other New Testament passages that the Spirit plays an obvious role in salvation. Not only does the Spirit prepare people for salvation (Jn 16:8), but the reception of the Spirit is an integral part of salvation (Rom 8:9). The reception of the Spirit is also clearly connected to salvation in Luke-Acts. On the day of Pentecost Peter proclaims that all who repent and are baptized in the name of Jesus for the forgiveness of their sins *will receive the gift of the Holy Spirit*, because the promise of the Spirit is *for all whom the Lord our God will call* (Ac 2:38-39). The last phrase in Peter's proclamation is obviously intended to recall the last line of Joel's prophecy, *And everyone who calls on the name of the Lord will be saved* (Jl 2:31; Ac 2:21).

A problem occurs with the interpretation of these passages if we assume that the function of the Spirit is the same for these New Testament authors. This is not the case. Paul and John connect the active presence of the Spirit to the work of salvation. In other words the Spirit is connected to salvation because the Spirit does the saving work. However, Luke does not address the issue of how the saving work is accomplished in the life of the believer. According to Luke, the condition necessary for salvation to occur is repentance and the tangible proof that salvation has occurred is the presence of the Spirit producing prophetic signs.

Two functions of the Spirit are easily discernible from these observations. First, the tangible presence of the Spirit in the lives of believers is proof of God's approval and their salvation. This function corresponds with Luke's strategy to give certainty to his readers. The Spirit ensures reliability. If a character in the story is inspired and led by the Holy Spirit, the other characters in the story and the readers know that their words and acts are reliable and represent God's will.

The second function of the Spirit corresponds to the characters' experience with the Spirit in the story. The Spirit enables them to produce prophetic signs. According to chapter 4, these two functions are closely related. We know that Luke's characters are inspired and led by the Spirit if their words and actions resemble those of Old Testament prophets. These Spirit empowered characters within the story are considered to have received a prophetic anointing similar that of Moses, Elijah or Elisha. The Spirit's function, then, in the life of the believers in Luke-Acts is to anoint them, enabling them to exercise prophetic ministries.

Spirit-experience metaphors

Having established the framework for Luke's presentation of the Spirit and the function the Spirit plays in Luke's strategy, we are in a better position to understand the vocabulary he uses for Spirit experiences in Luke-Acts. Luke uses a variety of metaphors, mostly borrowed from the Septuagint (a Greek version of the Old Testament including the Apocrypha), to describe the activity of the Spirit in the life and ministry of the characters in Luke-Acts. Since the Spirit is invisible and his activity is invisible, biblical authors use comparisons or metaphors to describe his activity. Occasionally, the comparisons are explicitly stated. For instance, Luke tells us that *the Holy Spirit descended on him* [Jesus] *in bodily form like a dove* (Lk 3:22). Most of the time, the comparison or analogy is not explicitly stated. For example, when Jesus quotes Isaiah and says, *The Spirit of the Lord is on me, because he has anointed me*, he is not literally speaking of the Spirit being transformed into some sort of liquid which is poured out on Jesus' physical body. Jesus is using an analogy. The onset of the Spirit's influence in the life of Jesus is likened to the gesture of anointing with oil. Just as the oil is visibly or manifestly poured out on the head of a person being anointed (see, for example, Ex 29:7), the Spirit manifests his presence in the life of that person. A clear example of this relationship is David's anointing. When *Samuel took the horn of oil and anointed* David, *from that day on the Spirit of the Lord came upon David in power* (1 Sam 16:13). Both of the key Old Testament prophecies discussed above (Is 61.1-2; Jl 2.28-32) use this analogy of anointing. Isaiah's prophecy,

which Jesus quoted, talks about Jesus being anointed with
the Spirit. Joel's prophecy, which Peter quoted, talks about
the Spirit being *poured out* on the disciples.

Luke appears to have chosen most of his metaphors
to correspond with these two very important end-time
prophecies. First of all, there is a series of spatial metaphors which allude to
the physical gesture of anointing. Besides the two verbs already mentioned,
"anointed" (Lk 4:18; Ac 10:38) and "poured out" (Ac 2:17-18, 33; 10:45),
there is a whole series of metaphors referring to the movement of the Spirit
from above down to the individual. Just as oil descends, falls or comes on or
upon one who is anointed, so the Spirit descends (*katabainô*, Lk 3:22), falls
(*epipiptô*, Ac 8:16; 10:44; 11:15) and comes (*erchomai*, Lk 1:35; Ac 1:8; 19:6)
on or upon (*epi*) characters in Luke-Acts. After descending from above, the
Spirit is said to be on or upon (*eimi epi*, Lk 2:25; 4:18) the individual.

A study of the use of these terms in the Septuagint is very enlightening.
Luke appears to have borrowed most of his vocabulary to describe Spirit experiences from this version.[18] The only expression used by Luke but not found
in the Septuagint is "baptized with the Spirit."[19] One of Luke's favorite spatial
metaphors, the Spirit "on" (*epi*) someone, is used much more frequently for
Spirit experiences than any other spatial metaphor in the Septuagint.[20]

Although Luke is undoubtedly indebted to the Septuagint for his Spirit
vocabulary, he is very selective in his choices. It is revealing to note the Septuagint expressions Luke does not use. He does not employ the expression
to "leap on"[21] (*hallomai, ephallomai*) used for some of the judges and the first
kings of Israel (Jgs 14:6, 19; 15:14; 1 Sam 10:6, 10; 11:6; 16:13), probably because the expression is too closely associated with empowerment for military
exploits. He does not use the expressions "to put the Spirit on" (*epitithêmi, epi*,
Nb 11:17, 25; Is 44:3) or the "Spirit rested on" (*anapauô epi, epanapauomai*, Nb
11:25, 26; 2 Kgs 2:15; Is 11:2). This is surprising, since Luke probably alludes
to passages where these expressions are used (Lk 10:1; cf. Nb 11:25-29; Lk

---

[18] A. George, "L'Esprit Saint dans l'œuvre de Luc," *Revue Biblique* 85, 1978, p. 528; Odette Mainville,
L'Esprit dans l'œuvre de Luc, Héritage et Projet 45, ed. André Charron, Richard Bergeron and Guy
Couturier, Ville Mont-Royal, Québec, Éditions Fides, 1991, p. 323-32. See her bibliographic
references supporting this affirmation, n. 5, p. 323-24.

[19] Roger Stronstad, *The Prophethood of All Believers: A Study in Luke's Charismatic Theology*, JPTSS 16, ed.
John Christopher Thomas, Rickie D. Moore and Steven J. Land, Sheffield Academic Press, 1999, p. 26.

[20] Nb 11:17, 25, 26, 29; 23:7; Jgs 3:10; 11:29; 14:6, 19; 15:14; 1 Sam 10:6, 10; 11:6; 16:13; 19:20, 23;
2 Kgs 2:9, 15; 2 Chr 15:1; 20:14; Jl 3.1, 2; Is 11:2; 32:15; 42:1; 44:3; 59:21; 61:1; Ez 2:2; 3:24; 11:5.

[21] Translated *come upon in power* in the NIV.

24:49; cf. 2 Kgs 2:14-15). I suggest that this choice reflects Luke's desire that his Spirit-experience expressions more closely reflect the analogy of anointing. Finally, Luke uses none of the Old Testament expressions referring to the Spirit "in" (*en*) or "in the midst of" (*en mesô*) his people. In the Septuagint the Spirit was in Joseph (Gn 41:38), in Balaam (Nb 24:2), in Joshua (Nb 27:18), in Israel (Is 63:11) and in the midst of Israel (Hag 2:5). The other half of the uses of this expression in the Septuagint are found in the prophecies of Ezekiel referring to end-time kingdom restoration (Ez 11:19; 36:26, 27; 37:6, 14). Since Luke is also concerned with the fulfillment of end-time prophecies, one might expect him to use these expressions. But this is not the case. Neither are there any apparent allusions to these passages. These expressions are found in Paul's letters (Rom 8:9, 11; 1 Cor 3:16; 6:19; 2 Ti 1:14), but not in Luke-Acts. This is another indication that Luke and Paul are probably not looking at the same passages or talking about the same things.

A second series of metaphors in Luke-Acts alludes to God's end-time *promise* in Joel's prophecy to *give* his Spirit to all people. At the end of Luke's gospel, Jesus tells his disciples that he will send *on* (*epi*) them *the promise of his Father* (Lk 24:49). The use of the preposition "on" is unusual for sending a promise but consistent with the other Spirit expressions in Luke-Acts. At this point in the story, the Spirit is implied in this promise but not mentioned. In Jesus' immediate instructions, however, he uses another term which is closely associated with the Spirit in Luke-Acts: power. The disciples are told to stay in the city until they *have been clothed with power from on high* (Lk 24:49; cf Lk 1:35; 4:18; Ac 1:8). At the beginning of the book of Acts, Jesus repeats his instructions telling his disciples to *wait for the gift* his *Father promised, which you have heard me speak about* (Ac 1:4). This time he makes two references to the Holy Spirit. *In a few days*, says Jesus, the disciples *will be baptized with the Holy Spirit* (Ac 1:5). When the disciples misunderstand this prophetic word, Jesus clarifies the expression, telling his disciples that they *will receive power when the Holy Spirit comes on* (*epi*) them (Ac 1:8).

The logical sequence of these statements and the repetition of terms clearly indicate that what the Father has "promised" to send "on" the disciples is the Holy Spirit. The following chart shows how carefully Luke has placed these terms in parallel sequences. Bold print in this chart is used to show obvious parallels presented in a chiastic pattern (AB/BA and ABCDE/ED-CBA). Luke 24:49 is repeated in the chart because it shows chiastic parallels with both Jesus' instructions in Ac 1:4-5 and the explanation of those instructions in Ac 1:8. A detailed study of the second chiasm in this chart reveals that the only element from Luke 24:47b-49 not closely paralleled in Acts 1:8 is the command to "stay in the city" which is paralleled in Ac 1:4. The phrase *I am going to send* [on][22] *you what my Father has promised* (Lk 24:49a) is clearly parallel with the phrase *when the Holy Spirit comes on you* (Ac 1:8b). The promise of the Father is undoubtedly to send the Holy Spirit on the disciples.

Chart 6: Parallels between Luke 24 and Acts 1

Luke 24	Acts 1
[49] *I am going to send* [on] *you*	
A) *what my Father has promised;*	B)[4]*Do not leave Jerusalem, but wait for*
B) *but stay in the city until*	A) *the gift my Father promised,*
you have been clothed with power from on high.	[5] *For John baptized with water, but in a few days you will be baptized with the Holy Spirit.*
[47] *repentance and forgiveness of sins will be preached in his name*	
A) *to all nations,*	E) [8] *But you will receive* ***power***
B) *beginning at* ***Jerusalem.***	D) *when the Holy Spirit comes* ***on you;***
C) [48] *You are* ***witnesses*** *of these things.*	C) *and you will be my* ***witnesses***
D) [49] *I am going to send* [***on***] ***you*** *what my Father has promised; but stay in the city*	B) *in* ***Jerusalem***
E) *until you have been clothed with* ***power*** *from on high.*	A) *and in all Judea and Samaria, and to the ends of the earth.*

In these two chapters, Luke employs a literary technique called recapitulation and resumption, often used in New Testament times to knit two volumes together.[23] First, Luke repeats a number of themes in the second volume to recapitulate what he wrote in the first volume (Ac 1:1-3), and

---

[22] We have added the preposition "on" to the NIV translation to better represent the Greek phrase. It is presumably left out of the NIV because of the awkwardness of sending a promise on someone. The unusualness of the expression gives further support to the proposed synonymous parallel.

[23] Aune, p. 117, informs us that Polybius, Strabo, Diodorus, Josephus, and Herodian all used the same technique.

then he resumes the story where he left off (Ac 1:4-11). His first volume had to do with what Jesus began to do and teach: the choice of his disciples, his suffering, resurrection and instructions he gave his disciples just before his ascension. In the resumption, Luke reiterates Jesus' instructions concerning the Holy Spirit and the disciples' witness. Then he expands on the account of his ascension. The chart above shows how carefully Luke repeats Jesus' two basic instructions concerning the Holy Spirit and the disciples' witness in exact opposite order. Jesus instructs his disciples to wait in Jerusalem until they have had the experience with the Holy Spirit which the Father has promised (Lk 24:49; Ac 1:4-5). When they have had this experience, they are to be his witnesses from Jerusalem to the ends of the earth (Lk 24:47-49; Ac 1:8). The two chiastic structures above are well supported by the use of terms in parallel. The metaphors used to describe the disciples' experience with the Spirit are presented in parallel and thus synonymous. The disciples receive the Holy Spirit which the Father has promised and sent. Thus, they are baptized with the Spirit and clothed with power from on high.

Peter makes the connection between the promise of the Father and the Holy Spirit even clearer. First, he quotes a prophecy from Joel in which God promises to *pour out* his Spirit "*on*" all people (Ac 2:17-18). Then, after a series of explanations concerning Jesus' resurrection, Peter again summarizes his explanation of the perceptible phenomena on the day of Pentecost, *He* [Jesus] *has received from the Father the promised Holy Spirit and has poured out what you now see and hear* (Ac 2:33). Then Peter tells those who repent and are baptized that they will also *receive the gift of the Holy Spirit* because the "promise" is for all (Ac 2:38-39). Expressions such as the *gift* or *giving* of the Spirit (Lk 11:13; Ac 2:38; 5:32; 8:18; 10:45; 11:17) and *receiving* the Spirit or the gift of the Spirit (Ac 1:8; 2:38; 8:15, 17; 10:47; 19:2) are clearly linked in Jesus' final instructions (Lk 24:49; Ac 1.4-8) and Peter's Pentecost discourse (Ac 2:1-4, 17-18, 33, 38-39) to God's promise in Joel's prophecy to pour out his Spirit. It is perfectly logical, according to Luke's strategy, that these expressions are intended to call attention to the fulfillment of this prophecy throughout Luke-Acts.

Therefore, the vast majority of expressions used to describe Spirit experiences in Luke-Acts are easily explained by Luke's conviction that these experiences demonstrate the fulfillment of his two key end-time prophecies involving anointing with the Spirit. Jesus is anointed with the Spirit (Lk 4:18-19; Is 61:1-2) and his disciples are anointed with the Spirit (Ac 2:17-21; Jl 3:28-31). Luke's vocabulary is made to order for describing individuals and groups who are anointed with the Spirit. It should probably be noted that the actual term, "anointed," is only used to describe Jesus (Lk 4:18; Ac 10:38), presumably in order to maintain a clear distinction between his identity as the Christ, the Messiah or Anointed One, and those who are simply anointed for ministry. But, if one expression could summarize Luke's description of Spirit experiences in Luke-Acts, it would be "anointed with the Spirit," with the understanding that it refers to a prophetic anointing, an empowering experience for prophetic ministry. In other words, the Spirit empowers the disciples to speak prophetic words and do prophetic acts like the great prophets of the Old Testament.

Only three Spirit-expressions in Luke-Acts are not easily explained with the analogy of anointing. A detailed examination of the two most debated expressions, baptized with the Spirit and filled with the Spirit, is reserved for chapters 6 and 7. The only other expression is *clothed with power from on high* (Lc 24:49). Being clothed (*enduô*) with power or with the Spirit is another expression borrowed from the Septuagint (Jgs 6:34; 1 Chr 12:18; 2 Chr 24:20; Ps 92:1). Even though the metaphor is not specifically derived from the analogy of anointing, it is definitely compatible with it. The spatial relations remain the same. The Spirit comes from above and is "on," not "in," the individual. In fact, "clothed" is a somewhat appropriate metaphor for anointing, since an entire horn was filled with oil and poured out upon the one being anointed (1 Sam 16:1, 13). The psalmist describes Aaron's anointing with these words, *It is like precious oil poured on the head, running down on the beard, running down on Aaron's beard, down upon the collar of his robes* (Ps 133:2). But saying that the anointed person was "clothed" in oil would surely be an exaggeration.

There is, however, a better explanation for Luke's use of this expression, since it is used in close association with the ascension. Jesus is *taken up into heaven* shortly after he leaves instructions for his disciples to wait in the city until they have been *clothed with power from on high* (Lk 24:49, 51). The same two themes are repeated in rapid succession at the beginning of Acts with different words. Jesus promises the disciples that they will receive the power of the Holy Spirit just before he is taken up into heaven (Ac 1:8-9). Even though different terms are used for the ascension in these passages (*anapherô* Lk 24:51, *epairô* Ac 1:9, *analambanô* Ac 1:2, 11; 2 Kgs 2:9-11),[24] the paral-

---

[24] The ascension was already mentioned in a passage filled with allusions to Elijah and Elisha in Lk 9:51-62. The use of synonyms is a common feature in Luke's writing, Cadbury, *Features*, p. 91-93.

lel with the transfer of the Spirit from Elijah to Elisha is difficult to miss. *Clothed with power from on high* probably alludes to Elijah's cloak which *fell from above on Elisha* (2 Kgs 2:13, translation from the Septuagint) as Elijah was being taken up into heaven. Elisha picked up the cloak and used it to perform the same miracle Elijah had just performed, demonstrating that the Spirit of Elijah was now "on" him (2 Kgs 2:11-15). This expression is probably one more Spirit-experience metaphor pointing to a prophetic anointing like that of the great prophets of the Old Testament.

Prophetic anointing

In this chapter, a large amount of evidence has been presented to support the idea that the vast majority of the expressions used in Luke-Acts to describe experiences with the Spirit are derived from the analogy of prophetic anointing. Luke's characters are depicted as anointed prophets, pronouncing prophetic words and performing prophetic acts. Like the prophets of old, they are mighty in word and deed. God has poured out his Spirit on his servants, making them all prophets like the great prophets in the Old Testament.

We have yet to examine the meaning of the two most controversial expressions for experiences with the Spirit: baptized with the Spirit and filled with the Spirit. Do these expressions also refer to prophetic anointing? Given Luke's strategy to demonstrate the fulfillment of his two key prophetic anointing prophecies and his tendency to use vocabulary consistent with those prophecies, it would be surprising to find out that these expressions referred to any other reality. We would certainly need clear evidence to support any other conclusion. In the next two chapters we will discover that the evidence does in fact point to the same conclusion. Baptized with the Spirit and filled with the Spirit are synonymous expressions for the same reality of prophetic anointing.

Chapter 6

Baptized with the Spirit

*T*he interpretation of the expression "baptized with the Spirit" is not only a controversial issue, but an extremely important one in many Christian circles. It is probably the most distinctive doctrine of the Pentecostal and charismatic movements. Non Pentecostal groups are probably just as adamant about their interpretation of this polarizing expression. The debate tends to make people take sides and draw immovable lines in the sand, defining their positions. I am not opposed to strong convictions on biblical doctrines, especially on ones which have such a huge influence on the spiritual life of the church. However, I feel that all too often the various sides of the debate are so busy defending their position that they do not take seriously legitimate biblical inconsistencies highlighted by arguments presented in opposing viewpoints.

In order to give perspective to the debate, I would like to use an illustration from little-league baseball. Imagine a high fly ball hit to short-left-center field. The center fielder, the left fielder and the short stop all start running toward the ball. They have all learned well from their coach to call it. Each one is yelling at the top of his lungs, "I've got it!" The only problem is that they cannot hear each other because they are all yelling so loudly. You can guess the outcome. If you were to capture it on video, it would make a great submission to "America's Funniest Home Videos."

If we compare this illustration to the situation in our churches today, the outcome is not so laughable. It seems that, when it comes to being baptized with the Holy Spirit, everyone is so busy yelling, "I've got it," that we are in danger of letting the ball drop and not benefiting from all God wants to do in and through us to draw the nations to himself. One says, "I've got it because I speak in tongues." Another says, "I've got it because we get everything God has for us at conversion." Still another says, "I've got it because I prayed with faith to receive it." But which of our churches is experiencing God's power like the community of believers in the book of Acts? Maybe you think that God does not intend for us to experience the same phenomena today. But which of us has no further need to seek God's power in his or her life? Which of us can truly say, "I've got it, and I need not ask for more?" Should we not keep on seeking God for all the help he has to offer? Isn't a part of that seeking process listening to other viewpoints and reexamining the Scriptures to see if what they say is true (Ac 17:11)? With this in mind, I invite you to take another look at how Luke uses the expression "baptized with the Holy Spirit."

The meaning of "baptized with the Holy Spirit" in John the Baptist's preaching (Lk 3:15-17)

The people were waiting expectantly and were all wondering in their hearts if John might possibly be the Christ. [16] John answered them all, "I baptize you with water. But one more powerful than I will come, the thongs of whose sandals I am not worthy to untie. He will baptize you with the Holy Spirit and with fire. [17] His winnowing fork is in his hand to clear his threshing floor and to gather the wheat into his barn, but he will burn up the chaff with unquenchable fire."

The expression "baptized with the Holy Spirit" is only used three times in Luke-Acts: once in the Gospel (Lk 3:16), and twice in Acts (Ac 1:5; 11:16). In Luke's Gospel, John prophesied that one more powerful than he would baptize his listeners *with the Holy Spirit and with fire* (Lk 3:16). We have already studied how the use of the verb "to baptize" in the Septuagint, the various metaphors employed by John, and the logic of the passage all lead to the inevitable conclusion that John used this expression to refer to end-time judgment. The expression to *baptize with the Holy Spirit and with fire* evokes an intense image of the unrepentant being overwhelmed and blown away by the wind of the Spirit and destroyed by fire.

This interpretation falls right into line with popular end-time expectations in Jesus' day. John expected the strong wind of the Spirit to disperse Israel's enemies, permitting the restoration of the kingdom of Israel under the leadership of her warrior-king Messiah. So then, John's contrast is not between two different aspects of initiation: its symbol and its reality. It is between two different aspects of end-time judgment: preparation for that judgment and the reality of that judgment. John baptized repentant individuals with water to prepare them for the coming judgment. But Jesus would enact that coming judgment by baptizing all people with the Holy Spirit and fire, separating the unrepentant for destruction by fire and ushering the repentant into the kingdom.

John is a reliable prophetic voice and his prophecy will be fulfilled. His prophecy only repeats what other inspired voices have already predicted in the Old Testament and in Luke's narrative. In the beginning chapters of Luke's gospel, the angel Gabriel predicted that Jesus would sit on *the throne of his father David* and *reign over the house of Jacob forever* (Lk 1:32-33; 2 Sam 7:16). Zechariah prophesied that Jesus would bring *salvation from our enemies and from the hand of all who hate us* (Lk 1:71). New Testament authors, including Luke, place the fulfillment of these events at the return of Christ (Lk 12:35-13:5; 17:22-37; 19:11-27; 20:9-18; 21:5-36; Ac 3:21; 10:42; 17:30-31; 24:25).

John's mistake, and that of his contemporaries (including Luke's readers), was to believe that Jesus, the Messiah, would fulfill these prophetic expectations right away. The fact that Jesus did not immediately fulfill John's prophecy according to John's expectations does not call into question John's inspiration. As an inspired prophet, his prophetic words are reliable, but he himself is fallible. His understanding is dependant on the knowledge and revelation available to him. Who could have guessed that the Messianic prophecies contained in the same Old Testament passage and sometimes even in the same sentence would be fulfilled in stages? John's understanding of end-time prophecies and that of his contemporaries (including Luke's readers), needed modification. John needed to understand that the Spirit had anointed Jesus, not as a great warrior, but as a great prophet, empowering him to fulfill the prophetic aspects of Isaiah's end-time messianic prophecy (Lk 7:22).

The meaning of "baptized with the Holy Spirit" in Acts

In both passages in Acts in which the expression "baptized with the Holy Spirit" is repeated, the characters hearing the expression must also modify their end-time expectations. The disciples need to modify their understanding of the function of the Spirit in the end-time community. Peter's listeners need to modify their understanding of the beneficiaries of end-time salvation. Popular Messianic expectations in Jesus' day provide the background necessary to comprehend the need for these modifications. Israel was waiting for a Spirit-endowed leader to conquer her Gentile enemies and *restore the kingdom to Israel* (Ac 1:6).

It is within this context of modifying end-time expectations that we must understand Jesus' and Peter's use of the expression "baptized with the Holy Spirit." In neither case is the speaker attempting to define the believer's experience with the Spirit. The speaker is redefining or modifying his audience's expectations concerning the fulfillment of end-time prophecies. In the process of doing this, the role of the Spirit is also redefined. Luke's purpose in including these details is to explain and demonstrate the fulfillment of end-time prophecies, not to develop a theology of the Spirit.

Thus, although we can learn some things from these passages about the believer's experience with the Spirit, we must not try to infer too much. We must understand them within the context of Luke's literary work. Because the expression is so rarely used and because it is not explicitly defined in Scripture, there is a huge risk of reading our own ideas into the metaphor. We can greatly reduce this risk if we limit our conclusions to what can be legitimately derived and inferred from its literary context.

These limitations can put a damper on both Pentecostal and non-Pentecostal interpretations. The non-Pentecostal may want to emphasize the initiatory aspect of water baptism and conclude that the baptism with the Spirit initiates the believer into Christian life, making the experience analogous to new birth. The Pentecostal may look at the same analogy and conclude that the believer is initiated into the Spirit-filled life. The non-Pentecostal may consider the spatial meaning of the term and decide that the metaphor describes the believer's plunge into the realm of life with the Spirit. The Pentecostal may decide that the same spatial considerations point to a greater involvement with the Spirit, believing that the Spirit resides in the believer from the point of conversion, but that he envelops and fills the believer who is baptized with the Spirit. All of these analogies are somewhat plausible. But, since neither Jesus, nor Peter, nor Luke exploit these analogies explicitly in their arguments, interpreters who use them are simply guessing at possible meanings.

The author of Luke-Acts is not interested in any of these analogies. In the first place, he does not exploit them. This means that he does not explain the metaphor in terms of one of these analogies or even use one of these analogies to describe an experience with the Spirit somewhere else in the text. In the second place, none of these analogies would serve any purpose in Luke's strategy for demonstrating the fulfillment of end-time prophecies. And finally, and perhaps most importantly, these interpretations do not correspond to any analogy in John the Baptist's use of the expression, where the context gives more clues to its interpretation. Although the meaning of the expression is most likely modified in Acts to represent a different type of fulfillment than what John expected, it only makes sense that the analogy remains at least similar. In John's use of the expression, baptism with the Spirit is analogous to the wind separating the chaff from the grain. The emphasis is not on initiation or on any relationship with the Spirit, but on the powerful influence of the Spirit. We should look for a similar emphasis in the other two repetitions of John's metaphor, an emphasis on the powerful influence of the Spirit.

The new meaning which Jesus gives to John's prophecy (Ac 1:4-8)

> On one occasion, while he was eating with them, he gave them this command: "Do not leave Jerusalem, but wait for the gift my Father promised, which you have heard me speak about. ⁵ For John baptized with water, but in a few days you will be baptized with the Holy Spirit." ⁶ So when they met together, they asked him, "Lord, are you at this time going to restore the kingdom to Israel?" ⁷ He said to them: "It is not for you to know the times or dates the Father has set by his own authority. ⁸ But you will receive power when the Holy Spirit comes on you; and you will be my witnesses in Jerusalem, and in all Judea and Samaria, and to the ends of the earth."

The repetitions of John the Baptist's prophecy in Acts appear to emphasize more positive effects than John's original intended meaning. John emphasized the frightening effects of being baptized with the Spirit on the unrepentant. Jesus refers to the powerful effects of the Spirit on his disciples. This aspect is not entirely absent from John's original prophecy. In John's analogy, after being separated from the chaff destined for the fire, the wheat is "gathered" into the barn (Lk 3:17). This gathering undoubtedly refers to those who are set apart, approved by God and gathered into God's end-time community to experience his promised salvation.[1]

A closer examination of how Jesus modified John's saying will help us to understand his new emphasis. Here are the major changes:

1. The prophet changes. It is no longer John who prophesies. Jesus prophesies using most, but not all, of John's prophecy (Ac 1:5).

2. The focus changes. John focuses on the task of the baptizer, *he will baptize you with the Holy Spirit* (Lk 3:16). Jesus focuses on the results experienced by the baptized, *you will be baptized with the Holy Spirit* (Ac 1:5).

3. The baptism changes. John talks about being baptized *with the Holy Spirit and with fire*. Jesus removes the element of fire so closely associated with judgment in the gospel (Lk 3:9, 16, 17; 9:54; 12:49; 17:29).

4. The time of fulfillment is specified. John does not say when the baptism will occur. Jesus tells his disciples that they will be baptized *in a few days*. Logically, the fulfillment has to be what occurred on the day of Pentecost. It is the only Spirit experience recorded by Luke which occurred within a few days.[2] It is probably not coincidental that both elements used in John's metaphor are also present in the Pentecost event. Surely Luke is demonstrating that John's prophecy is being fulfilled in an unexpected manner when he writes, *Suddenly, a sound like the blowing of a violent **wind** came from heaven and filled the whole house where they were sitting. They saw what seemed to be tongues of **fire** that separated and came to rest on each of them* (Ac 2:2-3) Even though Jesus avoids repeating the image of fire because of its association with end-time judgment, Luke includes it in a context which clearly does not refer to end-time judgment. The mention of tongues of fire seems to be a symbolic

---

[1] Notice the repetition of the verb "gather together" (*sunagō*) for the community of believers in Acts, 4:31; 11:26; 14:27; 15:6, 30; 20:7, 8.

[2] Some ancient manuscripts actually add the words "until Pentecost," clarifying how long they needed to wait. See Barrett, vol. 1, p. 75.

representation of Spirit-empowered speaking in other tongues in the next verse (Ac 2:4).

5. The recipients of the prophetic message change. John addressed his prophecy to *all* his listeners (Lk 3:16). Jesus' prophecy is addressed to *the apostles he had chosen* (Ac 1:2).

6. The understanding needing modification changes. In the gospel Jesus corrected John's expectation concerning the Messiah's Spirit-anointed task (Lk 7:21-22). In Acts Jesus corrects the disciples' expectations concerning their own Spirit-empowered task. To understand this last change we need to follow the logic of the passage.

Jesus' mention of John the Baptist's prophecy leads the disciples to ask a question. Luke writes, *So when they met together, they asked him, "Lord, are you at this time going to restore the kingdom to Israel"* (Ac 1:6)? Notice the causal link *so* (*oun*, sometimes translated "therefore") connecting Jesus' reiteration of John's prophecy and the disciples' question. Why would these prophetic words motivate the disciples to ask a question about the restoration of the kingdom to Israel? If John's prophecy were understood to refer to the gift of the Spirit at conversion or to some sort of Pentecostal anointing, it would be difficult to imagine some sort of causal link with the restoration of the kingdom to Israel. We would be forced to conclude that the disciples purposely decided to change the subject and that Jesus changes the subject back again in the following verses. Given the explicit logical connection, this is surely not the case. The disciples' question is another indication that John the Baptist's hearers understood him to announce the coming of a Spirit-empowered warrior-king Messiah, who would now destroy the enemies of Israel and establish his kingdom. In this context, the disciples' question is completely understandable.

His disciples probably understood that they would enjoy the spoils of Jesus' coup d'état. After all, Jesus promised to *confer* on them *a kingdom*. They were to *sit on thrones, judging the twelve tribes of Israel* (Lk 22:29-30). Their question is probably an expression of joyful anticipation. Their hope for riches and glory was demolished when Jesus died. Now that Jesus is risen and talking about the kingdom, hope for such blessings is renewed.

Jesus modifies these expectations in the following two verses. First, he modifies their expectations concerning the time of the restoration of the kingdom. Note that he does not nullify the disciples' understanding of John's prophecy. As with John in the gospel, the problem is not with the concept but with the timing. The disciples thought that the time of restoration was near, because Jesus said that they would be baptized with the Spirit in a few days (Ac 1:5). So, they ask Jesus if he is going to restore the kingdom *at this time* (Ac 1:6). Jesus replies, *It is not for you to know the times or dates the Father has set by his own authority* (Ac 1:7). His response not only corrects their timing but also their understanding of what he just said. If the disciples are not to know the time for the restoration of the kingdom, then what Jesus predicted to occur in a few days does not refer to that restoration. But, if Jesus was not referring to the restoration of the kingdom, then what did he predict? Jesus answers this question in the following verse, where he modifies the disciples' expectations concerning what is in store for them. It is not time for them to sit on thrones and rule. They will not at this time be baptized with the Spirit to enable them to reign in power with the Messiah. They will be baptized with the Spirit to enable them to be witnesses *to the ends of the earth* (Ac 1.8).

This causal connection of needing the power of the Holy Spirit *in order to* carry out the task of witnessing to the nations is not explicitly stated. However, there are at least three very strong reasons for inferring a causal relationship between the endowment with the power of the Holy Spirit and the disciples' function as Christ's witnesses.

The first reason is that the logical progression of the passage leads to this conclusion. In the natural ebb and flow of narration, there is a logical connection between one statement and the next. The most common logical connections are cause and effect relationships. The first statement in some way prepares for or causes the second. The second causes the third, and so forth, creating a chain of cause and effect relationships. Sometimes the relationship is better described by saying that the second statement is a result or consequence of the first. Sometimes the order is reversed and the second statement explains or substantiates what was said in the first statement. This ebb and flow between cause and effect can be explicitly stated by the author, using some sort of connecting word or phrase, or the connection may simply be assumed.

The chart on the following page diagrams the logical flow of Jesus' conversation with his disciples in Acts 1:4-8. Some of the clauses in the summary of the text have been left out to reflect the simplest form of the logic.

Chart 7: The logical flow of Acts 1:4-8

Connection	Summary of the text
	Jesus tells his disciples to wait for the promise of the Father.
"For" or "because"	They will be baptized with the Holy Spirit in a few days.
"So" or "Therefore"	The disciples ask if Jesus will now restore the kingdom to Israel.
"Jesus said to them" (an implied answer to their question)	No, but they will receive power when the Holy Spirit comes on them
"and" (result implied)	They will be his witnesses

The first two connections are explicitly stated. Jesus tells his disciples to wait for the promise of the Father (effect) because (*hoti*) they will be baptized with the Holy Spirit in a few days (cause or reason). Because Jesus tells the disciples they will be baptized with the Holy Spirit in a few days (cause), *therefore* (*oun*), the disciples ask if Jesus will now restore the kingdom to Israel (effect or result). The last two connections are implied by the author but not explicitly stated. The disciples ask a question (cause) and Jesus gives the answer (effect). If the author had written, "Jesus answered and said" or "Jesus replied," the logical relationship would be explicit. Because Jesus' words immediately follow the disciples' question, the reader naturally assumes this is Jesus' answer to their question. A similar natural assumption should be made between the last two statements. The disciples will receive power when the Holy Spirit comes on them (cause) enabling them to be his witnesses (effect).

Concerning the last implicit connection in this chart, Michel Quesnel points out that the conjunction "and" followed by a verb in the future tense is a classic grammatical construction to indicate a causal connection.[3] Luke uses this construction frequently (Ac 2:17-18, 38-39; 13:11; 16:31; 18:10; 21:24; 28:27-28). To illustrate this grammatical concept, let's consider a simplified example. If my wife says, "I went to the store yesterday and bought some eggs," I might assume the cause and effect relationship that she went to the

---

[3] Michel Quesnel, *Baptisés dans l'Esprit: Baptême et Esprit Saint dans les Actes des Apôtres*, Lectio Divina 120, Paris, Cerf, 1985, p. 46. F. Blass and A. Debrunner, *A Greek Grammar of the New Testament and Other Early Christian Literature*, trans. Robert W. Funk, University of Chicago Press, 1961, p. 227, n. 442 (3).

store in order to buy eggs; but I might be wrong. She may have gone to the store for some other reason and remembered we needed eggs when she saw some in the store. However, if we place the event in the future, the likelihood of a cause and effect relationship is much greater. If my wife says, "Tomorrow I will go to the store and buy some eggs," it is pretty safe to assume that at least one of her goals in going to the store is to buy eggs. She does not need to explicitly state her purpose. The purpose is understood in the sequence of her statements. In a similar way, the purpose for receiving the power of the Holy Spirit is understood in the sequence of Jesus' statements. The disciples receive the Holy Spirit so that they can effectively witness to the nations.

The second reason for inferring a cause and effect relationship between the disciples' endowment with the power of the Holy Spirit and their mission as witnesses is a similar logical progression in the parallel passage at the end of Luke's gospel. Jesus tells his disciples that repentance and forgiveness will be preached to all nations and that they are witnesses of these things (Lk 24:47-48). After describing such an overwhelming task, we might expect Jesus to tell them to get busy doing it. Instead, he tells them to wait in the city until they have been clothed with power from on high (Lk 24:49). If we ask why the disciples should wait for this power from on high, the logical conclusion is that they will need this power for their mission to the nations.

The third reason for inferring this cause and effect relationship is that the empowering of the Holy Spirit is the only available explanation in the text for the disciples' renewed courage and ability to preach the gospel and testify. There is no evidence of such courage between the resurrection and Pentecost. Before Pentecost, Peter denies the Lord three times (Lk 22:54-62). Even after the resurrection, we find the disciples secluded in a room praying (Ac 1:13-14), not on the streets witnessing to the truth of the resurrection. However, after Pentecost, Peter preaches repentance and the forgiveness of sin, and he gives powerful testimony concerning the resurrection (Ac 2:32, 38). According to the pattern revealed in chapter 5, speaking the word of God with boldness and power is a common characteristic of all Luke's Spirit-endowed characters.

We are now able to summarize Jesus' twofold response to his disciples' misunderstanding of end-time events and the new meaning which he has infused into John the Baptist's prophecy. It is perhaps easier to comprehend his response in a more explicit reconstruction of his logic. Jesus responded with the following logic.

When I said you would be baptized with the Holy Spirit in a few days, I was not talking about the political restoration of the kingdom to Israel. You should not even worry about when that will take place. The Father has that under control and will bring it about in his good time. But I was referring to the power of the Holy Spirit which you will receive to enable you to be my witnesses to the ends of the earth (Ac 1:7-8 author's paraphrase).

Luke's account clearly demonstrates that Jesus' disciples received this empowering and began their mission of witnessing to the nations on the day of Pentecost. Not only do we find the same metaphoric symbols of wind and fire used to describe the Holy Spirit's empowering (Ac 2:1-4), but this empowering, expressed through the gift of speaking in other tongues, enables the disciples to witness to people from *every nation under heaven* (Ac 2:5-11). The new meaning which Jesus gives to John's prophecy when he tells his disciples that they will *be baptized with the Holy Spirit* is undoubtedly that they will receive the Spirit's empowering for witnessing to the nations.

The new understanding acquired by Peter concerning John's prophecy (Ac 11.15-17)

> As I began to speak, the Holy Spirit came on them as he had come on us at the beginning. [16] Then I remembered what the Lord had said: "John baptized with water, but you will be baptized with the Holy Spirit." [17] So if God gave them the same gift as he gave us, who believed in the Lord Jesus Christ, who was I to think that I could oppose God?

When the Holy Spirit came on the household of Cornelius, Peter remembered what Jesus said about being baptized with the Holy Spirit (Ac 11:15-16). This is the third and last time the expression is used in Luke-Acts. The coming of the Spirit is described four times in the book of Acts (Ac 2:1-4; 4:31; 10:44-47/11:15-16; 19:6). The expression "baptized with the Spirit" is used on only two of these occasions (Ac 1:5 in anticipation of Pentecost and here in Ac 11:16). We need to ask why this is so. If the expression were as closely associated with conversion as it is in the non-Pentecostal viewpoint, we would expect it to show up in some other conversion accounts, both in Acts and in the rest of the New Testament. If it were as closely associated with a second blessing with the Spirit after conversion as it is in the Pentecostal viewpoint, we would expect it to show up in the other two accounts in Acts and perhaps a few other places in the New Testament. Arguments from silence such as this should not be overly emphasized in interpretation, but its absence is troublesome. If the expression is understood within the logic of Luke's strategy, a clear explanation is easily perceivable.

Within the narrative, neither Peter nor Luke answers the question why the expression "baptized with the Spirit" is used so infrequently. We must infer our answers from the context. Two logical answers fit the context of Luke's strategy. First of all, we need to look at what Peter is attempting to do in Acts 11. He is being called on the carpet by circumcised believers for eating with Gentiles. Peter defends himself by revealing how God demonstrated his own approval of Gentile incorporation into the community of end-time believers. His first argument is God's miraculous leading up to and including his preaching the gospel in the house of Cornelius (Ac 11:4-14). His second argument is that their experience with the Spirit is like that of the disciples at Pentecost. Peter carefully establishes a parallel between the two encounters with the Spirit using three different expressions. He says, *the Holy Spirit came on them **as he had come on us at the beginning*** (Ac 11:15). He also states that *God gave them **the same gift as he gave us*** (Ac 11:17). In between these two statements, Peter recalls the expression used by Jesus just before his own experience: *you will be baptized with the Holy Spirit* (Ac 11.16).

Peter surely includes the expression "baptized with the Spirit" here to accentuate the parallels between the Gentiles' experience in the house of Cornelius and the disciples' experience at Pentecost. It should also be pointed out that Luke is not a passive recorder of these events. He demonstrates his involvement in this strategy using parallel vocabulary in the description of the event by the narrator. The narrator mentions that *the **gift** of the Spirit* was ***poured out*** on the Gentiles (Ac 10:45). Like "baptized with the Spirit," these two expressions are only used for these two events in Luke-Acts. On both occasions Luke also records that they spoke in tongues (Ac 2:4; 10:46) and declared the greatness of God (Ac 2:11; Ac 10:46). Luke concludes the description of the event with a statement by Peter, *They have received the Holy Spirit **just as we have*** (Ac 10:47).

Although the details in the preceding paragraph explain why the expression "baptized with the Holy Spirit" is used for the episode in Cornelius' house, they do not explain why it is not used in the other two descriptions of Spirit anointing in the book of Acts (Ac 8:15-17; 19:6). Both of these events also have clear parallels with the Pentecost episode. In Acts 8, the Samaritan disciples also *receive* the Holy Spirit which *comes upon* them. Afterwards, there are also visible signs of this reception (Ac 8:18). In Acts 19, the Ephesian disciples also speak in tongues and prophesy.

The three repetitions of the expression "baptized with the Holy Spirit" in Luke-Acts can all be explained in the light of the literary context of Luke's goal to give assurance to his readers (Lk 1:4) and within the historical context of popular messianic expectations which made such assurance more difficult. Luke's readers, along with the majority of Jews and god fearers at the time of Christ's first appearing, probably understood end-time prophecies to predict the coming of a David-like warrior-king Messiah, who would destroy Israel's Gentile enemies and reestablish a David-like kingdom. Not only did Jesus and his disciples fail to fulfill these expectations, but the movement they started was becoming more and more Gentile in its composition. Luke needed to show that this movement was the fulfillment of end-time prophecies and had God's approval. He demonstrated this by describing the powerful and visible manifestations of the Spirit which God used to validate these conclusions.

John's prophecy concerning the Messiah's task of "baptizing with the Holy Spirit" plays an important role in this strategy. In its original context (Lk 3:15-17), the expression reflects the popular expectations of Luke's readers also held by John the Baptist. John anticipated a warrior-like Messiah who, with the overwhelming power of God's Spirit, would deliver Israel from her Gentile enemies and restore the kingdom to Israel. Jesus corrected John's understanding of his messianic task, explaining how he fulfilled other messianic prophecies (Is 61:1-2; Lk 4:18-19; 7:22-23) and announcing the postponement of the fulfillment of more popular expectations for a future date (Lk 12:35-13:5; 17:22-37; 19:11-27; 20:9-18; 21:5-36; Ac 3:21; 10:42; 17:30-31; 24:25).

John's expression is brought up two more times with the same strategic goal of modifying messianic expectations. Jesus brings it up in order to modify his disciples' expectations of the immediate restoration of the kingdom to Israel (Ac 1:5-6). Jesus again reveals that the fulfillment of those expectations must be postponed until some indefinite future date (Ac 1:7). Having adopted John's words and made them into his own prophecy (Ac 1:4-5), Jesus gives new meaning to John's expression. At this point in time the Spirit is not sent to provide overwhelming power to destroy Israel's Gentile enemies, but to provide overwhelming power to spread the gospel to the nations (Ac 1:8). The disciples understood the first part of this new paradigm on the day of Pentecost. They understood that they had been empowered for witnessing and preaching the gospel. However, it is not until Peter's experience in the house of Cornelius that they understood the second part. They must have understood their mission to be to take the gospel to dispersed Israel. In the house of Cornelius, Peter finally gets it. And so, he recalls Jesus' prophecy about being "baptized with the Spirit" (Ac 11:16). He understands now that the Spirit's overwhelming power is intended to enable them to carry the gospel to Gentile nations and not just to dispersed Israel.

Luke is very consistent in his use of the expression "baptized with the Spirit." In Luke-Acts, it is only used in contexts where the Spirit-empowered mission of the Messiah and his disciples is misunderstood. He probably does this because the expression was so closely associated with that misunderstanding in the church's beginning. This makes perfect sense if John did in fact use the term to refer to end-time judgment. The early disciples would have been familiar with John the Baptist's teaching. The fact that some form of John's saying is found in all four gospels shows that the traditions for this episode were well known.

This re-creation of Luke's logic also explains why the expression "baptized with the Holy Spirit" is not used more widely, either in Luke-Acts or in the rest of the New Testament. Because of its similarity to popular expectations, early believers were probably more familiar with the meaning given by John the Baptist than with the new specialized meaning given to the expression by Jesus. Saying that someone was "baptized with the Spirit" would have been tantamount to saying that they had been winnowed out for destruction by the powerful wind of the Spirit. This was not what the early disciples were trying to communicate. Luke wanted to communicate that they were endowed with the power of the Holy Spirit for the purpose of spreading the gospel to the ends of the earth. Although the specialized meaning of John's saying did actually express this, more popular understandings of the expression would have introduced confusion for Luke's readers. Thus, Luke is careful to only use the expression to correct the misunderstanding associated with it.

Understanding "baptized with the Holy Spirit" in Luke's portrayal of John

Some readers may not be comfortable with the idea of Jesus correcting John the Baptist, but actually the need for modifying and updating John the Baptist's message lends coherence to Luke's entire presentation of John's character and to every reference to him in Luke-Acts. Luke consistently portrays John the Baptist as a great Old Testament-like prophet whose understanding of the fulfillment of end-time prophecy needs modification to bring it up to date with its actual fulfillment in Jesus. The comparison between John and Jesus in the opening chapters sets the stage for modifying the message of such an important prophetic figure by demonstrating the superiority of Jesus (Ac 1:5-2:52). The theme of Jesus' superiority over John is maintained throughout Luke's two-volume work. John was widely considered to be a great prophet (Lk 9:7, 19). In fact, Jesus presents John as *more than a prophet* and the greatest among *those born of women*. But he says, *the one who is least in the kingdom of God is greater than he* (Lk 7:26-28). Jesus also says, *The Law and the Prophets were proclaimed until John. Since that time, the good news of the kingdom of God is being preached* (Lk 16:16; cf. Lk 4:43).[4] John prepared the way for the proclamation of the kingdom of God and, like the prophets of old, announced the good news of its coming. Jesus, however, proclaimed the good news of the kingdom of God in word and deed. He did not just announce its coming. He demonstrated it.

If we follow the clues in Luke's gospel carefully, it is easy to understand why John's teaching and preaching needed updating. His teaching and preaching occurred before Jesus began his ministry (Lk 3:2-20). We learn from Luke's account of Jesus' ministry and teaching that he introduced innovative interpretations of the Scriptures which were hard to understand (Lk 8:10; 9:45; 18:34). In the end, Jesus needed to open the minds of his disciples *so that they could understand the Scriptures* (Lk 24:45). John's disciples, who may not have heard some of Jesus' explanations, also needed to update their understanding and sometimes even their experience (Ac 18:24-19:6).

What do some of these updates look like? John's disciples, and those of the Pharisees, often fasted and prayed (Lk 5:33). Jesus' disciples are not to follow the same model. While it is not clear what Jesus has in mind, he does give clear indication that drastic change is in order. With the arrival of the Messiah, everything changes. Like an old garment or an old wineskin the old ways must be replaced with the new (Lk 5:34-39).

One of Jesus' updates on prayer is revealed a little later in Luke's account. Jesus' disciples ask him to teach them to pray *just as John taught his disciples*

---

[4] The meaning of this verse is difficult to determine because the Greek time markers "until" and "since that time" could be understood either to include or exclude John from the period of proclaiming the law and the Prophets. If we look at repetitions of the term "to proclaim good news," we note that John does announce good news (Lk 3:18), but then, so do angels in the time period before John (Lk 1:19; 2:10). In Luke the 'good news of the kingdom of God" is not proclaimed until Jesus (Lk 4:43; 8:1). Luke appears to make a distinction between the good news of the future coming of the kingdom announced by the law, the prophets, the angels and John and the proclamation of the kingdom of God by word and deed in the ministry of Jesus and his disciples.

(Lk 11:1). Since we do not have an example of John's teaching on prayer, it is difficult to pinpoint how Jesus' teaching updates that of John's, but the coming of the kingdom of God is clearly a key. Jesus instructs his disciples to pray, *your kingdom come* (Lk 11:2). Jesus' teaching on prayer culminates in instructions for the disciples to ask the Father to *give the Holy Spirit* (Lk 11:13). In some ancient manuscripts, a request for the Holy Spirit to come upon believers follows or precedes the request for the coming of the *kingdom* in the Lord's Prayer (Lk 11:2).[5] While this phrase was probably not in the original, its addition to the text by early copyists surely indicates the importance given to the phrase at the end of this episode. The fact that the final request for the gift of the Spirit differs from the details given in Matthew (Mt 7:11) may also indicate the importance of this phrase for Luke.[6] It is probably significant that Jesus and his disciples do actually receive the Holy Spirit in response to prayer in Luke-Acts (Lk 3:21-22; Ac 1:14 with 2:1-4; 4:31; 8:15-17; 9:11-17; 10:4-46; 19:6).[7]

We have already studied how Jesus needed to update John and his own disciples concerning their understanding of the Messiah and his kingdom (Lk 7:22-23; Ac 1:6-8). Jesus was anointed, not to rule over the nations, but to mightily proclaim the kingdom of God in word and deed. Jesus' disciples were not to be baptized with the Spirit so that they could participate in Jesus' rule over the nations, but so that they also could mightily proclaim the good news of Jesus Christ to the nations.

Jesus' disciples also needed to update their understanding of water baptism, which they had inherited from John. John preached *a baptism of repentance for the forgiveness of sins* (Lk 3:3; Ac 13:24) telling people to believe in *the one coming after him* (Ac 19:4). The disciples continue preaching a baptism of repentance (Ac 2:38). In fact, Luke draws a parallel between John's preaching and Peter's by repeating several key expressions. Notice the repetition of exhorting the people *with many other words*, the *crooked* ways of the people and the need for salvation (Lk 3:5-6, 18; Ac 2:40). Nevertheless, one very important aspect of baptism is modified in Acts. Since the identity of

---

[5] Found in the minuscule 700 and in quotes by Gregory of Nyssa, Tertullian and Marcion.

[6] Commentators argue on whether Jesus originally said "give good things" or "give the Holy Spirit." Often it is felt that Luke modified the saying because of his emphasis on the Holy Spirit. See, for example, C. F. Evans, p. 487. Jesus probably said both phrases and both authors are summarizing what Jesus said at this point. That Luke chose this detail because of its pertinence in his account seems likely.

[7] In Ac 19:6 the author only mentions the laying on of hands. I am assuming that this gesture was accompanied by prayer as it was in Ac 8:15-17 and 13:3.

the one coming after John is revealed to be Jesus (Ac 19:4), believers are baptized *in the name of Jesus Christ* (Ac 2:38; 8:16; 10:48; 19:5).

Two other episodes demonstrate the need for updating John the Baptist's teaching. They are found back to back in Acts chapters 18 and 19. Apollos was powerfully used by God to teach *about Jesus accurately* and *speak boldly in the synagogue*. These details provide evidence that he was already empowered by the Holy Spirit. However, *he knew only the baptism of John* and needed Priscilla and Aquila to explain *to him the way of God more adequately* (Ac 18:25-26). In Acts chapter 19 the contrast between Jesus' disciples and some of John's disciples is emphasized again. John's disciples did not know about the gift of the Holy Spirit or even about the arrival of Jesus, the Messiah. Paul, a disciple of Jesus, informed John's disciples about Jesus, re-baptized them in the name of the Lord Jesus, laid hands on them and presumably prayed for them, and then *the Holy Spirit came on them and they spoke in tongues and prophesied* (Ac 19:1-6). The repetition of needed modifications for John and his disciples throughout Luke-Acts provides strong evidence that these last two episodes are included in Luke's account for this same reason. These two episodes probably represent various levels of need among John the Baptist's disciples during apostolic times.[8] Some already knew much about Jesus the Messiah and had already experienced the power of the Spirit in their lives. They only needed a little instruction. Others had never heard of Jesus, their long-awaited Messiah, and knew nothing of the Spirit-empowered life. They needed much more.

"Baptized with the Spirit" and synonymous expressions in Luke-Acts

In the previous chapter we looked at two series of metaphors which Luke used to point to the fulfillment of Joel's prophecy concerning the prophetic anointing on God's end-time community (Joel 2:28-31). Spatial metaphors allude to the physical gesture of anointing with oil: anoint, pour out, come, descend, fall or be upon. Another series of metaphors allude to God's promise in Joel's prophecy to pour out his Spirit: the promise of the Father or the gift of the Spirit, which is sent and received.

The evidence in this chapter clearly points to the conclusion that "baptized with the Holy Spirit" is another synonymous expression for the vari-

---

[8] Barrett, vol. 2, p. 885.

ous Spirit-anointing experiences described in Acts. First of all, the chain of logic in Ac 1:4-8 clearly connects *baptized with the Holy Spirit* to some of the above anointing metaphors. Jesus tells his disciples to *wait for the promise of the Father* because they will *be baptized with the Holy Spirit in a few days* (Ac 1:4-5). *Baptized with the Spirit* is synonymous here with *the promise of the Father*. Both expressions refer to the event which will occur in a few days and for which the disciples should wait. Also, when Jesus corrects his disciples' understanding of the phrase *you will be baptized with the Holy Spirit*, he describes the same future event with other anointing metaphors. *You will receive power when the Holy Spirit comes upon you* is a clarification of the more enigmatic phrase, *You will be baptized with the Holy Spirit* (Ac 1:5, 8).

Secondly, the expression "baptized with the Holy Spirit" describes the same events as the two series of Spirit-anointing metaphors we have already studied. Both the timing and the details of the Pentecost event clearly indicate that the disciples' experience with the Spirit on the day of Pentecost is a fulfillment of Jesus' prophecy that they would be *baptized with the Holy Spirit*. It is the only experience with the Spirit recorded by Luke occurring within *a few days* (Ac. 1:5). The repetition of wind and fire with the subsequent witness to the nations (Ac 2:1-11) clearly allude to John's prophecy recalled by Jesus and explained in Acts 1:4-8. Peter also defines the same Pentecost event as the fulfillment of Joel's prophecy promising Spirit anointing. Peter explains to the crowds that the Pentecostal experience with the Spirit *is what was spoken by the prophet Joel* (Ac 2:16). All of the metaphors used by Peter in this passage refer back to this same event. God promises to *pour out* his Spirit on all people. Those who repent will *receive* this *gift of the Spirit*, because the *promise* is for all (Ac 2:17-18, 33, 38-39).

Some of the same metaphors are also used synonymously with the expression *baptized with the Spirit* in Luke's account of the Gentile experience with the Spirit in the house of Cornelius. The Spirit is *poured out* and *comes upon* the Gentile believers leading Peter and the other Jewish believers to conclude that the Gentiles had received the same *gift*, and thus, they were *baptized with the Spirit* (Ac 10:44-45; 11:15-17)

All of these details lead to the almost inevitable conclusion that Jesus used John's expression of being baptized with the Holy Spirit to refer to the disciples' prophetic anointing with the Spirit of God, to their endowment with prophetic power in order to fulfill their mission as witnesses for Christ to the nations. Luke does not use his various Spirit-experience expressions to distinguish between different experiences with the Spirit. All of his expressions refer to the same Spirit-anointing experiences. The various expressions merely emphasize different aspects of the same events or experiences. Some expressions emphasize the coming of the Spirit from God upon the disciples. Others emphasize God's promise to pour out his Spirit on the disciples in prophetic anointing, preparing them for prophetic ministry. *Baptized with the Spirit* emphasizes the overwhelming power and influence of the Spirit when He comes upon the disciples, enabling them to fulfill their prophetic ministries.

A brief evaluation of Pentecostal and non Pentecostal positions

It is clear from the preceding discussion that the non-Pentecostal interpretation of "baptized with the Spirit," equating the expression with conversion or new birth, does not fit Luke's account. Not only does the expression refer to an event occurring after the disciples' conversion, but the logical sequence of expressions and events clearly connect this expression with an empowering prophetic anointing.

Prophetic Spirit anointing in Luke-Acts is the proof used by Luke to demonstrate that groups of believers belong to the end-time community approved by God. It is thus also proof of their conversion. But it is not a description of their conversion or their new birth. New birth is not a concept used by Luke and he describes conversion in terms of repentance and turning to God apart from any experience with the Spirit (Lk 15:10; Ac 5:31; 11:18; 26:18, 20). Baptism with the Spirit is a result of conversion and not a description of it. In Luke-Acts, baptism with the Spirit is an anointing with the Spirit to enable those who are converted to spread the good news of Christ (Ac 1:8). So, when Peter promises the gift of the Holy Spirit to those who repent and are baptized in the name of Jesus (Ac 2:38-39), he is not promising them they will experience new birth as a result of their repentance. He is promising his listeners that, if they convert to Christ, they will receive the proof of their incorporation into the end-time community of believers: the prophetic Spirit anointing promised by the prophet Joel (Ac 2:17-18).

There is a basic congruence between the Pentecostal position and the details found in Luke-Acts. The expression "baptized with the Holy Spirit" does represent a post-conversion experience of empowering for witness in Luke-Acts. However, the Pentecostal position, through its particular emphasis on this expression and on the sign of speaking in tongues, tends to introduce several problems into the equation. Because the term "baptism" is so closely associated with Christian initiation, an emphasis on being baptized with the Holy Spirit as a second experience tends to limit the concept to some sort of initiation into a Spirit empowered life. While this is actually the case in the two occurrences of the expression in Acts, the expression is also used synonymously with other Spirit-empowering expressions which do not always indicate an initiation. This creates a difficulty with the text which we will examine in the next chapter on being filled with the Spirit.

A detailed examination of Luke's use of this expression reveals that it was not intended either to be so closely associated with initiation or to be used so frequently. Because of its association with end-time judgment in John the Baptist's preaching, it was probably used very infrequently in the early church. When Luke did use the expression, it was in order to demonstrate the fulfillment of John's prophecy in an unexpected manner. The expression was not intended to emphasize initiation but the overwhelming impact of the Spirit in the life and witness of the believer.

The Pentecostal insistence on speaking in tongues as the initial evidence for the baptism in the Holy Spirit has probably been the most controversial element in their doctrine. In defense of Pentecostals, I would argue that it is both biblical and spiritually healthy to seek visible manifestations of the Spirit (1 Cor 14:1; Ac 4:29-30). However, the insistence on tongues has all too often resulted in settling for too little. Speaking in tongues is probably the least convincing prophetic gift for outsiders, unless of course the tongues are understood by their listeners as on the day of Pentecost. There is no way the listeners can verify that these unintelligible sounds are from God. They could just as easily be fabricated in the imagination of those who speak. In the eyes of the unbeliever, tongues-speakers seem to be babbling away in nonsensical sounds. This is not a problem if the community of believers manifests other more convincing gifts of the Spirit. But, when Pentecostals declare this gift to be the sign of the baptism with the Spirit, they give tongues-speakers tacit permission to stop seeking the power of the Holy Spirit. Why continue to seek what you already have?

Baptized by one Spirit (1 Cor 12:13)

Before wholeheartedly adopting the interpretation presented in this chapter of the expression "baptized with the Holy Spirit," one other passage containing the same vocabulary must be considered. The same terms *en pneumati* (with, by or in the Spirit) are used in a sentence in 1 Corinthians 12:13, where the main verb is also "to baptize." The interpretation of this verse is important because it is commonly used to affirm that all Christians are baptized with the Spirit, eliminating the possibility of the expression referring to any subsequent experience.[9] Paul, however, does not use this vocabulary in the same way as the gospel writers. The expression is not identical because the word order is different. In the gospels and in Acts, *en pneumati* immediately precedes (Ac 1:5) or follows (Mt 3:11; Mk 1:8;[10] Lk 3:16; Jn 1:33; Ac 11:16) the verb "to baptize." In 1 Corinthians the preposition *en* is separated from the noun *pneumati* by the adjective "one," and the entire expression is separated from the verb "to baptize" by the words "you all into one body." A wooden translation of the Greek reads, "For *en* one *pneumati* we all into one body were baptized." I purposely left the words *en pneumati* in transliterated Greek because the translation of these terms is highly debated and must be determined by an examination of the context.

Before examining the context, it should be pointed out that word order is not as important in Greek as it is in English, since the function of words is determined in Greek more by the form of the word than by its position in the sentence. The conclusion that the same expression is used here cannot be refuted simply on the basis of word order. Greek writers tend to use word order for emphasis. The expression *en pneumati* appears to be emphasized in 1 Corinthians 12:13 by its position at the beginning of the sentence. The significance of this observation will become clear when we take a look at Paul's emphasis on the Spirit's activity in the preceding passage.

The various versions are divided on the translation of these words. The King James, Revised Standard, New American Standard and New International versions use "by one Spirit" in the translation. The New Revised Standard and the Jerusalem Bible use "in one Spirit."[11] The arguments have to do with the grammatical construction of *en pneumati* and the context of the passage where it is found.

The preposition *en* followed by a noun in the dative case (*pneumati* in this verse) can be used both in a locative sense to indicate the location or sphere where the action of the verb takes place (in one Spirit) or in an instrumental

---

[9] See, for example, Stott, p. 27.
[10] Mark inserts the word "you" in between *en pneumati* and the verb "to baptize."
[11] For a list of various authors supporting each of these translations see Dunn, p. 128, note 37.

sense to indicate the means by which or possibly the agent by whom the action of the verb takes place (by one Spirit).[12] Typically, New Testament authors use the preposition *hupo* with the genitive case to refer to a personal agent and *en* with the dative case to refer to an impersonal means. Greek grammarians consider the use of the dative referring to a personal agent to be extremely rare.[13] This is a legitimate argument against an instrumental meaning for this construction in 1 Corinthians 12:13, since the Holy Spirit functions as a person in the New Testament.

However, it should be pointed out that the vocabulary used to refer to the Spirit in the New Testament is often impersonal.[14] Paul exhorts the Ephesians to be filled with the Spirit, not with wine (Eph 5:18). How is one to be filled with a person? In Acts, Peter talks about the Spirit being poured out on the day of Pentecost (Ac 2:17). Do you pour out a person? In the sentence parallel to the one we are considering (1 Cor 12:13b), Paul says that *we were all given the one Spirit to drink.* How does one drink a person? These impersonal expressions do not contradict the concept that the Holy Spirit functions as a person in the New Testament. They merely demonstrate that New Testament authors can speak of the Holy Spirit with both personal and impersonal expressions. Perhaps we should understand the Spirit in this passage to be the "instrument" God uses to baptize believers into the body of Christ, "even though he is a person."[15] God is the personal agent acting by his Spirit to accomplish his will.

The expression *en pneumati* is frequently used in the New Testament to refer to God's powerful agency enabling his servants. Jesus does not drive out demons by (*en*) Beelzebub, but by the Spirit (*en pneumati*, Mt 12:27-28). David spoke by the Spirit (*en pneumati*) in the Psalms (Mt 22:43; Mk 12:36). Simeon comes into the temple by the Spirit (*en pneumati*) at just the right moment to see the Christ (Lk 2:27). The Corinthians were washed, sanctified and justified by the Spirit (*en pneumati*, 1 Cor 6:11). The mystery of

---

[12] Brooks and Winbery give 14 different possibilities for the use of the preposition *en* with a noun in the dative case in the New Testament, p. 61. Only three of these possibilities provide a reasonable translation in the context of 1 Cor 12:13: locative of sphere, instrumental of means and instrumental of agency.

[13] Brooks, p. 44; Wallace, p. 163; Robertson, p. 590.

[14] Joseph A. Fitzmyer, "The Role of the Spirit in Luke-Acts," *The Unity of Luke-Acts*, ed. J. Verheyden, Leuven University Press, 1999, p.179, attributes this non personified manner of speaking about the Holy Spirit to Luke's affinity with the Old Testament concept of the Spirit.

[15] Wallace, p. 374. Wallace understands Christ to be the unnamed agent, but the passive voice without a named agent points to God's agency in a more general sense rather than to one person in the Godhead. Wallace chooses this interpretation because he connects Paul's use of these terms with John the Baptist's prophecy, where Christ is the baptizer. There is no need to infer that Paul is referring to John the Baptist's prophecy.

Christ is revealed to the apostles and prophets by the Spirit (*en pneumati*, Eph 3:5). *En pneumati* is used four times in the immediate context of 1 Corinthians 12 to refer to God's enabling power. *No one who is speaking by the Spirit (en pneumati) of God says, "Jesus be cursed" and no one can say, "Jesus is Lord," except by the Holy Spirit (en pneumati,* 1 Cor 12:3). A few verses later, faith and gifts of healing are both given by the Spirit (*en pneumati*, 1 Cor 12:9).

Not all Greek grammarians are comfortable with an instrumental understanding of this expression. For example, A. T. Robertson, whose massive Greek grammar is considered the standard reference for biblical research, believes that "all of the N. T. examples of *en* can be explained from the point of view of the locative."[16] While it is possible to explain these verses in a locative sense by saying that it is because these individuals are 'in the sphere' of the Spirit that they are able to do what they do, a locative translation does not seem to convey the intended meaning. Even Robertson admits that, "It is not always easy to draw the line of distinction between the locative and instrumental in Greek"[17] and that an instrumental translation may be the best for the "resultant idea."[18] Translators agree that the expression "by the Spirit" best translates the intention of most of these passages, especially the four examples in the preceding passage in 1 Corinthians 12.[19] What occurs in these passages occurs by the power of the Holy Spirit.

The context of 1 Corinthians 12 brings us to the same conclusion for verse 13. The author repeats the notion of the Spirit's operation in the life of the believer in practically every verse of the passage using a variety of grammatical constructions. There are different gifts, ministries and workings, but there is only one Spirit, one Lord and one God who *works* all of them (12:4-6). The author then switches to the passive voice to enumerate some of these gifts, ministries and workings. *To each one the manifestation of the Spirit is given* (12:7). A word of wisdom is given *through the Spirit* (*dia tou pneumatos*, 12:8). A word of knowledge is given *by means of the same Spirit* (*kata to auto pneuma*, 12:8). Faith and gifts of healing are given *by the Spirit* (*en*

---

[16] Robertson, p. 590.

[17] Robertson, p. 526.

[18] Robertson, p. 590.

[19] Ervin, *Conversion*, p. 99. KJV, NKJV, RSV, NRSV, NAB, NASB, NIV and JB all use an instrumental expression ("by the Spirit," occasionally "through the Spirit") for Mt 12:28 and 1 Cor 12:3 and 9. NJB has "in the Spirit" for 1 Cor 12:3. Most of these translations also use an instrumental expression in Mt 22:43; Mk 12:36; Lk 2:27 and 1 Cor 6:11. The following exceptions have "in the Spirit": NASB – Mt 22:43; Mk 12:36; Lk 2:27; NKJV – Mt 22:43; NAB – Lk 2:27; 1 Cor 6:11; RSV and NRSV – 1 Cor 6:11.

pneumati, 12:9). Other gifts are then mentioned with the inference that they are derived from the same source (12:10). The author then switches back to the active voice to repeat the notion, stating that *one and the same Spirit works all these things* (12:11). The grammatical forms are varied, but the concept remains the same throughout the passage. It is the same Spirit who works in all believers enabling them to exercise various gifts, ministries and workings. The notion of the Spirit's unique agency underlies the entire passage.

Paul then uses the metaphor of the human body to continue his teaching on unity with diversity (12:12-26). In light of the preceding context, the repetition of *en pneumati* in the emphatic position at the beginning of verse 13 would naturally be understood to refer to the same agency of the Holy Spirit already emphasized multiple times in the preceding passage. Paul is taking his arguments for unity one step further. In verses 4 through 11, Paul affirms that all the gifts in operation within the church were given by one Spirit. Beginning with verse 12, he affirms that the church itself is a product of the Spirit. Those now exercising the gifts of the Spirit were also incorporated into the church by one and the same Spirit. They *were all baptized by one Spirit into one body.*

There are several good reasons for adopting this translation of *en pneumati* in 1 Corinthians 12:13. First of all, the instrumental use (by the Spirit) of this expression four times in the preceding passage (12:3[2x]; 12:9[2x]) is the strongest evidence that an instrumental meaning is also intended in verse 13. Secondly, there is no clear allusion to John the Baptist in this verse. Every other time a New Testament author refers to being "baptized *en pneumati*," there is a clear allusion to John the Baptist's preaching (Mt 3:11; Mk 1:8; Lk 3:16; Jn 1:33; Ac 1:5; 11:16). It is interesting to note that every occurrence in the New Testament of the expression "baptized with water" is found in these same passages. It would appear that New Testament authors felt the need to specify the medium for baptism when they needed to distinguish between water baptism and another baptism. Otherwise water baptism was assumed.[20] Thirdly, if my conclusions concerning the original meaning of John the Baptist's prophetic saying are correct, early Christians probably associated the expression "baptized with the Spirit" with end-time judgment rather than with Christian initiation.

---

[20] There are 77 occurrences of the verb "to baptize" in the N.T. 15 of those use the construction *en* plus a noun in the dative form to indicate the medium. Of those 15, 14 clearly allude to John the Baptist's preaching. Of the 62 remaining occurrences, 28 clearly assume water baptism. Either water or a source of water is mentioned in the context (Mk 1:5, 9; Mt 3:6; Jn 1:23, 28; 10:40; Ac 8:36, 38; 10:47) or the baptizer is clearly human (Mk 1:4; Lk 3:7, 12, 21[2x]; 7:29, 30; Jn 1:25; 4:2; Ac 8:12, 13, 16; 1 Cor 1:13, 14, 16[2x], 17; 15:29[2x]). Spirit baptism is not clearly assumed in any reference where it is not specifically mentioned.

To which baptism, then, does this passage refer? Rather than looking at the expression "baptized *en*" something to answer this question, we should be looking at the expression "baptized *into* (*eis*)" something. On several other occasions, Paul uses the expression "to baptize into (*eis*)" something. In Romans 6:3 and Galatians 3:27, Paul talks about being baptized into (*eis*) Christ. These are more likely parallels to Paul's expression *baptized into one body* in 1 Corinthians. According to the text, these phrases were all written by the same author (Rom 1:1; 1 Cor 1:1; Gal 1:1). The body into which the Corinthians were baptized is also described as *the body of Christ* (1 Cor 12:27). The expressions *baptized into* (*eis*) *the name of Jesus* (Ac 8:16; 19:5) and *into* (*eis*) *the name of the Father and of the Son and of the Holy Spirit* (Mt 28:19) are probably also parallel. Paul does not use either of these specific expressions in his writings; but he begins addressing the issue of unity in 1 Corinthians with a discussion of baptism, in which he emphasizes the fact that none of the Corinthians were baptized into (*eis*) his name (1 Cor 1:13, 15), presumably because they were baptized into Christ's name.

The closest parallel to the expression *baptized into one body* (1 Cor 12.13) is probably the expressions *baptized into Jesus Christ* and *into his death* (Rom 6.3). In both references, believers are baptized into (*eis*) something associated with their union in Christ. Both instances are probably an allusion to water baptism. However, in both cases, the author probably has in mind the spiritual reality represented in the ritual rather than the spiritual effects accomplished through the ritual. In Romans, the descent under water and subsequent rising represent the death and resurrection of the believer with Christ. Paul goes on in the following chapters to describe how the Spirit enables the believer to live out what is represented in this ritual, namely resurrection life and freedom from sin (Rom 6:4-7; 8:1-17). In 1 Corinthians, the result is emphasized rather than the symbols. The Spirit enables believers to become a part of Christ's body and function within it. Believers are "initiated 'into (*eis*) the one body' through water baptism, which from the spiritual standpoint is administered *by* the Spirit."[21] In conclusion, the mention of baptism *en pneumati* in 1 Corinthians 12:13 does not refer to John's prophetic saying. Paul is referring to the work of the Spirit associated with water baptism, incorporating the believer into the body of Christ, and not to a baptism in or with the Spirit.

---

[21] Ervin, *Conversion*, p. 99.

The use and meaning of the expression "baptized with the Holy Spirit" in the New Testament

In the New Testament, the expression "baptized with the Holy Spirit" is only used in the four gospels and Acts. In the original use of this metaphor, John the Baptist refers to the overwhelming power of the Spirit in end-time judgment to blow away the unrighteous, separating them from the righteous to await fiery judgment, allowing the righteous to freely enjoy the blessings of the kingdom. This original meaning still awaits fulfillment at the return of Christ.

Luke refers back to this expression in John's prophecy in a manner consistent with his strategy to show how end-time prophecies were fulfilled in unexpected ways. Even though Jesus and his disciples did not destroy the enemies of Israel nor restore the kingdom to Israel in accordance with popular end-time expectations, Luke demonstrates how they did fulfill end-time prophecies. Just as Isaiah's messianic end-time prophecy was fulfilled in an unexpected manner through the anointed ministry of Jesus, so also John's end-time prophecy was fulfilled in an unexpected manner through the anointed ministry of Jesus' disciples.

In Acts "baptized with the Holy Spirit" refers to the prophetic anointing of Jesus' disciples predicted by Joel. This anointing enabled them to fulfill their function as witnesses for Jesus Christ in full prophetic power. Like the great prophets of the Old Testament they proclaimed God's message with boldness in the face of tremendous persecution and performed signs and wonders to confirm this message. For Jesus' disciples and other groups in Acts, this anointing was subsequent to their conversion. For Luke, this anointing is proof of the disciples' incorporation into God's end-time kingdom community and thus of their salvation. But it is not an integral part of or an alternate description of their conversion. It is a part of their salvation in the larger sense of the word in that it is one of the blessings promised for end-time salvation.

Even though speaking in tongues occurs on both occasions in Acts where the expression "baptized with the Holy Spirit" is used, this gift is not 'the sign' of the baptism with the Holy Spirit. This supernatural phenomenon is one of the signs confirming the disciples' prophetic anointing. For the early disciples, some sort of prophetic sign was necessary to confirm this prophetic anointing. According to Luke, the presence of God's Spirit in the life of the believer was not assumed at conversion; it was confirmed by a prophetic sign.

The presence of the Spirit without a manifestation of some tangible sign is unknown to Luke. I will have more to say about this in chapter 8. But first, we must examine one other metaphor used to describe Spirit experiences in Luke-Acts: the expression "filled with the Spirit."

Chapter 7

Filled with the Spirit

"Filled with the Spirit" is Luke's preferred metaphor for describing Spirit experiences. He talks about being filled with the Spirit no less than fourteen times in Luke-Acts. There is only one other occurrence of the expression "filled with the Spirit" in the entire New Testament (Eph 5:18). Nowhere in the New Testament is this metaphor explained. Its meaning is assumed. Even though we use similar metaphors in modern English, we cannot presuppose that Luke or Paul meant the same thing we do. Its meaning must be inferred by its use in context and by any literary or historical background material which might give us a clue. So, we will start our investigation in Luke-Acts, where we have more contexts to give us clues. Then we can look at Paul's one use of the same expression. But, before we do this, we need to look at the meaning of metaphors in general.

The meaning of metaphors

A metaphor is a figure of speech in which a word or phrase literally denoting one kind of object or idea is used in place of another to suggest a likeness or analogy between them. For example, if we say that a person is "drowning in money," we do not mean that they are in danger of dying from a lack of oxygen because their money is literally suffocating them. The metaphor is

147

simply a colorful way of saying that someone has a lot of money. The likeness
or analogy has to do with the quantity of water or money involved. Just as it
usually takes a lot of water to drown a person, a person who is "drowning in
money" has a great quantity of money.

Taking metaphors too literally can create wrong and often very comical
meanings. When Jesus said, *You are the light of the world* (Mt 5:14) he did not
literally mean that our bodies would radiate light. We instinctively know this
about most metaphors. The literal meaning makes no sense, so we assume a
figurative meaning. For the metaphor "filled with the Spirit," we instinctively
know that the Holy Spirit does not somehow transform himself into a liquid
in order to fill our bodies from head to toe. However, we may assume a more
literal interpretation for some uses of the metaphor without realizing it.

Both Pentecostal and non Pentecostal interpreters do this. Non Pentecostal interpreters may want to use the analogy of filling to infer a process.
Just as a container is filled with a pitcher of water in some sort of process, it
has been assumed that being filled with the Spirit is a continual process and
that individual believers are more or less filled with the Spirit according to
how far along they are in the process. Alfred Kuen, for example, compares
being filled with the Spirit to a reservoir slowly being filled by a tranquil
source of water.[1] The classic non Pentecostal viewpoint sees this process of
infilling occurring as the believer surrenders more and more of his or her life
to the lordship of Jesus Christ.

Pentecostal interpreters, on the other hand, may want to use the analogy of filling to explain the need for more than one filling. Multiple fillings
are necessary because we leak. We may experience the power of the Holy
Spirit, but sin and the cares of this world cause us to become ineffective and
need new infillings. Others may talk about being filled with the Spirit to the
point of overflowing, believing that the fullness of the Spirit should result in
Spirit-empowered outreach to others.

What is the problem with these analogies? They seem logical enough.
They also have a ring of truth about them. Surely we would agree that believers need to surrender more and more to the lordship of Christ and that the
Spirit plays a part in this process. It is equally true that sin and the cares of
this world can have an ill effect on our spiritual lives producing a need for renewal. Surely the Spirit also has a role to play in this renewal. Luke certainly
emphasizes the role of the Spirit in the outreach of the church.

---

[1] Kuen, p. 121.

The problem is that these analogies are not used by biblical authors to define the expression "filled with the Spirit." So, interpreters are only guessing at the meaning of the expression when they use them. It is true that these guesses are probably 'inspired' by other biblical passages. The process of surrender connected with increased spiritual maturity is most likely inspired by Paul's concept of "walking by the Spirit" (Rom 8:4-17; Gal 5:16-25). The concept of the loss of spiritual effectiveness through the deceitfulness of sin and the need for spiritual renewal could be inspired by a number of passages (Mt 13:22; Heb 3:13; Jas 4:4-10). The overflowing influence of the Spirit is surely inspired by Jesus' prophecy concerning the Spirit in John's gospel (Jn 7:38-39).

The real problem is not that interpreters are teaching non biblical concepts, but that they are teaching biblical concepts with the wrong vocabulary. The danger in this is that we miss the real meaning and implications of Luke's fullness vocabulary. If we use other New Testament authors to define Luke's concept of the fullness of the Spirit, we are in real danger of bypassing what Luke wants us to understand. We cannot afford to take the shortcut of our own imagined analogies. Luke's understanding must be inferred from the context of Luke-Acts.

Luke's use of Spirit-fullness vocabulary

Two different Greek words are used for the concept of Spirit fullness in Luke-Acts, *pimplēmi* (Lk 1:15, 41, 67; Ac 2:4; 4:8, 31; 9:17; 13:9) and *plēroō* (Lc 4:1; Ac 6:3, 5; 7:55; 11:24; 13:52). Attempts at differentiating between the two terms are unconvincing.[2] It is far more likely that Luke's use of two different terms reflects a stylistic tendency. Luke uses far more vocabulary than any other New Testament author and he is particularly fond of using synonyms. Henry J. Cadbury says that the "studied variation and exchange of synonyms" is a "distinct feature" of Luke's style of writing.[3] Thus, for ex-

---

[2] Blocher, for example, has tried to differentiate between a sudden influx of the Spirit (*pimplēmi*) and a more durable saturation with the Spirit (*plēroō*) producing Christian character, p. 21-24. This hypothesis has several problems. 1) Blocher is obligated to create a third category of "intermediate filling" for two uses of *pimplēmi* (Lk 1:15; Ac 9:17) where a "more durable dispensation of the Spirit" is discernable. 2) He also affirms that bold proclamation is a "dominant note" in the episodes where the disciples experience a sudden influx of the Spirit. Bold proclamation is clearly a durable trait of Spirit-empowered individuals in Luke-Acts (Ac 28:31). 3) He is obligated to adopt a more unlikely translation for the participle *plēstheis* (Ac 4:8; 13:9).

[3] Cadbury, *Features*, p. 92.

ample, we find in the story of Ananius and Saphira (Ac 5:1-11) two words for "property" (*ktêma*, 5:1 and *chorion*, 5:3), three words for "sell" (*epôlêsen*, 5:1, *prathen*, 5:4 and *apedosthe*, 5:8) and two words for "young men" (*neôteroi*, 5:6 and *neaniskoi*, 5:10). Cadbury has shown that this kind of variation "can be illustrated in great profusion."[4] These synonyms are not meant to convey any shift in meaning. They are used simply to avoid monotony.

Luke does, however, use various grammatical forms to make a distinction between sudden Spirit-empowering events and the powerful abiding influence of the Spirit. Elizabeth, Zachariah and Jesus' disciples were all suddenly "filled" (aorist indicative) with the Spirit and endowed with prophetic gifts such as prophecy, tongues, and boldness in proclaiming God's word (Lk 1:41, 67; Ac 2:4; 4:31). Jesus and his disciples were also described as being "filled" with (aorist participle, Ac 4:8; 13:9) or "full" of the Spirit (adjective, Lk 4:1; Ac 6:3, 5: 7:55; 11:24). The disciples are later described as being continuously "filled" (imperfect indicative) with joy and the Holy Spirit (Ac 13:52). The other two verbal forms used to indicate Spirit-fullness in Luke-Acts anticipate future endowments. John will be filled (future indicative, Lk 1:15), and Ananias prays for Paul that he might be filled with the Spirit (aorist subjunctive, Ac 9:17). The actual fillings anticipated in these verses are not recorded by Luke. However, an enduring fullness is surely implied in John's case, since he is to be filled *from his mother's womb.*

The meaning of "filled with the Spirit" in Luke-Acts

How can we legitimately determine the meaning of the expression "filled with the Spirit," since it is not defined in the New Testament? Its meaning must be inferred from historical and literary contexts. The best source for the historical context of this expression is certainly the Septuagint. This known source for some of Luke's inspiration contains several examples of similar Spirit-fullness expressions. The best source for literary contexts is, of course, Luke-Acts, where all but one of the New Testament Spirit-fullness expressions are found. Several verbal forms are used to describe Spirit-filling events. These are found together with a number of synonymous expressions used to describe the same events. Luke also uses various forms to describe an enduring state of Spirit-fullness. The sequence in the use of Spirit-fullness

---

[4] Cadbury, *Features*, p. 93.

expressions is important for discerning the relationship between Spirit-filling events and the enduring state of Spirit-fullness. Finally, a comparison of Spirit-fullness expressions with other fullness expressions in Luke-Acts should help in discerning what this metaphor was intended to convey.

"Filled with the Spirit" in the Septuagint

There is clear evidence that Luke used the Septuagint, or Greek version of the Old Testament. All of his Old Testament quotations were taken from this version.[5] We have already seen in previous chapters that the majority of Luke's Spirit-experience vocabulary is derived from Old Testament passages, in particular Isaiah's prophecy concerning a future anointed leader (61:1-2) and Joel's prophetic promise of anointing for God's end-time community (3:28-31). It only makes sense to look for Septuagint parallels to help clarify the meaning of the fullness of the Spirit.

There are only eight occurrences of Spirit-fullness expressions in the Septuagint.[6] Technically there are no uses of the two exact words used by Luke for Spirit fullness. However, all eight occurrences use a compound form of the verb *pimplēmi* used by Luke. *Empimplēmi* (sometimes written *empiplēmi*) is formed by adding the preposition *en* (with or in) to the verb. The addition of this preposition really changes nothing in the meaning of the expression, since the meaning of the preposition is already communicated by the genitive or dative case of the noun which follows. During the *koinē* period in the evolution of the Greek language, a period which included both the translation of the Septuagint and the redaction of the New Testament, there was a shift toward adding prepositions to older verbs to render them more "vivid and expressive."[7] The Septuagint verb *empimplēmi* is simply an embellished form of *pimplēmi*, the verb used by Luke. Luke also uses this compound verb, but not in conjunction with the Spirit (Lk 1:53; 6:25; Ac 14:17). Given Luke's tendency to borrow vocabulary from the Septuagint, it is plausible to think that one or more of these passages provides some basis for Luke's concept of being "filled with the Spirit."

Four of the eight occurrences appear to have little or no significance for

---

[5] Robertson, p. 99.
[6] Ex 28:3; 31:3; 35:31; Dt 34:9; Sir 39:6; 48:12; Mic 3:8; Is 11:3.
[7] Robertson, p. 163. Winer-Masson, *A Grammar of the New Testament Greek*, 1859, p. 127. Robertson places the *koinē* period between 300 B.C. et 330 A.D., p. 43.

Luke's theology of the Spirit. One of them clearly does not refer to the Spirit of God (Jb 15:2). Three others speak of artisans filled with *the Spirit of God, with skill, ability and knowledge in all kinds of crafts* (Ex 28:3; 31:3; 35:31). There is no counterpart to this type of enabling in Luke's narrative. It is interesting to note that references to the Spirit's enabling of these artisans is lacking in Josephus' account of this passage (*Antiquities* 3:200). This probably represents the tendency in intertestamental Judaism to limit the Spirit's activity almost exclusively to prophetic inspiration.[8] Even though Luke attributes other activities to the Spirit, such as the powerful exercise of signs and wonders, his theology of the Spirit, with its strong emphasis on prophetic anointing, more closely resembles that of his Jewish contemporaries than that of Paul or the apostle John.

All of the four remaining examples in the Septuagint of being filled with the Spirit appear to provide significant clues to understanding Luke's use of this expression. In Isaiah 11:3, it is the anointed descendant of David, a clearly messianic figure, who is "filled with the Spirit," like Jesus in the gospels. In Sirach 39:6 and Micah 3:8, being "filled with the Spirit" results in prophetic wisdom, proclamation and praise, just as it does in Luke-Acts.[9]

The other two Spirit-fullness expressions are particularly significant, because they use the same grammatical construction as Luke, and because they are related to Luke's important theme of the transfer of the Spirit's enabling from one Spirit-filled leader to another. In the first instance we read, *Joshua son of Nun was filled with the Spirit/spirit*[10] *of wisdom because Moses had laid his hands on him. So the Israelites listened to him and did what the LORD had commanded Moses* (Dt 34:9). On three different occasions Luke refers to Spirit-filled leaders laying their hands on others so that they might receive the gift of the Spirit. Peter and John were sent from the Jerusalem church to a new group of believers in Samaria. *When they arrived, they prayed for them that they might receive the Holy Spirit, … Then Peter and John placed their hands on them, and they received the Holy Spirit* (Ac 8:14-17). When Simon, one of the believers in Samaria, saw that *the Spirit was given at the laying on of the apostles' hands, he offered them money* so that he might obtain the same power (Ac 8:18-19). Ananias prayed and laid his hands on Saul (Paul) for him to receive

---

[8] Menzies, p. 54-56.

[9] Shepherd, p. 118.

[10] All of the major English translations read "spirit." The NIV gives the alternative "Spirit" in a footnote. The French translation, Nouvelle Edition de Genève, has "l'Esprit." Neither Greek nor Hebrew makes this distinction. The meaning must be determined by context.

his sight and be filled with the Holy Spirit (Ac 9:12, 17). Paul, in turn, laid his hands on the Ephesian disciples for them to receive the gift of the Holy Spirit (Ac 19:6). The above incident with Moses and Joshua, recorded in Deuteronomy, is the closest parallel in the Old Testament to these passages, making it a likely source of inspiration for this practice in the book of Acts.

The second significant passage concerns the transfer of the Spirit's enabling power from Elijah to Elisha. "When Elijah was concealed by a whirlwind, Elisha was filled with his Spirit/spirit" (Sir 48:12).[11] Prophecy and the exercise of miraculous wonders were the result (Sir 48:13-14). The multiple and clear allusions to the prophetic ministries of Elijah and Elisha in Luke-Acts make this parallel particularly pertinent. Jesus performs miracles, heals the sick and raises the dead (Lk 7:22). The transfer of the Spirit from Jesus to his disciples takes place after his ascension (Ac 2:33). Jesus' disciples then perform miracles, heal the sick and raise the dead in the power of the Spirit. All of these events are paralleled in the Elijah and Elisha stories. Now, in Sirach's account of these stories, we find another important parallel. When the transfer of the Spirit takes place, both Jesus' disciples and Elijah's disciple are described as being "filled with the Spirit" (*eplêsthêsan pneumatos*, Ac 2:4; *eneplêsthê pneumatos*, Sir 48:12). Even the fact that Elisha is filled with his Spirit, if we understand "his" to refer to the Spirit which was upon Elijah, has its parallel in the book of Acts, because the Holy Spirit is also referred to as the *the Spirit of Jesus* (Ac16:7).

These two Spirit-transfer parallels in the Septuagint provide the most likely basis for understanding Luke's use of "fullness" vocabulary to describe encounters with the Spirit.[12] The same vocabulary and grammatical constructions are used to describe these encounters. The same methods are used to bring about these experiences. The various encounters occur in similar situations with similar results. The Spirit is passed on from one prophet to the next with the result that the new prophet begins to function in the power of the Spirit like his predecessor. All these factors lead to the same conclusion. "Filled with the Spirit" is another synonymous expression referring to prophetic anointing. Jesus is a prophet like Moses and Elijah in that his prophetic anointing is passed on to his disciples in an experience which is described as being "filled with the Spirit" (Ac 2:4, 33).

---

[11] My translation of the Septuagint.
[12] Josephe A. Fitzmeyer, "The Role of the Spirit in Luke-Acts," *The Unity of Luke-Acts*, ed. J. Verheyden, Leuven University, 1999, p. 179.

"Filled with the Spirit" and synonymous expressions in Luke-Acts

Like the expression "baptized with the Spirit," "filled with the Spirit" is also used synonymously to describe the same events. Practically every expression Luke uses to describe encounters with the Spirit in Luke-Acts is used to describe what happened on the day of Pentecost. In anticipation of the events, the disciples are told to wait for *power from on high* which they are about to *receive*, a *gift* which the *Father has promised* (Lk 24:49; Ac 1:4, 8). This is to be a fulfillment of John's prophecy that they will be *baptized with the Holy Spirit* (Ac 1:5). When the fulfillment of these prophetic promises actually occurs, none of these expressions are used to describe the experience. Instead, the Spirit is said to descend or *fall upon* them (Ac 2:2-3; 11:15), and they are *filled with the Spirit* (Ac 2:4). When Peter explains what has just happened, he adds another expression. He says that the Spirit has been *poured out* on them in fulfillment of Joel's end-time prophecy (Ac 2:17-18, 33). He also repeats the idea that they have *received* the *gift* of the Holy Spirit, which the *Father has promised*, indicating that the Father's promise is the same as that prophesied by Joel (Ac 2:33, 38-39; 10:47).

All of the above expressions refer to the prophetic anointing which God promised to pour out on all his servants in the last days according to Joel's prophecy. In Luke-Acts, this anointing appears to have taken place suddenly in some sort of crisis experience. Elizabeth was suddenly filled when she heard Mary's greeting and immediately began to utter prophetic praise (Lk 1:41). Zachariah was suddenly filled at the birth of his son, John the Baptist, and immediately began to prophesy (Lk 1:67). Jesus' disciples were suddenly filled on the day of Pentecost and began to speak in tongues (Ac 2:2-4), a gift which Peter understood as a manifestation of prophesy (Ac 2:16-18). The believers were again suddenly filled with the Spirit when the place where they were meeting was shaken and they spoke the word of God boldly (Ac 4:31).

If we accept the use of synonymous phrases as true parallels to the expression "filled with the Spirit," the new believers in Samaria were suddenly filled with the Spirit when Peter and John prayed and laid their hands on them (Ac 8.15-17). Those in the house of Cornelius were suddenly filled with the Spirit while Peter was still preaching, and they immediately began speaking in tongues and praising God (Ac 10:44-46). The same would be true for the disciples in Ephesus. They were suddenly filled with the Spirit when Paul laid his hands on them, and they spoke in tongues and prophesied (Ac 19:6).

The pattern of all these episodes is clear and consistent. They all experience a sudden encounter with the Spirit and then immediately exercise some sort of tangible prophetic gift, demonstrating the power of their prophetic anointing. This pattern resembles that of numerous encounters with the Spirit in the Old Testament. We have already mentioned the experiences of Joshua and Elijah. Several others fit the same pattern. When the Spirit rested upon the 70 elders of Israel, they prophesied (Nb 11:25-29). When he came mightily upon Saul, he also prophesied (1 Sam 10:10-11;[13] 19:23). He came upon some of Saul's envoys and they also prophesied (1 Sam 19:20). When the Spirit came upon David, there is no mention of any immediate tangible prophetic gift (1 Sam 16:13). However, in the following episode, David's music has the power to drive out Saul's evil spirit (1 Sam 16:23), and his psalms were definitely considered to be prophetically inspired by the Spirit in Luke-Acts (Ac 1:16; 2:29-30; 4:25). David's capacity to drive out Saul's evil spirit is certainly the closest parallel in the Old Testament to the New Testament practice of casting out evil spirits, also a function of those who were empowered by the Spirit (Lk 4:14, 36; 7:21; 11:15-26; Ac 5:16; 8:7; 19:12-17). Luke appears to understand and describe New Testament experiences in terms of the vocabulary and prophetic experiences he has learned from the Septuagint. He sees the move of the Spirit in the early church as a renewal and expansion of Old Testament prophetic anointing. This is explicitly stated in Peter's quotation of Joel's prophecy and demonstrated throughout Luke's two-volume work by his choice of Spirit-anointing and fullness expressions.

The continuous state of Spirit fullness in Luke-Acts

Luke employs several other expressions to describe a more continuous state of Spirit fullness. The most common expression employs the adjective *plêrês*. Jesus was *full of the Holy Spirit* when he *returned from the Jordan* (Lk 4:1). The seven men chosen to distribute food to poor widows were full of the Spirit (Lk 6:3). Twice Stephen is described as being full of the Spirit (Ac 6:5; 7:55). Barnabas was also full of the Spirit (Ac 11:24). Another

---

[13] The term used here in the LXX (*hallomai*) is not used by Luke for an experience with the Holy Spirit, perhaps because it is so closely associated with military exploits in the LXX (cf. Jgs 14:6, 19; 15:14; 1 Sam 11:6), and Luke wants to avoid the image of a Messiah warrior-king. Luke uses it to describe a 'military' exploit of a man with an evil spirit (Ac 19.16).

unquestionable example of a more continuous state of Spirit fullness is the statement that the *disciples were* [continuously] *filled (eplêrounto) with joy and the Holy Spirit* (Ac 13:52).[14]

In four of the above six examples, the statement that individuals were 'filled with' or 'full of' the Holy Spirit "is coupled with some second quality (6.3 = wisdom; 6.5 and 11.24 = faith; 13.52 = joy) in such a way that the quality in question is seen to derive from the Spirit."[15] For example, Stephen and the other men chosen to distribute food are *full of the Spirit and wisdom* (Ac 6:3). That this wisdom is derived from the Spirit becomes clear from the related statement that Stephen's opponents *could not stand up (anthistêmi) against his wisdom or the Spirit by whom he spoke* (Ac 6:10). This statement is a fulfillment of two prophecies given by Jesus. To prepare them for the coming persecution he told his disciples, *the Holy Spirit will teach you at that time what you should say* (Lk 12:12). He also told them not to worry about what to say, for *I will give you words and wisdom that none of your adversaries will be able to resist (anthistêmi) or contradict* (Lk 21:15).

Because two of the above qualities are also found in Paul's list of the fruit of the Spirit (Gal 5:22), some interpreters believe that Luke is talking about a similar process and have hypothesized that these passages support the idea of a progressive growth in fullness and its accompanying qualities.[16] The concept of progressive growth producing the fruit of the Spirit fits the metaphors used by Paul. Not only does the production of fruit imply a period of growth, but the other Spirit expressions in the same passage also suggest a process. Paul exhorts the Galatians to *live by the Spirit* (Gal 5:16) just before mentioning the fruit of the Spirit and to *keep in step with the Spirit* (Gal 5:25) just after.

The metaphor "filled with the Spirit" could possibly imply a gradual process, but it is not a foregone conclusion. A vessel can be filled gradually over time or suddenly in one moment. The time required depends on the source filling the vessel. Our studies up to this point favor a more sudden filling. Luke's vocabulary is intense. The source of filling in Luke-Acts is more like an overwhelming flood or a violent wind (Lk 3:16; Ac 1:5; 2:4) than a trickling stream or a gentle breeze. All of the episodes describing the act of being filled with the Spirit are sudden and powerful (Lk 1:41, 67;

---

[14] The NIV does not include the term continuously. I have added it to emphasize the continuous meaning of the imperfect tense used here. The NASB translates the term with "continually filled."

[15] Turner, p. 408.

[16] Turner, p. 409-411.

Ac 2:4; 4:31). Believers did not contain the Spirit. They were completely overwhelmed by the Spirit and the results were immediately and powerfully evident.

Does the sequence of vocabulary and events suggest a different process for expressions describing the state or condition of Spirit-fullness? Do the more adjectival expressions imply a more gradual filling? The hypothesis of progressive fullness seems plausible, but it is not explicitly taught using fullness vocabulary anywhere in the New Testament. Luke also gives no examples of believers who are partially filled with the Spirit. In Luke-Acts we find believers who have not yet "received" the Spirit (Ac 8:16; 9:17; 19:2), and we find those who are full or have been filled with the Holy Spirit (Ac 2:4; 4:8, 31; 6:3, 5; 19:6, etc.). There is no mention in Luke-Acts of any carnal Christians who have some influence of the Spirit in their lives, but who are not yet full.

Instead of assuming that Paul and Luke are describing the same reality, let's examine Luke's Spirit-fullness expressions in contexts where they are associated with qualities related to Christian maturity. For example, the disciples chosen to distribute food to widows must be *full of the Spirit and wisdom* (Ac 6:3). Is this wisdom derived from their Christian growth or a more miraculous gifting from the Holy Spirit? The example given in the episode immediately following this description supports the second conclusion. Stephen's adversaries were unable to *stand up against his wisdom or the Spirit by whom he spoke* (Ac 6:10). Jesus prophesied that these words of wisdom would be given to his disciples *at that time*, when it was needed (Lk 12:12; 21:15). This example of Stephen's Spirit-endowed wisdom immediately following the description of him being described as *full of the Spirit and wisdom* does not appear to be wisdom which Stephen acquired over time as he matured in his Christian walk. It is described as a powerful manifestation of wisdom exceeding human capabilities and thus attributed to the supernatural influence of the Spirit.

One could ask why these leaders needed supernatural wisdom to distribute food. But Luke also included an episode in the preceding chapter where supernatural knowledge was needed in the distribution of wealth. Peter received supernatural knowledge that Ananias and Saphira *lied to the Holy Spirit* concerning the money they had received for the sale of property (Ac 5:3). He asked Saphira, *How could you agree to test the Spirit of the Lord* (Ac 5:9)? The early believers had an acute awareness of the Spirit's direct involvement in the life and function of the church. It is completely logical that its leadership would want to ensure the continuation of such Spirit-directed leadership by requiring those who replaced them in this service to exhibit some of the same direct influence of the Spirit.

Stephen was also *a man full of faith and the Holy Spirit* (Ac 6:5). Was this faith an unshakeable assurance in God, the fruit of his continued dependence on the Holy Spirit over time? Or was it an incredible faith to do miracles, demonstrated at various times at the initiative of the Holy Spirit? The immediate context again provides the best clue to answer this question. Three verses later Luke tells us that, *Stephen, a man full of God's grace and power, did great wonders and miraculous signs among the people* (Ac 6:8). The fact that *power* is so closely associated with the Spirit in Luke-Acts (Lk 1:35; 4:18; Ac 1:8) supports the connection already evident in the sequence of the details related in this story. Again, we see that the immediate context favors the idea of a supernatural gifting of faith rather than a faith acquired through the influence the Spirit over time.

We should take into consideration one more Spirit-fullness expression, because it involves a quality listed as a fruit of the Spirit. When persecution arose and Paul and Barnabas were expelled from the region of Pisidian Antioch, Luke tells us that *the disciples were filled with joy and with the Holy Spirit* (Ac 13:52). The verb tense (imperfect) indicates more than a single event. It refers to some kind of continuous activity. The context is not clear enough to define this activity precisely. Some of the possibilities would include an emphasis on describing what was in the process of occurring, what occurred repeatedly or what occurred continuously. Should we conclude from this observation that this joy was acquired over time through the imperceptible influence of the Spirit, the fruit of continued obedience to the Lord? Or is it more likely that Luke sees here a miraculous endowment of joy? The second hypothesis is more likely for two reasons. First of all, the disciples filled with joy and the Holy Spirit were new believers (Ac 13:48-49). They would not have had time to develop this fruit. Secondly, Luke's emphasis throughout his entire two-volume work is on the immediate tangible evidence of the Holy Spirit. It is more likely that he sees in the joy of these disciples evidence of the supernatural empowering of the Holy Spirit. They are filled with joy when circumstances called for fear and apprehension.

Spirit-fullness expressions in narrative sequence

One of the problems facing interpreters is that Spirit-filled individuals are described as being filled with the Spirit more than once. How are we to understand these 'multiple' fillings? What happens to individuals who are filled with the Spirit? Do they remain full? Can they lose their fullness? If they can lose their fullness, how do we explain the more continuous expressions of fullness? Answers to these questions need to explain all of these expressions in context. I propose looking at all these expressions in narrative sequence.

John the Baptist is the first individual in Luke's narrative to be "filled with the Spirit." The angel of the Lord announces to Zechariah that John *will be filled with the Holy Spirit even from birth* (Lk 1:15). The verb used is the future indicative of *pimplēmi*. The emphasis in this sentence is on the early beginning of this experience, *even from birth* or more literally, "even from his mother's womb." But the result is obviously a continuous state of fullness. It is inconceivable that John was filled momentarily for a specific task at birth. In chapter 3, John is presented as a prophet of the Lord, proclaiming God's message to Israel. His fullness with the Spirit announced in chapter 1 anticipates this ministry.

In the next two examples, both Elizabeth and Zechariah "were filled with the Holy Spirit" and immediately endowed with prophetic speech (Lk 1:41, 67). The aorist indicative of *pimplēmi* is used. The aorist presents the event as a "snapshot" in contrast with the present or imperfect which views the event as an "ongoing process."[17] This does not imply that the results of this event do not continue. In fact, there is good reason to believe that this is an ingressive aorist, which simply means that the aorist tense stresses the entrance into a state of being.[18] This use of the aorist is quite common, especially with verbs describing a state of being.[19] Since the first reference to being filled with the Spirit implied an entrance into a state of fullness (Lk 1:15), the reader would most naturally assume that the next two uses of the same verb refer to a similar event, unless there were some information to contradict such an understanding. There is no such information in Luke's account. It should also be noted that every occurrence of the verb *pimplēmi* (*empimplēmi*) in the Septuagint with respect to the Spirit results in a more enduring state of fullness.[20]

---

[17] Wallace, p. 554-55.

[18] Ervin, *Baptism*, p. 45.

[19] Ervin, *Baptism*, p. 45; Dana, p. 196.

[20] Ex 28:3; 31:3; 35:31; Dt 34:9; Sir 39:6; 48:12; Mic 3:8; Is 11.3, see Turner, p. 167. It is not clear whether Sir 39:6 or Is 11:3 refer to the Spirit or the spirit, but they do refer to a more enduring state of fullness. Even though Turner acknowledges this consistent use of the verb in the Septuagint, he affirms that Luke uses it to "designate short outbursts of spiritual power/inspiration, rather than the inception of long-term endowments of the Spirit" (p. 168).

The fourth example of Spirit fullness in Luke-Acts is a description of Jesus. He was *full (plêrês) of the Spirit* when he *returned from the Jordan and was led* (imperfect tense) *by the Spirit in the desert* (Lk 4:1). The adjective *plêrês* and the continuous action of being led by the Spirit both infer a continuous state of fullness. When and how was Jesus filled? The answer must be inferred from context. Luke uses five expressions in rapid succession to describe Jesus' experience with the Spirit: 1) The *Spirit descended on him* during his baptism at the Jordan (Lk 3:22); 2) He returned from the Jordan *full of the Spirit* (Lk 4:1); 3) He was *led by the Spirit* (Lk 4:1); 4) He returned to Galilee *in the power of the Spirit* (Lk 4:14) and 5) He read the passage from Isaiah stating, *The Spirit of the Lord is on me, because he has anointed me* (Lk 4:18). Two of these expressions have verbal links with Jesus' baptism experience and probably refer back to it. *Jesus, full of the Spirit, returned from the Jordan,*[21] the place where the Spirit descended on him (Lk 3.3). The clear implication is that he was filled with the Spirit when the Spirit descended on him. Jesus also stated that the Spirit was *on* him, because he had anointed him. When did this anointing take place? It most likely refers back to the Spirit descending *on* him at his baptism (Lk 3.22). These conclusions will become even clearer when we look at the parallel experience of Jesus' disciples. The other two expressions probably refer to the effects of Jesus' fullness of the Spirit acquired at his baptism. He was led by the Spirit and operated in the power of the Spirit.

The next individuals to be filled with the Spirit in Luke's narrative are Jesus' disciples on the day of Pentecost. *All of them were filled with the Holy Spirit and began to speak in other tongues as the Spirit enabled them* (Ac 2:4). I have already referred to the large number of synonymous phrases used to refer to this one event. It bears repeating that the same types of expressions used to describe Jesus' encounter with the Spirit are also used to describe the disciples' encounter. The Holy Spirit also came *on* the disciples (Ac 1:8). This descent of the Spirit on the disciples was also represented by a visible sign (Ac 2:3). The disciples, like Jesus, were all *filled* with the Spirit (Ac 2:4). Their experience is also described with anointing vocabulary (Ac 2:17-18, 33). There is no question about when the disciples were filled with the Spirit. Like Jesus, they were all filled when the Spirit descended on them (Ac 2.3-4).

The next episode in Luke-Acts containing Spirit-fullness expressions

---

[21] This reference to Jordan at the beginning of this episode is not found in the parallel accounts of Matthew and Mark.

concerns some of the same disciples. Peter and John were used by God to heal a crippled beggar near the temple (Ac 3:1-7). This miracle sparked a series of events. First, Peter used this miracle as a springboard for preaching the gospel and many turned to Christ. This greatly disturbed some of the religious rulers so they arrested them and asked for an explanation. Peter, *filled* (aorist participle) *with the Holy Spirit* began to preach to them with great boldness (Ac 4:8-13). The difficulty with the interpretation of this expression has to do with the various uses of the aorist participle. Participles in Greek are verbal adjectives and can emphasize either a verbal or an adjectival aspect.[22] If the adjectival aspect is emphasized, the participle tells us something about Peter. He is filled with the Spirit. Used as an adjective, Peter's condition resembles that of Stephen, who spoke wisdom by the Spirit because he was "full" of the Spirit (Ac 6:3, 10). Peter's preaching here is another fulfillment of Jesus' prophecy. Just as Jesus predicted, Peter was *brought before synagogues, rulers and authorities* (Lk 12:11; Ac 4:4-7). Luke mentions Peter being "filled with the Spirit" to indicate that the Spirit is teaching him what to say, just as Jesus predicted (Lk 12:12). The aorist participle *plēstheis* appears to have the same function in this episode with Peter as the adjective *plērēs* has in the episode with Stephen. Luke recognizes an individual is Spirit-filled when he exercises a prophetic function.

If the verbal aspect of the participle is emphasized in this passage, it may tell us something about when the action took place. Peter was filled with the Spirit some time before he spoke, just previous to speaking, or perhaps, simultaneously as he spoke.[23] F. F. Bruce attempts to draw a distinction here between the use of the aorist participle in this passage, "denoting a special moment of inspiration, and the use of the adjective ('full') to denote abiding character of a Spirit-filled man."[24] This distinction, however, is inconsistent with Luke's usage of these terms elsewhere, since he also uses the adjective "full" in the context of a momentary event. Stephen is "full" (adjective) of the Spirit, when he sees a vision of Jesus at the right hand of God (Ac 7:55). In these two episodes the participle and the adjective perform the same function. They both indicate the source of the individual's prophetic experience which follows. Visions and prophetic speech were typical results of the Spirit's influence in the Old Testament and promised to the end-time commu-

[22] Wallace, p. 616.
[23] Wallace, p. 623-25.
[24] Bruce, p. 99.

nity in Joel's prophecy (Ac 2:17-18; Jl 2:28-29). Even if we decide that the participle is adverbial, the most common understanding of a temporal aorist participle is that the action of the participle is antecedent to the action of the main verb "to speak."[25] For this verse it would mean that Peter's filling with the Spirit occurred at some time previous to this event.

We must again ask when Peter was filled. The most obvious answer is that he was filled at Pentecost, because Luke states explicitly that they were all, including Peter, filled with the Holy Spirit at Pentecost (Ac 2:4). This is the most likely answer to this question whether we consider the participle to be adjectival or adverbial. If it is adjectival, there is no other previous mention of Peter's infilling with the Spirit in the text. If this participle is adverbial, surely it refers to the event already mentioned by Luke. If Luke wanted his readers to understand a simultaneous event or one which occurred immediately prior to Peter's speaking, he would have needed to use an indicative verb instead of the more ambiguous participle.

The next repetition of Spirit fullness creates a problem for those who hold to the position that believers can only be filled with the Spirit one time. Presumably, only a few hours after Peter is said to be *filled with the Holy Spirit* (Ac 4:8), he is part of a group of believers who *were all filled with the Holy Spirit* (Ac 4:31). Howard Ervin has attempted to explain why Peter and John should not be included in the *all* who were filled that day.[26] How can Peter be filled with the Spirit and later in the same day need to be filled with the Spirit again? Could he have lost his fullness so quickly? The problem with this type of reasoning is that it places too much emphasis on the literal meaning of the metaphor "filled with" something. We will return to these questions after examining other uses of the same metaphor in Luke-Acts.

We find the aorist participle, employed to describe Peter's state of fullness, used in a similar manner to describe the apostle Paul. Ananias prays that Paul might *be filled* (aorist subjunctive) *with the Holy Spirit* (Ac 9:17). Presumably this occurs at that time. The event is not recorded by Luke. Later in the narrative, Paul is said to be *filled* (aorist participle) *with the Spirit*, when he pronounces a curse on Elymus, the magician (Ac 13:9). If we ask when Paul was filled, the most likely answer is when Ananias prayed for him. With this episode there is an interesting conceptual link between the

---

[25] Bruce, p. 624. Simultaneous action is also possible. Dunn concludes that it had to occur "immediately prior to" Peter's act of speaking, p. 71. Dunn has been ably refuted by Ervin, *Conversion*, p. 36-37.

[26] Ervin, *Baptism*, p. 53-54.

two passages. When Ananias prays for Paul to be healed and filled with the Spirit, Paul was blind and his eyesight is restored. In the later passage, when Luke reminds us that Paul is filled with the Spirit, Paul curses Elymus with blindness (Ac 13:11).

Most of the remaining examples of Spirit fullness in Luke-Acts concern individuals who are described as "full" of the Holy Spirit using the adjective *plērēs* with no previous mention of when they were filled. There are three references to the seven men chosen to distribute food to widows. They must all be *full of the Spirit and wisdom* (Ac 6:3). Stephen is *full of faith and the Holy Spirit* (Ac 6:5). Luke then reminds us that Stephen is *full of the Holy Spirit*, when he sees a heavenly vision (Ac 7:55). Luke probably mentions the fullness of the Spirit here to remind his readers that this is a fulfillment of Joel's prophecy that *your young men will see visions* (Ac 2:17). Finally, Barnabas is described as *full of the Holy Spirit and faith* when he is sent to encourage the church in Antioch (Ac 11:24).

When were these men filled with the Spirit? No previous encounter with the Spirit is specifically mentioned for these individuals, so there is no obvious answer. Yet, the narrative sequence in the account of Jesus' experience and in that of his disciples encourages the reader to assume a similar experience for these other disciples. If Jesus and his disciples, and later Paul, all had some sort of powerful first encounter with the Holy Spirit and then afterwards were described as full of the Spirit, the reader is ready to assume that those who are described as full of the Spirit also had some sort of powerful encounter. Luke describes no other paradigm for being filled with the Spirit. Modern readers might assume a different paradigm, especially if their own experience lacks any such powerful encounters with the Spirit. But Luke's account in Acts gives us the impression that early believers would have no trouble with this assumption. We cannot, however, determine when or where these men were filled with the Spirit. They may have been among the 120 who were all filled on the day of Pentecost (Ac 1:15; 2:4). Or they may have been at the prayer meeting when *the place where they were meeting was shaken. And they were all filled with the Holy Spirit* (Ac 4:31). Or they may have been filled at some other moment not included in Luke's account. The point is that Luke's account leads us to believe that every Spirit-filled believer had some sort of powerful encounter with the Spirit, which Luke would describe with the metaphor "filled with the Holy Spirit."

In the last use of Spirit-fullness vocabulary in the book of Acts, we are told that the disciples in Pisidian Antioch *were filled* (imperfect tense) *with joy and with the Holy Spirit* (Ac 13:52). The imperfect tense focuses on the process and portrays the action as it unfolds.[27] Some sort of continuous process or repetitive action is to be understood.[28] The New Amercan Standard version translates this verb with a continuous meaning. "The disciples were continually filled with joy and with the Holy Spirit." There are two ways of understanding a possible repetitive action in this verse. Either the same disciples were being "filled *again* and *again*" with joy and with the Holy Spirit, or different disciples were being "filled *one after another*."[29] Any of these translations are possible. However, a more continuous meaning is probably intended here, with the idea that their phenomenal continuous joy was a result of them being continuously full of the Spirit. Luke is not concerned with these disciples' reception of the Spirit or any previous experience with the Spirit. His purpose is to demonstrate that the expansion of the end-time community of believers among the Gentiles is sanctioned by God, even though it is rejected by Jewish leaders (Ac 13:45-50). His point is that, even though Paul and Barnabas were persecuted and expelled from the region (Ac 13:50), their ministry was validated by God. The ongoing phenomenal joy experienced by their disciples in the face of such persecution was clear evidence of the powerful influence of the Holy Spirit. Luke probably also included this detail as another parallel to Jesus, who was also *full of joy through the Holy Spirit* (Lk 10:21).

Other fullness expressions in Luke-Acts

The expression "filled with" something or "full of" something is not limited to Spirit-fullness in Luke-Acts. The metaphor is used by Luke to communicate various conditions. These non-Spirit fullness expressions may shed some light on what Luke intends to communicate by indicating that individuals were Spirit-filled. Luke uses both the verbs *pimplêmi* and *plêroô* (to be filled) and the adjective *plêrês* (full) to describe a variety of emotions and qualities. Individuals were filled (*pimplêmi*) with rage (Lk 4:28; 6:11), fear (Lk 5:26), wonder and amazement (Ac 3:10), jealousy (Ac 5:17; 13:45) and confusion (Ac 19:29). They were also filled (*plêroô*) with wisdom (Lk 2:40) and joy

---

[27] Wallace, p. 541.
[28] Wallace, p. 546-48.
[29] Ervin, *Baptism*, p. 56-57, Ervin's italics. Ervin gives Mt 3:6 as an example. Those who confessed their sins were obviously not baptized by John again and again but one after another.

(Ac 2:28). Satan filled (*pleroō*) Ananias' heart, prompting him to lie to the Holy Spirit (Ac 5:3). Others were full (*plērēs*) of leprosy (Lk 5:12), grace and power (Ac 6:8), good works and acts of charity (Ac 9:36), deceit (Ac 13:10), and rage (Ac 19:28).

None of these expressions are used to describe a progressive process. They are all used to describe a condition. Jesus' listeners were filled with rage when they heard Jesus extolling the faith of Gentiles included in God's plan of salvation with the inference that they were being excluded (Lk 4:24-28). Luke's emphasis here is not on the process of "filling" but on their enraged condition. The expression *filled with rage* is simply a more animated, more powerful way of saying "they were enraged." Those who are filled with fear are exceedingly afraid. Those who are filled with wonder and amazement are extraordinarily amazed. Those who are filled with jealousy are extremely jealous. It follows that those who are filled with the Spirit also exhibit some sort of extreme condition. They are powerfully influenced by the Spirit, overwhelmed by the Spirit. This is what makes this expression a good substitute for the expression "baptized with the Spirit" (Ac 1:5; 2:4). They both refer to the overwhelming influence, impact and power of the Spirit on those who receive the gift of the Spirit.

On several occasions, Luke demonstrates this overwhelming influence by way of contrast. Jesus was full of the Spirit (Lk 4:1) and started his ministry of proclamation and healing in Galilee in the power of the Spirit (Lk 4:14-44). His compatriots in Nazareth were filled with rage and tried to kill him (Lk 4:28). Jewish leaders were filled with jealousy when they saw the success of the early disciples' preaching (Ac 5:17; 13:45). The disciples were filled with joy and the Holy Spirit (Ac 13:52). Satan filled the heart of Ananias so that he lied to the Holy Spirit concerning the distribution of aid to the poor in Jerusalem (Ac 5:3). The Jerusalem church is then asked to choose seven leaders "full of the Holy Spirit" and wisdom to administrate the distribution of this aid (Ac 6:3). The emphasis here is on the source of inspiration and influence. Ananias is powerfully influenced by Satan. The seven must be powerfully influenced by the Holy Spirit.

Source of influence is an important issue in Luke's strategy. Luke must demonstrate that Jesus is the Anointed One and that his disciples are approved by God. There is no question that powerful acts are being performed. People are healed and delivered from demons. The dead are raised. The word of God is powerfully proclaimed in tongues unknown to those proclaiming it. Opponents try to discredit these deeds by attributing them to other influences. His detractors claim that Jesus casts out demons *by Beelzebub, the prince of demons* (Lk 11:15). Jesus explains that he drives them out *by the finger of God* (Lk 11:20).[30] Some attribute the disciples' exuberant praise in unknown tongues to drunkenness (Ac 2:13). Peter explains that their source is the prophetic anointing of the Holy Spirit (Ac 2:16-18).

The meaning of Spirit-fullness expressions in Luke-Acts

Luke uses the expression "filled with the Holy Spirit" to describe the powerful and overwhelming influence of the Holy Spirit in the life and ministry of those who have received this gift. In Luke-Acts, the Spirit's influence is always powerful and overwhelming. Every Spirit-filled individual in Luke-Acts is described in powerful and overwhelming terms. They prophesy and perform signs and wonders. The wisdom of their arguments is irrefutable. Their joy is unassailable. Their faith and courage is unstoppable. All of these powerful effects are attributed to the influence of the Holy Spirit, which Luke frequently describes with fullness vocabulary.

"Filled with the Spirit" is derived from an Old Testament expression which Luke has adopted to describe this overwhelming influence. He uses it to affirm to his readers that the powerful acts and qualities exhibited in the lives of Jesus and his disciples are the result of the empowering influence of the Holy Spirit. In a manner similar to its use in the Septuagint, "filled with the Spirit" is used to describe powerful encounters with the Holy Spirit enabling those who are "filled" to function as prophets. As in the Old Testament, Spirit-filled individuals continue to function in the enabling power of the Spirit after their initial filling. It is therefore a very suitable synonymous expression for all the various prophetic anointing episodes in Luke-Acts. Because of two very important Septuagint examples (Dt 34:9; Sir 48:12), "filled with the Spirit" is particularly appropriate for describing the transfer of power from one Spirit-filled prophetic figure to another.

The study of non-Spirit fullness expressions leads to the conclusion that "filled with the Spirit" describes the source and intensity of their empower-

---

[30] This is probably an allusion to Ex 8:15, where the Egyptian magicians ascribe signs and wonders performed by Moses to "the finger of God." Some think that Luke is trying to avoid the idea of the Spirit empowering individuals to cast out demons (see, p. ex., Menzies, p. 112-13, 161-63), but it is more likely Luke's desire to highlight the "prophet like Jesus" motif which motivates this choice of words.

ing rather than the process of their experience. This solves the enigma of how Peter can be filled, then full, and then filled again with the Spirit (Ac 2:4; 4:8, 31). When the Holy Spirit came upon him at Pentecost, he began to speak in other tongues. Luke recognized that the exercise of the gift of tongues was due to the overwhelming influence of the Holy Spirit. This was Peter's first encounter with the Spirit and it occurred in a powerful event. A powerful wind filled the house and tongues of fire descended and came to rest on each of them. So, Luke uses a verb to describe the experience. He was *filled with the Holy Spirit* (Ac 2:4). Later, when Peter courageously proclaims the gospel to hostile religious leaders in Jerusalem, Luke recognizes in this prophetic ability the powerful influence of the Holy Spirit and recalls that Peter is *filled with the Holy Spirit* (Ac 4:8). Thus, Luke uses a participle to describe his condition of Spirit-fullness which enabled him to do what he did. Finally, when the place where they were praying was shaken and the disciples experience renewed courage to speak the word of God boldly, Luke understands that this is again due to the overwhelming influence of the Holy Spirit. Since this occurs in another powerful event, Luke uses a verb again to describe the experience. *They were all filled with the Holy Spirit* (Ac 4:31). Since the expression describes the source and intensity of their experience rather than the process, there is no need to determine when they lost Spirit-fullness. Luke is just describing another intense experience brought about by the powerful influence of the Holy Spirit.

How does "filled with the Spirit" compare with the other expressions used by Luke to describe experiences with the Spirit? Almost all of Luke's expressions are used for the disciples' experience with the Spirit on the day of Pentecost. Howard Ervin insists that all these terms are equivalent because they all refer to the same event.[31] His logic is not entirely correct. His reasoning merely proves that they are synonymous. They are not necessarily equivalent. They could and do refer to different perspectives concerning the same event. Some of the expressions refer to the arrival of the Holy Spirit, his descent upon believers or the reception of the Spirit by believers. Many allude to the fulfillment of Joel's prophetic promise of the gift of Spirit anointing. However, Luke does not distinguish between the reception of the Spirit and prophetic anointing with the Spirit. Those who receive the Spirit demonstrate prophetic anointing through powerful words and acts, and it is understood that those who do not demonstrate prophetic anointing have

---

[31] Ervin, *Baptism*, p. 25.

not received the Spirit (Ac 8:15-19; 19:1-6). This fact introduces a difficulty with the Pauline theology of the Spirit, which we will examine in chapter 8.

The expression "filled with the Spirit," however, is not entirely equivalent to Spirit-reception or Spirit-anointing expressions in Luke-Acts, because it refers not so much to the event itself as to the powerful effects of Spirit reception-anointing.[32] It is the only expression used by Luke more than once for the same individuals. Individual believers who were filled with the Spirit continue to demonstrate the powerful effects of being Spirit-filled and therefore, are said to be "full" of the Spirit. They can also have other powerful experiences with the Spirit where they are again "filled with the Spirit." In Luke-Acts, therefore, "filled with the Spirit" is both continuous and repeatable. It simply means that the influence of the Spirit is powerfully visible in the life and ministry of the believers.

The meaning of "filled with the Spirit" in Ephesians 5:18

The metaphor of Spirit fullness is only used one time in the New Testament outside of Luke-Acts. Paul exhorts the saints in Ephesus to *be filled with the Spirit* (Eph 5:18). Does Paul use this expression in the same way Luke does? Do we need to modify our understanding of Luke's expression on the basis of what Paul teaches? The answers to these two questions are interdependent. If the metaphor "filled with the Spirit" had acquired some sort of fixed meaning before the redaction of the New Testament, then it should be evident that both authors use the expression in the same manner. However, if they use the expression differently, there is no need to change our understanding of one author on the basis of the other. We do, however, need to base our understanding of the overall work of the Spirit on the teachings of multiple New Testament authors. To discern the answers to these questions we need to examine both the similarities and the differences in the use of this expression in Luke-Acts and Ephesians.

---

[32] "Baptized with the Spirit" also refers to the powerful effects of the Spirit, and could be an equivalent to "filled with the Spirit" in Luke's theology. Luke's infrequent use of this expression does not permit us to draw this conclusion with certainty. Even though the expression emphasizes the powerful effects of the Spirit, it is only used for initial experiences in Luke-Acts. This is most likely because of its popular association with end-time judgment and not because of its association with an *initial* reception, but some sort of initiatory idea cannot be ruled out.

Differences

As in the case with the metaphor "baptized with the Spirit," Paul does not use the same Spirit-fullness expression as Luke. For fullness of Spirit, Luke always places the term "Spirit" in the genitive case (*pneumatos* 14 times). This is true no matter which term or grammatical form he uses for fullness. Paul, however, places the term "Spirit" in the dative case (*pneumati*) preceded by the preposition *en*. As we have already seen in Paul's use of "baptized *en pneumati*," this grammatical construction can create a certain amount of ambiguity. *En pneumati* could, among other possibilities, have an instrumental meaning. Just as the Corinthians were "baptized by one Spirit," Paul could be saying here that the Ephesians must be "filled by the Spirit." This would be a repetition of a similar idea expressed two chapters earlier, where Paul prays for the believers to be strengthened *through his Spirit* with the ultimate goal that they may *be filled to the measure of all the fullness of God* (Eph 3:16-19; cf. 1:23). Daniel B. Wallace, in his excellent grammatical work *Greek Grammar Beyond the Basics*, defends this translation and calls the predominant translation, "filled with the Spirit," "grammatically suspect." According to Wallace, there are no clear examples in biblical Greek where a verb of filling followed by *en* plus the dative case indicates content ("filled with").[33] Whether we adopt an instrumental translation or not, "filled with the Spirit" is clearly not a fixed expression used by both Luke and Paul.

The expected results of Spirit filling are also not equivalent. Luke emphasized more phenomenal results. Spirit-filled believers were expected to exercise powerful prophetic gifts – inspired speech and miraculous signs and wonders. Inspired speech, particularly inspired praise, also appears to be included in Paul's list of expected results. The Ephesians were to speak to one another *with psalms, hymns and spiritual songs* and *giving thanks* (Eph 5:19-20). However, the phenomenal aspect of this speech is not clearly emphasized like it is in Luke's account. Paul also adds *submitting to one another in the fear of Christ* to his list of expected results (Eph 5:21).[34] The results in Luke-Acts are for the purpose of effective witness. The results in Paul's letter are aimed more at effective living in Christian community. They are to speak to one another and submit to one another.

---

[33] Wallace, p. 374-75, 93, n. 62, p. 94. He says there are only 3 clear examples where the simple dative case indicates content (Lk 2:40; Rom 1:29; 2 Cor 7:4), p. 374, n. 55).

[34] The imperative "be filled" is followed by 5 present participles indicating the results of being filled: speaking, singing, singing praise, giving thanks and submitting.

The means of achieving Spirit filling is also different. Luke emphasized the necessity of prayer. He is the only gospel writer who recorded Jesus' exhortation to pray to receive the gift of the Holy Spirit (Lk 11:13). Jesus himself was praying when *the Holy Spirit descended on him* (Lk 3:22). When they were waiting for the promise of the Spirit, the disciples prayed (Ac 1:14). When they wanted others to receive the same gift, they prayed and laid hands on them (Ac 8:15; 9:17; 19:6). Paul, however, commands the Ephesians to be filled with the Spirit, apparently indicating some sort of necessary cooperation. This command is expressed in Greek with a present imperative, indicating some sort of continuous action. There is no equivalent to this sort of cooperative continuous action in Luke-Acts.

How can we discern the nature and extent of the believer's cooperation inherent in Paul's command to the Ephesians to be filled with the Spirit? Our best clues must be inferred from the context of this passage, the literary context of this letter to the Ephesians and concepts taught by Paul in other letters. Paul's command to be continuously filled with the Spirit is placed within a series of exhortations to righteous behavior held together by exhortations to live or "walk" (*peripateô*, Eph 4:1, 17; 5:2, 8, 15) in a manner worthy of the Christian calling (Eph 4:1-6:9). Paul does not say how we should enlist the Spirit's help in this endeavor. The Spirit's involvement is simply assumed. Improper words and behavior grieve the Holy Spirit (Eph 4:29-31); but being filled with the Spirit results in righteous words and behavior (Eph 5:18-6:9).

Since Paul does not define this cooperation with the Spirit in his letter to the Ephesians, we are forced to speculate on the process by looking for a similar concept in some of Paul's other writings. Paul's clearest teaching on the cooperation between the Spirit and the believer to produce righteous words and behavior is found in his letter to the Romans. There he informs his readers that *the righteous requirements of the law* are "fulfilled" or "filled" (*plêroô*) by those who *walk* (*peripateô*) *according to the Spirit* (Rom 8:4). In this passage believers are exhorted to *have their minds set on what the Spirit desires* (Rom 8:5), to *put to death the misdeeds of the body* (Rom 8:13), and to be *led by the Spirit* (Rom 8:14). These are all descriptions of working cooperatively with the Spirit which could possibly be implied in Paul's command to the Ephesian believers to be filled with the Spirit, if indeed his readers were aware of his teachings on this subject.

There is, however, no parallel to this type of teaching in Luke-Acts. If our speculations about Paul's teaching are correct, they only emphasize the differences between what Luke means by the expression "filled with the Spirit" and what Paul means. Paul does not use the same expression. Even if "filled with the Spirit" is the correct translation, it does not convey the same meaning or have the same implications. We should be careful, therefore, not to interpret either author through the eyes of the other. Both Pentecostals and non Pentecostals are guilty of this. Non Pentecostals have a tendency to see Pauline sanctification in Luke-Acts and Pentecostals have a tendency to see Lukan Pentecostal anointing in Ephesians.

It is highly probable that the metaphor "filled with the Spirit" has a much more generic meaning which both authors use in their own way to convey more specific ideas. From the study of Luke's overall use of fullness metaphors we concluded that the expression is used to describe a condition. The more generic or simple meaning of "filled with the Spirit," which fits the contexts of both authors, is "to be powerfully and visibly influenced by the Spirit." This powerful influence is discernible for both authors in the tangible or visible results it produces. The means of achieving Spirit fullness and the description of the tangible results of that fullness changes from one author to the other. From a human viewpoint, believers observe the exercise of powerful prophetic gifts (Luke) or incredible changes in worship and behavior (Paul) and discern from this that individuals are powerfully influenced by or "filled with" the Spirit.

Similarities

Both Luke and Paul emphasize the source of influence in their use of this metaphor. In fact, both authors mention the same possible confusion of sources. When the disciples were filled with the Spirit and began to speak in unknown tongues, some in the crowd mocked them saying, *They have had too much wine* (Ac 2:4, 13). In response to this accusation, Peter declares, *These men are not drunk, as you suppose ... No, this is what was spoken by the prophet Joel* (Ac 2:15-16). Paul exhorts the Ephesian believers, *Do not get drunk on wine ... Instead, be filled with Spirit* (Eph 5:18).

It is difficult to believe that the repetition of these contrasting sources for perceivable modified behavior could be coincidental. There must be something in the exuberance of Spirit-inspired worship and behavior combined with unintelligible speech, or perhaps some other highly emotional forms of worship, which outsiders might mistakenly associate with a state of drunkenness. There are scriptural and extra-biblical texts which attest to this possibility. Paul tells the Corinthians not to speak in unknown tongues in public meetings lest outsiders think they are *out of their minds* (1 Cor 14:23). Eli thought Anna was drunk, when she poured her soul out to the Lord (1 Sam 1:13). Describing Saul's Spirit-inspired behavior as 'ecstatic,' when he prophesied 'in the buff' all day and all night, is certainly an understatement (1 Sam 19:24). It sure sounds like the behavior of a drunkard. Ernest Best lists a number of ancient references to religious leaders trying to induce spiritual ecstasy through drinking wine.[35] E. K. Simpson states that "manifestations of the Spirit in seasons of revival" have often been "accompanied by phenomena easily confounded with physical intoxication."[36]

Peter and Paul are both quick to correct this confusion of sources. Peter underlines the unlikelihood of drunken behavior at nine o'clock in the morning. Paul points out that drunkenness leads to debauchery, not divinely inspired worship and behavior. Both emphasize that the desired source of modified behavior is the Spirit of God, not alcoholic spirits![37]

Luke and Paul both also emphasize the results of this powerful influence. They do not emphasize the same results, but tangible and visible effects are a common factor in the use of this metaphor. These results are what triggers the description "filled with the Spirit." When observers are able to perceive powerful phenomena in the lives of individuals, they discern that these are the result of a powerful divine influence, and come to the conclusion that they are filled with the Spirit of God. Luke appears to limit these tangible, visible, Spirit-inspired phenomena to prophetic speech, signs and wonders and a few other phenomenal characteristics. Paul, on the other hand, includes more behavioral, less phenomenal characteristics among his discernable Spirit-inspired effects. Paul's ability to discern the powerful influence of the Spirit in a greater variety of tangible effects probably indicates some sort of progression in the early church's understanding of the Spirit's influence. We will examine this possibility more carefully in the next chapter.

---

[35] *A Critical and Exegetical Commentary on Ephesians*, Edinburgh, T&T Clark, 2001, p. 509. He lists Is 28:7; Philo, *Ebr* 147-48; *Vita Cont* 85, 89; Macrob *Sat* I 18:1; Hipp *Ref* 5.8.6f.

[36] E. K. Simpson and F. F. Bruce, *Commentary on the Epistles to the Ephesians and the Colossians: The English Text with Introduction, Exposition and Notes*, Grand Rapids, Eerdmans, 1965, p.125.

[37] This play on words in English is not derived from the Greek.

Chapter 8

Discovering the Spirit

$\mathcal{H}$ow does God communicate with us? For that matter, how does anyone communicate with anyone else? If we are to understand God or anyone else, there must be some amount of shared knowledge on which to base our communication. We must not only speak the same language, but understand symbols and metaphors in the same way. We must either know the same background information or provide it in our communication. For instance, earlier in the book I used an illustration from baseball to explain the importance of listening to each other. Even if you know all the vocabulary used in that illustration, but have no knowledge of the game of baseball, that explanation is unintelligible to you.

Progressive discovery

This necessity for common knowledge in order to communicate effectively creates a need for progressive communication. In teaching, we say that new knowledge must be based on and flow from old knowledge. We must proceed by logical steps from the known to the unknown. What are the logical steps which God has used to communicate with us? One must understand creation and the fall in order to comprehend the meaning of salvation. The Old Testament concept of substitutionary atonement is a necessary prerequisite for understanding the cross of Christ. God did not reveal all of these truths in one setting. He laid the foundations step by step. A correct understanding of any new truth is based on and dependant upon all the previous truth God has revealed. We must proceed from the known to the unknown. This process is called progressive revelation.

The other side of this coin is progressive discovery. God's servants are often slow to understand new revelation. This is why some things must be discovered and understood through experience. Jesus was very much aware of this process. He told his disciples that *many prophets and righteous men longed to see what you see but did not see it, and to hear what you hear but did not hear it* (Mt 13:17). God revealed many things to the prophets about a future time of deliverance. But it was the generation which actually began to experience this deliverance that was finally able to put the pieces of revelation together.

We have already discovered this process of progressive discovery in explanations concerning messianic expectations and the interpretation of John the Baptist's prophetic promise that the coming Messiah would baptize his listeners with the Holy Spirit and fire. John the Baptist and his contemporaries understood Old Testament messianic prophecies in the light of Israel's previous experience. They were expecting a messianic warrior-king like David who would execute God's end-time judgment. Jesus had to come and live out an entirely new model for us to be able to understand how God intended to fulfill this and other prophetic promises.

Jesus also told his disciples, *I have much more to say to you, more than you can now bear. But when he, the Spirit of truth, comes, he will guide you into all truth* (Jn 16:12-13). Jesus was informing them that the process of progressive discovery would continue. The disciples did not understand what Jesus told them about his death and resurrection until the events occurred (Lk 9:45; 24:44-46). The disciples understood more than the prophets of the Old Testament, because they saw first hand the fulfillment of their prophecies. But they understood less during Jesus' earthly ministry than they did after his resurrection.

This process of progressive discovery did not abruptly stop after the resurrection. The disciples did not suddenly understand everything there was to understand. Through his narrative, Luke gives us a window into this progressive discovery. We see how the disciples discovered the truths revealed in Scripture. For instance, on the day of Pentecost, Peter understood that what they were experiencing was the fulfillment of Joel's prophecy concerning the outpouring of the Spirit. However, he had to learn later through further experience that God's promise to pour out his Spirit *on all people* included

Gentile believers. His previous knowledge most likely led him to believe that the promise was for repentant Jews from every social class in Jewish society. God had to lead Peter step by step, through visions and visible manifestations of the Spirit's approval, to the conclusion that God *accepts men from every nation who fear him and do what is right* (Ac 10:35).

Progressive discovery of the Spirit

There is also clear evidence in the New Testament of a progressive discovery of the workings of the Holy Spirit. This is already evident within Luke's account as the disciples are forced to modify their conception of the role of the Spirit in inaugurating the kingdom. Initially, they understood the Spirit's role in terms of political and military empowerment for Jesus and his disciples to restore the kingdom to Israel (Ac 1:6). This faith in the Spirit's enabling is the only reasonable explanation for their readiness to take up the sword against Rome (Lk 22:49). Their willingness to go into battle is reminiscent of Jonathan's military boldness to do battle with the entire Philistine army with only one sword. He said, *Nothing can hinder the LORD from saving, whether by many or by few* (1 Sam 14:6). Saul and David both had extremely successful military exploits attributed to their being anointed with God's Spirit (1 Sam 10:10; 11:6-11; 16:13; 17:1-58). Jesus' disciples undoubtedly expected David's anointed successor to be endowed with the same sort of empowering to overthrow their Roman oppressors. Through Jesus' ministry and the events at Pentecost, the disciples discovered that the Spirit's New Testament role was not military empowerment for establishing a political kingdom but prophetic empowerment for proclaiming the gospel.

It is completely understandable that the disciples discover the Spirit progressively. They had very little previous knowledge of the Spirit. In Old Testament times the Spirit came upon a few chosen individuals, kings and prophets mostly, and empowered them for phenomenal tasks. Even their knowledge of these few individuals probably made these stories seem more to them like legends from a distant past than actual reality. There had not been any clear examples of such anointed individuals in Israel for hundreds of years. Luke tells about several individuals connected with the birth stories of Jesus and John the Baptist who were filled with the Spirit, but there is every indication that Jesus' disciples were unaware of these episodes. The disciples enter the story after these events occurred and most of these Spirit-filled individuals are not mentioned again in the narrative. Mary, the mother of Jesus, was there to witness these events, but Luke tells us that she *treasured all these things in her heart* (Lk 2:51). This sounds like insider information that Luke may have discovered during his research (Lk 1:3). The fact that these stories are not found in the other gospels lends support to the idea that these events were not common knowledge.

When the Holy Spirit came upon the disciples on the day of Pentecost and enabled them to speak in other tongues, this was a completely new experience. Peter and the other disciples immediately recognized that this was the fulfillment of Joel's end-time prophecy. They knew that God had poured out his Spirit on them in prophetic anointing. They knew that they had received the gift of God's Spirit. It is unreasonable, however, to expect them to understand all the New Testament implications of this event. It is unreasonable, for example, to expect Peter to be able to establish the norm for all future encounters with the Spirit, as James Dunn and others have proposed.[1] This assumption is probably the greatest hindrance to finding a coherent explanation for the various experiences with the Spirit in Luke-Acts. Just because Peter promised his hearers they would receive the gift of the Spirit, if they repented and were baptized in the name of the Lord Jesus, does not mean that he had discovered and established a universal chronological pattern for the immediate reception of the Spirit at conversion. This assumption goes way beyond the evidence and creates havoc for the coherence of Luke's theology.

The disciples continued to recognize the powerful influence of the Holy Spirit in the powerful and perceptible effects they experienced. Luke's presentation of the Spirit is characterized by this emphasis on perceptible effects from the beginning to the end of his two-volume work. Those who receive the Spirit or who are filled with the Spirit are endowed with prophetic speech. They prophesy (Lk 1:41, 67; Ac 2:17-18; 11:28; 19:6; 21:9) and speak in tongues (Ac 2:4; 10:46; 19:6). They proclaim the word of God with incredible boldness (Ac 4:31; etc.). They perform signs and wonders (Ac 2:22, 43; 5:12; etc.), healing the sick and delivering people from evil spirits (Ac 4:22, 30; 5:16; 8:7; 10:38; 19:11) and cursing those who oppose the gospel (Ac 13:9-11). They have visions (Ac 7:55) and revelations (Ac 21:11). They are led by the Spirit (Lk 2:26-27; 4:1; Ac 10:19; 11:2; 13:2; 16:6-7; 20:23). They were given supernatural wisdom to confound their adversaries (Ac 6:5, 10), miracle-working faith (Ac 6:5, 8) and unexplainable joy in the midst of

---

[1] Dunn, p. 90.

persecution (Ac 13:52). Every time Luke refers to the influence of the Holy Spirit, he also mentions some perceptible effect.

This emphasis on the tangible evidence of the Holy Spirit's influence in Luke-Acts is even recognized by non-Pentecostal interpreters. Max Turner, for instance, says that the Spirit in Luke-Acts "is virtually always ... the *self-manifesting* presence of God....When the Spirit 'fills' a person, it is compulsively, invasively, and with immediately-perceived effects."[2] A. George says that the activity of the Spirit is "always presented" with "tangible external effects."[3] Charles Talbert says that when Luke "speaks about the gift of the Holy Spirit in Acts, he is not talking about the secret inner work of God which convicts and converts, but rather about the moment of the Spirit's release in external manifestations."[4] Even James Dunn acknowledges that "Luke encourages his readers to think of the Spirit in terms of the effects of the Spirit's coming."[5]

What is more amazing, and more controversial, in Luke's presentation of the Spirit is that Luke's characters only recognized the activity of the Spirit when there were tangible effects to demonstrate his influence. If none of these perceivable effects of the Spirit were present, the early disciples concluded that individuals and groups had not yet received the gift of the Spirit (Ac 8:15-18). They did not recognize the influence of the Spirit without some perceivable extraordinary sign. According to J. H. E. Hull, the early disciples did not "differentiate between possession of the Spirit and awareness of it."[6] It is this perspective which gives coherence to Luke's theology of the Spirit. Every one of Luke's Spirit-experience episodes can be understood from this perspective, and two of them (the Samaritan and Ephesian episodes) do not make sense unless they are understood from this perspective.

The Samaritan episode

When Philip proclaimed Christ in Samaria, many Samaritans believed and were baptized. After this, Luke informs his readers that Peter and John came and *prayed for them that they might receive the Holy Spirit, because the Holy*

---

[2] Turner, p. 439-40, Turner's italics.
[3] "L'Esprit Saint dans l'œuvre de Luc," *Revue Biblique* 85, 1978, p. 530.
[4] *Reading Luke: A Literary and Theological Commentary on the Third Gospel*, New York, Crossroad Publishing Company, 1982, p. 43.
[5] Dunn, p. 9.
[6] Hull, p. 106.

Spirit had not yet come upon any of them (Ac 8:15-16). How could the disciples possibly come to such a conclusion? Luke's statement here appears to be in contradiction with what Paul teaches. If we compare the disciple's conclusion with what Paul teaches about the Spirit in his letter to the Romans, we run into theological difficulty. He states very clearly, *And if anyone does not have the Spirit of Christ, he does not belong to Christ* (Rom 8:9). A Christian has the Spirit, and therefore, must have received the Spirit. A few verses later Paul even uses the same vocabulary. He tells the Roman Christians that they have *received the Spirit of sonship* (Rom 8:15). Elsewhere he says, *We have not received the spirit of the world but the Spirit who is from God* (1 Cor 2:12). For Paul, this reception of the Spirit occurs at conversion, for he writes, *And you also were included in Christ when you heard the word of truth, the gospel of your salvation. Having believed, you were marked in him with a seal, the promised Holy Spirit* (Eph 1:13). We cannot read this immediate reception of the Spirit at conversion into Luke's narrative. It simply does not fit. Neither can we read Luke's version of the reception of the Spirit into Paul's letters.

We are again confronted with the dilemma of Paul and Luke using the same vocabulary to say different things. With the expressions "baptized *en pneumati*" and "filled *en pneumati*," at least the different things were not contradictory. With the reception of the Spirit, they appear to contradict each other. Paul affirms that a believer receives (*lambanō*) the Spirit at conversion (Rom 8:15). Luke gives instances of converted believers who have not received (*lambanō*) the Spirit (Ac 8:15-16). What are we to do with this dilemma?

Various solutions have been proposed to deal with this discrepancy. We will look at 5 of these solutions. The first two were already mentioned in chapter 2.

1. James Dunn has proposed that the Samaritan believers were not really Christians. He finds several details in Luke's account which might indicate that their response to Philip's preaching was "defective." According to Dunn, the Samaritans responded enthusiastically to the miracles performed by Philip, but without much discernment. They gave mental assent to what Philip was saying, but without much commitment. The example of Simon the magician, who still needed to "repent," proves that their faith was deficient.[7] As I pointed out in chapter 2, Luke's vocabulary is too clear to entertain Dunn's

[7] Dunn, p. 63-66.

proposal. Luke uses the same vocabulary here as elsewhere to describe conversion. They *accepted the word of God*. They *believed* and were *baptized into the name of the Lord Jesus* (Ac 8:12-16).

2. Other interpreters prefer to speak of exceptions due to unusual historical circumstances, where there is a departure from the norm established by Paul (Rom 8:9) and mirrored in Peter's call to repentance (Ac 2:38-39). John Stott, for example, believes that, to avoid a perpetuation of the schism between Jewish and Samaritan believers, God may have "deliberately withheld the gift of his Spirit from the Samaritan believers" until "the genuineness of the Samaritan's conversion" was "acknowledged and confirmed" by an apostolic delegation.[8] Stott's proposal would only be logical if God were writing this story. If an imperceptible reception of the Spirit is assumed at conversion, God is the only one who would know that this did not occur. But Luke writes his narrative, not from God's perspective, but from that of the apostles. It is not logical to talk about any exception to the norm from the apostles' perspective or from Luke's perspective. If the norm of the reception of the Spirit at the moment of conversion had indeed been established, as Dunn and others have proposed, the disciples would have assumed that these Samaritan believers had received the Spirit. How would they have discerned that there was an exception? If a norm were assumed, there would be no need for discerning and no way of discerning the lack of Spirit reception, apart from some sort of supernatural revelation. Luke, who has a particular penchant for supernatural phenomena, has not recorded any such supernatural revelation for determining the lack of Spirit reception among the Samaritan believers. He simply tells us, as if it were clearly evident to all, that the Spirit *had not yet come upon any of them*. If Luke had understood the gift of the Holy Spirit to be automatically given at conversion, he would not have made this statement.

3. Other interpreters have proposed that the various viewpoints found in Luke-Acts represent viewpoints from different sources which Luke pieced together to write his narrative. Supposedly, according to one source believers were thought to receive the Spirit at baptism

---

[8] Stott, p. 33.

(Ac 2:38), according to another source at conversion (Ac 10:44) and according to another sometime later through the laying on of hands (Ac 8:15-17: 19:6).[9] Any such theory is pure speculation, since we do not have copies of Luke's sources. Given the importance of the Spirit's validating function in Luke's narrative, it seems highly unlikely that he would have pieced his sources together without correcting such discrepancies.

4. Pentecostal interpreters have addressed this issue by redefining Luke's concept of Spirit 'reception.' Robert Cunningham counsels fellow Pentecostals to "refrain from using" the expression "receiving the Spirit," since the "believer receives the Spirit when he is saved" (Rom 8:9) and because "context clearly shows this 'receiving' refers to Pentecostal baptism."[10] Howard Ervin makes a distinction between an "ontological" reception of the Spirit connected to the concept of a "new creation" (Jn 20:22) and a "functional" reception of the Spirit "distinguished by the charismatic manifestations that accompanied it" (Ac 1:8).[11] Both authors have correctly identified a difference in Luke's 'reception' of the Spirit and Paul or John's 'reception' of the Spirit. But they have not resolved the issue. The fact remains that the Samaritans "received" the Spirit sometime after conversion. There is no indication in Luke's text that they had previously "received" the Spirit in a manner congruent with Paul or John's theology.

5. I propose that the two different perspectives on receiving the Spirit come from a progressive development in the disciples' discovery of the Spirit. If we ask the question how the disciples came to the conclusion that the Samaritan believers had not yet received the Holy Spirit, the only logical answer is that they needed some sort of perceivable proof to verify this reception. In Luke's narrative, this proof is clearly the exercise of prophetic gifts. The early disciples only knew that they had received the Spirit, if the Spirit produced some sort

---

[9] Scott, p 89.

[10] "Writing About the Person and Work of the Holy Spirit," *Conference on the Holy Spirit Digest: A condensation of plenary sessions and seminars of the Conference on the Holy Spirit in Springfield, Missouri, August 16-18, 1982*, vol. 1, ed. Gwen Jones, Gospel Publishing House, Springfield MO, 1983, p. 273.

[11] Ervin, *Conversion*, p. 136, 139-40.

of phenomenal sign or effect. This is a perfectly logical conclusion based on Joel's prophecy and their previous 'Pentecostal' experience. Joel prophesied that those who received the gift of the Spirit would prophesy. When the disciples received the Spirit, they spoke in tongues, which Peter considered to be equivalent in some way to prophecy (Ac 2.4, 16-17). The disciples continued to experience prophetic gifts in the narrative which follows. No other model or paradigm is given in the narrative for receiving the Spirit. Thus, in the absence of any such prophetic effects, the disciples simply concluded that the Samaritan believers had not yet received the Spirit. The Samaritan believers had not received what Joel promised and what Jesus' disciples had experienced.

The concept of a progressive discovery of the Spirit's activity solves the apparent contradiction between Luke and Paul. In Luke's account, the early disciples understood the reception of the Spirit in terms of prophetic anointing according to Joel's end-time prophecy, and thus, only perceived the reception of the Spirit when there was some sort of prophetic phenomena to validate that reception. For Luke then, the reception of the Spirit meant the reception and demonstration of end-time prophetic anointing. Luke is very consistent and coherent in this presentation of Spirit reception and the Spirit's function.

Paul's theology of the Spirit is much more developed. He was not limited to prophetic anointing in his perception of the Spirit. He also sees the Spirit playing a role in helping believers develop godly character (Gal 5:16-26). This process begins at conversion. Thus, for Paul the reception of the Spirit is tied to our union with Christ and must occur when that union takes place at conversion (Rom 8:9-10).

The development of a theology of the Spirit through progressive discovery

Before we consider the logical implications of Luke's Ephesian episode, it might be helpful to imagine how the progressive discovery of the Spirit's activity might have developed in the early church. It is not possible to determine with any certainty exactly how this development occurred. We can, however, observe the different levels of development present in New Testament writings and take an educated guess at the progression.

Hermann Gunkel was one of the first authors in modern biblical scholarship to propose such a development. He noticed a distinct difference between Paul's teaching on the Spirit and the popular view of the Spirit found
in the book of Acts. According to Gunkel, the early Christian community
in the book of Acts attributed to the influence of the Holy Spirit whatever
could not have been the result of natural causes.[12] Experiences in the early
church rendered the presence of the Spirit an unquestionable reality.[13] According to Gunkel, the apostle Paul is to be credited with attributing a variety of other functions to the influence of the Holy Spirit, which neither
Judaism nor the primitive Christian community had previously ascribed to
the supernatural power of the Spirit.[14]

Other biblical interpreters have also emphasized the role of experience
in the development of the earliest Christian community's theology of the
Spirit. Ernest F. Scott says that "belief in the Spirit has always arisen out of
actual experience, and the primitive church did not arrive at it by brooding
over ancient texts and precedents." They did, however, look to those texts for
understanding their experiences.[15] Odette Mainville affirms that the awareness of the active presence of the Spirit was not the fruit of logical reflection
but "the fruit of experience… his works were *seen* and *heard*" (Ac 2:33).[16]

It is completely logical that the earliest Christian community first recognized the activity of the Spirit in the events and phenomena which could
only be explained by supernatural causes. Miracles, signs and wonders, prophetic speech, extraordinary wisdom, incredible faith, and unexplainable
joy were all tangible evidence of a power greater than they had previously
known. For the most part, this evidence corresponded to what they knew of
the Spirit from the Old Testament. When they put two and two together,
they described those first experiences with the Spirit using Old Testament
terms and concepts. This evaluation of the community's initial phase of discovery seems clear from Luke's account.

Other effects of the Spirit are not as phenomenal, and it is more difficult

---

[12] *The Influence of the Holy Spirit, The Popular View of the Apostolic Age and the Teaching of the Apostle Paul*, trans. by Roy A. Harrisville and Philip A. Quanbeck II, Philadelphia, Fortress Press, 1979, p. 20.
[13] Gunkel, p. 4.
[14] Gunkel, p. 71.
[15] Scott, p. 61.
[16] *L'Esprit dans l'œuvre de Luc*, Héritage et Projet 45, ed. André Charron, Richard Bergeron and Guy Couturier, Ville Mont-Royal, Québec, Fides, 1991, p. 317.

to determine how the early church may have discovered their source. For instance, it is not too difficult for believers to discern that God has helped them to change their character over time. Many believers today were drawn to Christ by the changed behavior of another Christian. However, without prior knowledge of the workings of the Spirit, it might be difficult to discern that this change actually took place through the abiding influence of the Holy Spirit. This may have taken the early church a longer time to discover. There is very little in the Old Testament or in Jewish intertestamental literature which would have led them to this conclusion. The Old Testament tends to emphasize the idea that righteous living comes from obeying God's law (Ps 119:9-11).

A notable exception to this tendency in the Old Testament is God's promise in Ezekiel that He will give Israel a new heart, replacing her heart of stone with a heart of flesh. Then he says, *And I will put my Spirit in you and move you to follow my decrees and be careful to keep my laws* (Ez 36:26-27). Although these verses appear to refer to the internal operation of the Spirit in changing lives, Robert Menzies points out, that for most of intertestamental Judaism, these verses referred to the end-time removal of an evil inclination which God made prerequisite to sending the gift of prophetic anointing.[17] Max Turner is in agreement with Menzies that this expectation of the gift of prophetic anointing was the predominant tendency in Judaism at that time. But he also points out that certain rabbinic texts revealed a tendency to attribute more ethical functions to the Spirit, notably the Aramaic translation of this passage in Ezekiel.[18] It is probably indicative that there is no apparent allusion to this passage in Luke-Acts, but Paul alludes to it (2 Cor 3:3). In fact, Paul's teaching on walking by the Spirit in order to fulfill the righteous requirements of the law (Rom 8:4) appears to be a New Testament parallel to this promise in Ezekiel.

At what point did the early church realize that the Holy Spirit was active in the work of conversion, given to believers at conversion, and continuously active in the believer's life from that moment? These activities are much less perceptible. At times the Spirit's presence and activity in these realms are, humanly speaking, completely imperceptible. It is highly probable that it took the church much more time to come to these conclusions concerning the less tangible activities of the Holy Spirit. It is also likely that these conclusions involved a greater degree of theological reflection. Therefore, it is

---

[17] Menzies, p. 95-101.
[18] Turner, p. 89, 123-24.

not surprising to find these aspects of the Spirit's influence in writings which exhibit a much greater degree of theological reflection. Paul's writings and John's gospel, the texts in which we find these concepts, are far more oriented toward theological reflection than Luke's narrative.[19] I propose that Luke's narrative represents a less developed theology of the Spirit derived from the early church's experience and from popular Jewish understandings of the Spirit based on Old Testament examples. It seems likely that Paul's writings reflect a more developed theology of the Spirit most likely derived from a longer, wider base of experiences in the early church and more prolonged reflection on some specific passages in the Old Testament, in particular Eze- kiel's prophetic promise that God would put his life-changing Spirit in us.

The Ephesian episode (Ac 19:1-6)

One historical difficulty needs to be addressed before we can wholeheart- edly adopt this explanation of the progressive discovery of the Spirit. In the Ephesian episode, the apostle Paul himself appears to express this less de- veloped theology of the Spirit. How could the same person teach that the Holy Spirit is given to believers at conversion and ask the question, *Did you receive the Holy Spirit when* [or after] *you believed* (Ac 19:2)? In chapter 4, we were forced to set aside Paul's theology of the reception of the Spirit at conversion in order to find a coherent understanding of this episode. For this understanding to be considered legitimate, we must attempt to explain this apparent incongruence. There are at least three possible solutions.

Solution 1: Paul asked this question without really meaning what he said. This is the general idea of James Dunn's proposal. He believes that "Paul's opening question was one of suspicion and surprise" and that Paul was not really asking whether these Christians "have received the Spirit" but "whether they are Christians."[20]

To evaluate Dunn's proposal, it is necessary to make a distinction between the vocabulary used by Luke and Dunn's vocabulary. Dunn uses the term "Christian" to refer to those who are a part of the community approved by

---

[19] Richard Zehnle argues that Luke's theology of salvation is also less developed and pre-Pauline, "The Salvific Character of Jesus' Death in Lukan Soteriology," *Theological Studies* 30 (1969), p. 420-44. His conclusion is derived from C. H. Dodd, *The Apostolic Preaching and Its Development*, London, Hodder and Stoughton, 1936, p. 25.

[20] Dunn, p. 86.

God to inherit salvation. In Luke's narrative this term is used only twice and only three times in the entire New Testament (Ac 11:26; 26:28; 1 P 4:16). Luke prefers to refer to 'Christians' as those who *believe (pisteuontes).*[21] Thus, when Paul refers to when the disciples in Ephesus *believed (pisteusantes)*, he is using Luke's normal terminology for becoming a 'Christian.' Therefore, according to Dunn's proposal, what Paul really meant to say by this question was, "Did you receive the Holy Spirit when you thought you believed, because all evidence points to the fact that you do not have the Holy Spirit and are, thus, not real believers." What kind of evidence could provoke such a conclusion, since, according to Dunn, the reception of the Spirit is instantaneous and automatic at the point of their conversion? Any such evidence would have to be drastic. In actual fact, there is no evidence in the text for such an imagined solution. Even if Paul were to draw such an unlikely conclusion, it would be nonsensical for him to inquire about their reception of the Holy Spirit. We do not ask those we believe to be non-Christians if they have received the Holy Spirit. Instead, we ask them something about their beliefs or about the reality of their relationship with the Lord. Dunn's proposal is clearly based on his theological presupposition that Paul could not really have said what Luke's account in Acts claims he said.

Solution 2: Paul did not really ask this question, but Luke used his own words to summarize what happened. This solution is based on the fact that what Paul is reported to have asked the Ephesian disciples is more congruent with what Luke's narrator would have said than it is with what the Paul of the epistles would have said.[22] The conclusion that a group of believers had not received the Spirit (Ac 19:2) is both reminiscent of the Samaritan episode as it was told by Luke's narrator (Ac 8:15-17) and incongruent with what Paul taught in his letter to the Romans (Rom 8:9). The reception of the Spirit following the laying on of hands (Ac 19:6) is also narrated in both the Samaritan and Ephesian episodes (Ac 19:6; 8:17). The mention of speaking in tongues as phenomenal proof of this reception (Ac 19:6) is reminiscent of both the Pentecost episode (Ac 2:4) and the episode in the household of Cornelius (Ac 10:45-46).

Is this conceivable? Could Luke have placed words in Paul's mouth, words which Paul never said? According to the narrative, Luke was not there

---

[21] Ac 2:44; 4:4, 32; 5:14; 8:12, 13; 9:42; 10:43, 45; 11:17, 21; 13:12, 39, 48; 14:1, 9, 23, 27; 15:5, 7; 16:1, 15, 31, 34; 17:12, 34; 18:8, 27; 19:2, 4, 18; 20:21; 21:20, 25; 22:19; 24:24; 26:18.
[22] Cf. Barrett, vol. 2, p. 894

when Paul had this conversation with the Ephesian believers. Thus, Luke had to narrate the story from information he received from his sources. Like any other author, Luke selectively chose from all the information he received from his sources those elements that would contribute to the message he was trying to convey. Considering the brevity of this account and the fact that Luke acknowledges elsewhere that he has summarized speech (Ac 2:40), it is certainly conceivable that Luke also summarized this conversation. Given the fact that Luke appears to follow the literary conventions of his day for writers of history, it is also conceivable that he was more concerned with reporting the "general sense" of what was "really said" than with quoting the individuals "word for word."[23] These literary concepts and assumptions support the theory that Luke could have narrated the story in his own words. However, even if we accept this speculative line of reasoning to solve the problem of incongruence, it is still difficult to imagine what the Paul of the epistles would have said which could be summarized accurately by the question used in Luke's narrative. We are forced to conclude that this solution is an attempt to circumvent the normal understanding of Paul's question in its immediate literary context because it is motivated by the theological presupposition that Paul could not have said what Luke's account claims he said.

Solution 3: Paul asked this question and meant it. He must have said this before he discerned and wrote about the possession of the Spirit at conversion. His theology of the Spirit must have changed or developed over time. Initially, like the other characters in Luke-Acts, he may not have recognized the presence of the Spirit without some tangible supernatural evidence. Given Paul's considerable experience in a wide variety of circumstances and his great capacity for theological reflection, it would not be surprising for him to introduce this new understanding of the reception of the Spirit at conversion. Perhaps he came to this conclusion after this episode in Ephesus. His encounter with the Ephesian disciples may have even served as a catalyst for his conclusion.

Is such a historical reconstruction chronologically conceivable from the historical details we have in Scripture? The answer to this question depends largely on when Paul wrote his various teachings about the Spirit. Not all of

---

[23] Lucian of Samosata, writing around 165 AD., counseled historians to let the language of a person making a speech "suit his person and his subject" (p. 71). He refers frequently to Thucydides as a model historian (p. 23, 29, 37, 55, 57, 67. 69). Thucidides believed it was too difficult to remember speeches "word for word." For the speeches in his history of the Peloponnesian Wars (431-411 BC.), his habit was "to make the speakers say what was in my opinion demanded of them by the various occasions, of course adhering as closely as possible to the general sense of what they really said," *Peloponnesian War*, The Crawley Translation, New York, Random House, 1982, (p. vii, xiv, 13, I, 22).

Paul's letters contain developed discussions on the Spirit's activity in the life of the believer. Do Paul's letters written after the Ephesian episode exhibit a more developed theology of the Spirit than those written before this episode?

Paul's clearest reference to the reception of the Spirit at conversion, found in his letter to the Romans (8:9), was most likely written after the Ephesian episode (circa 57 AD). The letter to the Romans was written while Paul was preparing a voyage to Jerusalem with aid for impoverished Christians, after which he proposed a trip to Rome and on to Spain (Rom 15:24-28). These circumstances match a description of Paul's plans in the book of Acts near the end of his third missionary journey at least two years after the Ephesian episode (Ac 19:10, 21).

Most of Paul's letters were likely written after the Ephesian episode. First Corinthians was written during his stay in Ephesus (Ac 19.8-10; 1 Cor 16:8, circa 55 AD). Second Corinthians was written after First Corinthians, possibly also from Ephesus (circa 56 AD). Ephesians, Philippians, Colossians and Philemon were probably written during Paul's imprisonment at Rome (Ac 28:30, early 60s AD). First and Second Timothy and Titus are believed to have been written after Paul's release from prison (circa 62 AD).[24] Three of Paul's letters, however, may have been written before the Ephesian episode; First and Second Thessalonians (circa 50 AD), which were probably written from Corinth before Paul's encounter with the Ephesian believers, and Galatians, for which the date of its redaction is more difficult to determine.[25]

Paul's Thessalonian correspondence contains no clear reference to the reception of the Holy Spirit at conversion and some assertions about the Spirit that closely resemble concepts prevalent in Luke-Acts. Paul tells the Thessalonians that the gospel came to them *not simply with words, but also with power and with the Holy Spirit* (1 Thes 1:5). As in Acts, their reception of this message was accompanied by phenomenal joy from the Holy Spirit (1 Thes 1:6; Ac 13:52). There is a similar awareness in both writings of the Holy Spirit's presence and activity in community life. Just as Ananias and Saphira do not lie to men, but to the Holy Spirit (Ac 5:3), so also those who reject Paul's message do not reject a man, but God who gives his Holy Spirit (1 Thes 4:8). Second Thessalonians, however, probably contains a reference to

---

[24] The dating of these letters is a complex issue which I do not have the time to address thoroughly in this work. Since my goal is merely to establish the possibility of a certain historical reconstruction, I have simply adopted some of the more conservative viewpoints expressed by Carson, p. 242, 283, 309, 321-22, 335, 372, 378, 382, 388.

[25] Carson, p. 293-94, 347.

the sanctifying work of the Holy Spirit (2:13).[26] Even though this reference appears to be more in line with Paul's later writings (Rom 6:19-22), it does not necessarily indicate that Paul believed in the immediate and automatic reception of the Spirit at conversion when he wrote it and, therefore, does not contradict what Luke claims Paul said in the Ephesian episode.

Paul could have discerned the Spirit's sanctifying influence in the life of the believer before he came to the conclusion that this function of the Spirit began at conversion. Given that early church leaders reacted quickly to remedy the lack of perceptible manifestations of Spirit reception and God's rapid response to their efforts (Ac 7:15-17; 19:2-6), long periods of time between conversion and visible manifestations of the Spirit were probably unusual. Paul could easily have maintained the same belief in the perceptible prophetic proofs of Spirit reception and recognized that the Spirit played a part in the sanctification of the believer.

The concept of the Spirit's activity in Paul's letter to the Galatians is very similar to what we find in his letter to the Romans. Paul talks about receiving the Spirit at the beginning of the Christian life (Gal 3:2-3, 5, 14). It should be pointed out, however, that Paul's argument in this sentence is convincing only if we assume a tangible manifestation of the Spirit as in Luke-Acts. Paul writes, *Did you receive the Spirit by observing the law, or by believing what you heard* (Gal 3:2)? If the reception of the Spirit is only assumed at conversion, this is a weak argument. The fact that Paul mentions the giving of the Spirit and the working of miracles in a similar question in verse 5 supports this assumption.[27] He writes, *Does God give you his Spirit and work miracles among you because you observe the law, or because you believe what you heard* (Gal 3:5)? The Spirit is also connected to sonship in both letters (Gal 4:6; Rom 8:15). Both Galatians and Romans talk about the righteousness that comes from the Spirit and contrasting qualities exhibited in the lives of those who are not led by the Spirit (Gal 5:5, 16-23; Rom 8:4-8). Both use the metaphor of "living" and "walking by the Spirit" (Gal 5:25; Rom 8:4-13).

---

[26] The verse is very ambiguous. It could also refer to the sanctification of the human spirit, Ben Witherington III, *1 and 2 Thessalonians: A Socio-Rhetorical Commentary*, Grand Rapids, Eerdmans, 2006, p. 232,

[27] Richard N. Longenecker, for example, says that from Gal 3:5 "we may infer that there were outward signs of some sort" to indicate the reception of the Spirit, *Galatians*, Word Biblical Commentary 41, ed. Ralph P. Martin, Dallas, Word Books, 1990, p. 102. See also F. F. Bruce, *The Epistle to the Galatians*, NIGTC, ed. I. Howard Marshall and W. Ward Gasque, Grand Rapids, Paternoster Press, 1982, p. 149, 151 and William Barclay, *The Letters to the Galatians and Ephesians*, rev. ed., Philadelphia, Westminster Press, 1976, p. 23-24.

Various dates have been proposed for the redaction of Paul's letter to the Galatians. Some believe the letter to have been written before the Jerusalem council (Ac 15) because Paul does not mention the decrees sent from this council and because Peter's separation from Gentile believers (Gal 2:12) is easier to understand if the event occurred before the council (circa 48 AD).[28] Others believe the letter was written during Paul's extended stay at Ephesus or even later (circa 55-57 AD).[29] One of the main reasons for adopting this later date is that the "style and thoughts expressed" in Galatians "show an affinity with the Corinthian correspondence and with Romans."[30] The following chart is undoubtedly over simplified, but it should help to visualize the chronological development of Paul's theology of the Spirit.

Chart 8: A chronology of Paul's letters in relation to the Ephesian episode

Paul's letters	Approx. Date	Theology of the Spirit
1 and 2 Thessalonians	50	Emphasis on powerful manifestations and possibly ethical transformation, Moment of reception not defined
Ephesian episode	**52**	Emphasis on powerful manifestations, Reception subsequent to conversion possible
1 Corinthians	55	Emphasis on powerful manifestations, Moment of reception not defined
2 Corinthians	56	Emphasis on ethical transformation, Reception at conversion implied
Galatians	55-57	
Romans	57	
Prison epistles: Ephesians, Philippians, Colossians, Philemon	Early 60s	Emphasis on ethical transformation, Reception at conversion implied
Pastoral epistles: 1 and 2 Timothy, Titus	After 62	

---

[28] Carson, p. 293.
[29] Raymond E. Brown, *An Introduction to the New Testament*, New York, Doubleday, 1997, p. 477.
[30] Carson, p. 293-94.

This brief survey of the chronological sequence of Paul's references to the Spirit demonstrates that the idea of development in his theology of the Spirit is certainly possible. If we accept a later date for the redaction of his letter to the Galatians, there is strong evidence that Paul's theology of the Spirit was more developed in his later writings. If Paul did, in fact, discover later in his ministry that Spirit reception took place at the moment of conversion, he probably made this discovery during his prolonged stay in Ephesus immediately following this troublesome encounter with the Ephesian believers documented in Acts 19, since shortly after this he wrote his letter to the Romans in which he articulated his newly-discovered understanding of the Spirit's activity.

Luke was not with Paul during this time period. He appears to have remained in Philippi when Paul and Silas went on to Thessalonica (Ac 16:12; 17:1) and did not rejoin Paul again until he passed back through Philippi after his extended stay in Ephesus (Ac 20:5-6). If our chronological reconstructions are accurate, Luke was not with Paul either when he made these new discoveries or when he wrote about them. This would help explain why Luke was unaware of Paul's later teachings on the subject.

This proposed reconstruction of the chronology of Paul's writings removes the last reasonable obstacle to adopting a view of the progressive discovery of the Spirit in the New Testament. There is no longer any need to perform mental gymnastics to make Luke's narrative teach Pauline doctrines on the Spirit. Luke portrays a picture of the disciples' initial discovery of the Spirit through powerful prophetic manifestations. Paul describes a more developed theology of the Spirit most likely acquired through extended theological reflection and a wider, more diverse experience with the Spirit.

Conclusions

How should we understand Spirit experiences in Luke-Acts in the light of the wider more developed picture of the Spirit's activities provided in the rest of the New Testament? In the first seven chapters of this book, we attempted to understand Luke's vocabulary within the context of his own work. I believe this to be the only way to correctly interpret what he wrote. However, if we are correct in describing Luke's presentation of the Spirit as less developed than Paul's, we may need to modify our overall understanding of the work of the Spirit, and evaluate how this overall understanding might change our understanding of the events within Luke-Acts.

We came to the conclusion that the various expressions for Spirit experiences in the book of Acts all relate to the fulfillment of Joel's end-time prophecy. They all refer to the prophetic anointing promised in this prophecy. This prophetic anointing produces tangible effects or visible manifestations of the power of God's Spirit in the lives and ministries of those who receive this gift: prophetic speech, signs and wonders, phenomenal wisdom and joy. The presence of these visible effects in the early church clearly established those who were divinely accepted into this promised end-time community of prophets. If a group of believers did not manifest any visible signs of the Spirit's anointing, Luke's early Christian community understood that those believers had not yet received the Holy Spirit.

In chapter 7 we also discovered how Paul uses some of the same vocabulary to say different things about the Spirit. For Paul the reception of the Spirit refers to the enabling presence and power of the Spirit acquired at conversion. Spirit filling refers not only to the powerful influence of the Spirit to inspire prophetic words and deeds but also to transform the character of individual believers.

In this chapter we have discovered that these differing viewpoints probably represent a progression in the early church's discovery of the Spirit. With this information, it is now possible to reinterpret the experiences of Luke's early disciples (not Luke's interpretation of those experiences) in the light of the more developed theology of the Spirit found in other parts of the New Testament. When Luke tells us that the Samaritan believers had not yet *received* the Holy Spirit (Ac 8:15-16), we must understand that they had not yet *received* the prophetic anointing promised in Joel's prophecy. They knew this because they had not yet manifested any prophetic signs which should accompany this anointing according to Joel's prophecy. They had, in fact, already *received* the Holy Spirit according to Paul's later definition of these terms. This reception was simply imperceptible and unknown to them at that time.

This understanding of Luke's text is not new. J. E. L. Oulton writes that what is meant by the expression "receiving the Holy Spirit" in the book of Acts is the manifestation of "the outward marvelous signs of the Spirit."[31] He also says, "It is clear that Ac 8.15-17 does not refer to the gift of the Holy

---

[31] Oulton, p. 238.

Spirit *simpliciter*,[32] but, as Hort points out, to His outward manifestation."[33] J. H. E. Hull says that this understanding is the "only possible way to bring Luke's interpretation into line" with the rest of the New Testament.[34]

We should probably also understand the apostles' reception of the Spirit on the day of Pentecost and the Ephesian disciples' reception of the Spirit when Paul laid his hands on them in the same manner.[35] The apostles most likely received the Spirit in Pauline fashion when Jesus breathed on them and said, *Receive the Holy Spirit* (Jn 20:22). The Ephesian disciples probably received the Spirit in Pauline fashion when they believed and *were baptized into the name of the Lord Jesus* (Ac 19:4-5) just prior to when Paul laid his hands on them, or perhaps sometime before that when they first believed (Ac 19:2).

---

[32] In a simple degree or manner, Oulton's italics.
[33] Oulton, p. 238.
[34] Hull, p. 108-09.
[35] Hull, p. 107, 115.

Chapter 9

Seeking the Spirit

I first discovered the power of the Spirit forty years ago in the experience I have shared at the beginning of this book. Since that time I have had the privilege of serving the Lord in five different countries on three different continents, and in four different languages. Wherever I have shared my experiences or taught on the subject of the Holy Spirit, I have found those who hunger and thirst to see the power of the Holy Spirit manifested in the church today as it was in the days of the Acts of the Apostles. This hunger is not limited to Pentecostal or Charismatic churches. All over the world Christians reading the book of Acts are filled with a growing desire to experience the power of the Spirit in their own lives. This is one reason why Pentecostal and Charismatic movements have had so much success.

Is this desire legitimate? Should we seek such experiences with the Spirit? Should we expect them? Or should we be content with the tremendous blessings God has already given us? How much should we expect to copy the examples of these first century disciples? Was their experience unique or repeatable? All these questions are concerned with the application of these texts. The ultimate goal of biblical studies is not more knowledge but the application of that knowledge. Jesus' own words remind us of this priority, *Blessed rather are those who hear the word of God and obey it* (Lk 11:28). But, when it comes to experiences with the Spirit in Luke-Acts, we are not looking at commands which must be obeyed. We are looking at examples which we might want to follow. Intuitively, we know that we should not follow every example in Scripture. For example, we know that we do not all need to wait *in Jerusalem* for the promise of the Father. This specific instruction was addressed to Jesus' disciples in Jerusalem. We are not in Jerusalem. It is illogical for us to go there and wait. But do we even need to wait at all for this promise? Let's make the question a little harder. Should we tell people to drop dead like Peter did to Ananias and Saphira? Questions like this should not be answered without careful consideration of the principles involved. Otherwise, we will end up applying only those parts of Scripture which suit our fancy.

In what way do these texts apply to us? Should we seek to reproduce the phenomenal experiences found in the book of Acts? Or should we only apply underlying principles to our lives and ministries? How do changes in historical, geographical and cultural settings influence the applicability of these texts? This process of evaluation and adaptation is the first step to application. Many people imagine that they are applying God's Word literally. In actual fact, every Christian wishing to apply the text of Scripture to life situations does this kind of evaluation and adaptation without even knowing it. How many interpreters do you know who have traveled to Jerusalem to wait for the promise of the Father? Interpreters talk about 'your Jerusalem' or 'our Jerusalem.' In saying this they are recognizing that the applicability of the text must be evaluated and adapted to fit a new context.

Contextualization

I like to call this process of evaluation and adaptation "contextualization," partly because the term is familiar to me as a missionary, but also because the term fits what we are trying to do. Missionaries recognize that details in the message we present to other cultures must be adapted in order to communicate the same message. For instance, it is incomprehensible to call Jesus "the bread of life" in a culture which does not eat bread. If we want the people from such a culture to understand the same implications in the message given by Jesus, it may be necessary to call him "the rice of life."

Contextualization occurs quite naturally. However, if we are not careful, we can end up with the message we want to hear rather than the message God wants to communicate. Luke has given us an excellent example of this process. John the Baptist and Jesus' disciples very naturally contextualized some of the prophecies of the Old Testament. God had promised to send an anointed descendant of David to deliver Israel from her enemies (Is 11:1-5). Since David was anointed and used of God to deliver Israel from her political oppressors through military exploits, John the Baptist and Jesus' disciples expected the Messiah to deliver them in a similar manner from their Roman oppressors. This was the message they wanted to hear, not what Jesus came to communicate. Jesus' disciples understood the need for contextualization. They knew that the promised deliverance was no longer from the Babylonian empire as it was in Isaiah's message (Is 13:1-14:23; etc.). They believed that God would operate in the same way against their new political oppressors. They correctly assumed that the identity of their oppressors would not be the same as it was in Isaiah's prophecy. They incorrectly identified their new oppressors and the means God would use to deliver them from those oppressors. The ultimate oppressor is Satan, and Christ delivered his people by casting out demons, healing the sick and ultimately by suffering the penalty for our sins on the cross of Calvary (Ac 10:38; 2 Cor 5:21).

In chapter 2 we saw the importance of understanding the text of Scripture within its literary and historical context. Context helps determine the meaning of terms and phrases. We have closely examined both the literary and historical context in our study of the meaning of terms and phrases in Luke-Acts. In contextualization we recognize that the historical context has changed. If we want the biblical message to have the same significance and impact as it did for its original readers, we must adapt the communication of that message. The logic of this affirmation is very simple. If the meaning of a text is determined by its literary and historical context and we proclaim the exact same words in a new context, the message will not be the same. The following chart will help to visualize this process.

Chart 9: The process of contextualization or application

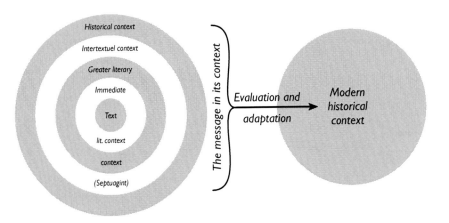

Historical context
Intertextuel context
Greater literary
Immediate
Text
lit. context
context
(Septuagint)

The message in its context

Evaluation and adaptation

Modern historical context

The task of the interpreter is to understand the biblical message within its original context and transmit the equivalent of this message into a new context. This task requires an evaluation of the differences between the two historical contexts and an adaptation of the message to fit the new context. This adaptation does not give us license to change the message to fit our own desires and purposes. The goal is for the message to have the same significance and impact as it had for its original readers.

Most discussions on contextualization emphasize the differences between contexts. We should not forget that the similarities are also important. The nature of sinful humanity, with its tendency toward selfishness has not changed. We are just as tempted to deviate from God's perfect plan as our ancestors in the Bible. Since most of the biblical message is intended to deliver us from this sinful human condition (salvation in every sense of the word), the things which have not changed far outnumber the things which have. This is why those who attempt to apply Scripture without consciously evaluating and adapting the text are usually not too far off the mark. Even so, a more conscientious approach should improve the effectiveness of Scriptural application. However, we must be careful to maintain an attitude of submission to God's word and not allow our sinful inclinations to 'explain away' the passages in Scripture which we find difficult or painful to apply.

Evaluation

The first step in the application of Scripture is an evaluation of the text's applicability to our context.[1] Since all Scripture is inspired by God and useful for our instruction (2 Ti 3:16), those of us who adhere to the Scriptures as the authoritative source for determining faith and practice do not question whether or not biblical texts are applicable today but how they are applicable. How does the text of Acts, written to ancient readers for their specific needs, apply to the church today? More specifically, how do the various experiences with the Spirit in the book of Acts apply to us? Can we and do we want to imitate the experiences of the early church? Two factors help to determine the answer to these questions: differences in historical situations and clues from the biblical texts.

---

[1] Robert A. Traina, *Methodical Bible Study: A New Approach to Hermeneutics*, Grand Rapids, Francis Asbury Press, 1985, p. 203-4.

A reduction in the manifestation of prophetic gifts

The greatest difference between the early church's experience in Acts and that of most of our churches today is a tremendous reduction in the manifestation of prophetic gifts. The book of Acts is characterized by signs, wonders and prophetic speech. Most churches today rarely see such gifts in operation. There are two plausible explanations for this disparity. Either God has decided to act differently or we are acting differently. It is less embarrassing for us if it is God who has changed. Thus, interpreters come up with reasons why God wanted to miraculously intervene more often in the early church. Perhaps the situation required more tangible proofs of God's approval than is needed today. If that is the case, God may not intend for us to repeat the experiences we read about in Acts. On the other hand, if we are the ones who have changed, these 'explanations' are merely excuses for our lack of Spirit anointing. It seems evident from these two entirely different interpretations that the observation of differences in historical situations is not sufficient for determining the applicability of these texts. We must look for clues from the text.

How can we distinguish between repeatable experiences and historical accounts or details tied specifically to the early church's context, which Luke did not intend for us to repeat or imitate? What experiences did Luke expect would be repeated or imitated among his readers? More specifically, did Luke expect his readers to be anointed with the Spirit and exercise prophetic gifts or did Luke intend for his readers simply to learn from these experiences? Are there any clues from the text to indicate Luke's expectations? At least two arguments from the text indicate that Luke expected his readers to have similar experiences with the Spirit.

1. Several of the prophetic statements made by Luke's characters were not completely fulfilled in Luke-Acts. For instance, Jesus said that *repentance and forgiveness of sins* would *be preached in his name to all nations* (Lk 24:47) and that his disciples would be his *witnesses…to the ends of the earth* (Ac 1:8). The fulfillment of these words began, but was not completed, in Acts. Spirit anointing was given to the disciples to accomplish this task (Ac 1:8). There is nothing in the text to suggest that Spirit anointing and the prophetic gifts which accompany that anointing are no longer needed for completing our God-given task. In fact Peter points out that the promise of Spirit anointing is *for all who are far off* (Ac 2:39). Paul's prophetic words at the end of the book

show that the task continues after the narrative ends. He says, *God's salvation has been sent to the Gentiles, and they will listen* (Ac 28:28)!

2. Joel's end-time prophecy, cited by Peter on the day of Pentecost, emphasizes that God's end-time community is to be characterized by a prophetic anointing with the resulting prophetic gifts (Ac 2:16-21). The *last days* referred to in Joel's prophecy have not yet come to an end. If the church ceases to exercise these prophetic gifts, Joel's prophecy ceases to be fulfilled. This may be one reason why effort was made in the narrative to remedy the lack of Spirit anointing among certain groups of believers. A community of believers today which does not exercise prophetic gifts is not fulfilling Joel's prophecy and is a contradiction to the message proclaimed by Peter and narrated by Luke. Logic requires that this situation be rectified.

An increase in the awareness of the various functions of the Spirit

The second difference between our historical situation and that of the early church which must be considered is the increase in our knowledge of the Spirit's operations. We now have the entire New Testament containing more developed ideas on the Spirit's activities. Even if Luke did expect his readers to repeat the Spirit experiences in Acts, should the more developed theology of the Spirit in the New Testament cause us to nullify or modify this expectation? Luke's characters prayed to receive the Holy Spirit. From Paul's teachings, we now understand that believers receive the Holy Spirit at conversion, sometimes without any perceptible proof of reception. Is it not logical, then, to cease praying to receive the Holy Spirit? Is there any further need to seek another experience with the Holy Spirit? At least six arguments support the idea of actively seeking the prophetic anointing described by Luke in order to complete the prophetic task which God has entrusted to the church today. (The first two arguments are already mentioned above.)

3. The apostle Paul also recognized the need for the power of the Spirit in order to accomplish the evangelistic task entrusted to the church. He talked about what God had accomplished through him "to lead the Gentiles to obedience by word and deed, by the power of signs and wonders, by the power of the Spirit" (Rom 15:18-19, New American Bible). His message and his preaching were not delivered *with wise and persuasive words, but with a demonstration of the Spirit's power*

(1 Cor 2:4). He also said, *Our gospel came to you not simply with words, but also with power, with the Holy Spirit* (1 Thes 1:5).

4. Certain passages in Paul's letters presuppose the exercise of prophetic gifts in the early church. Paul wrote to the Corinthian church saying, *For to each one the manifestation of the Spirit is given* (1 Cor 12:7). Paul wanted to *impart some spiritual gift* to the church in Rome (Rom 1:11). Timothy was given a spiritual gift *through a prophetic message when the body of elders laid their hands* on him (1 Ti 4:14; 2 Ti 1:6).

5. Luke's narrative gives the impression that the various communities in the early church were all characterized by a prophetic anointing with the demonstration of prophetic gifts. If prophetic gifts were exercised in the majority of Christian communities in Acts and the early church took steps to remedy the situation where communities did not demonstrate such powerful gifts (Ac 8:15-17), it should probably be assumed that the exercise of prophetic gifts was considered normative in the early church. Therefore, it is not surprising that the communities addressed by Paul are already anointed with the Spirit and exercise prophetic gifts. This could explain why there are no exhortations in Paul's letters to seek or pray for such an anointing.

6. It is difficult to believe that either Paul or the community of believers described by Luke would have been satisfied with a church not having any manifestations of prophetic anointing. Lukan communities would have concluded that the Spirit had not yet fallen on such a church and taken steps to remedy the situation. The Paul in Luke's narrative did not leave the Ephesian church in such a condition. In his letters Paul tells us that he exercised prophetic gifts and invited his readers to imitate him (1 Cor 4:16; 11:1; Phil 3:17; 2 Thes 3:7, 9). He explicitly encouraged the Corinthian church to imitate him in the exercise of the gifts of speaking in tongues and prophecy (1 Cor 14:5, 12-19), the two gifts most clearly associated with Spirit anointing in Luke-Acts. It is highly probable that the early church considered it 'normal' that Christian communities be anointed with the Spirit and exercise prophetic gifts. Those who think that the church has less need for such gifts today need to show how the situation has changed enough to allow for such an impoverishment in the powerful confirming evidence which accompanied the proclamation of the gospel in the Acts of the Apostles.

Adaptation

Even though we probably want to adopt Luke's expectations, it is probably advisable to change the vocabulary he used in order to avoid confusion. We must adapt the message to fit our current historical situation. There is significant biblical evidence that the church should still expect and seek to be prophetically empowered by the Spirit of God for the task of worldwide evangelism. We should have experiences with the Spirit and accompanying results similar to those of the early church. However, it is no longer logical or advisable to pray for the reception of the Holy Spirit as the apostles did in the book of Acts. Having come to this conclusion from the wider New Testament understanding of the reception of the Holy Spirit, Pentecostals and Charismatics pray for a baptism in or with the Holy Spirit. Although Luke avoided using this expression too often, most likely because of its popular association with end-time judgment, it is technically correct to use it to describe the experiences we are hoping to repeat. Because the expression is so popular, it is probably wise to continue using it. However, we need to be aware of the fact that the ambiguity of the expression in the New Testament leads to some confusion as to its meaning. If we could turn back the clock and restart the Pentecostal movement, the expressions "prophetic empowerment" or "prophetic anointing" give a much clearer idea of the meaning of this essential experience.

Application – Seeking the Spirit

Having established the continuing need for prophetic anointing, we must now look at the means for acquiring this experience with the Spirit. The church today has just as much need as the disciples in the first century for this prophetic empowering to fulfill its task of bearing testimony to the nations (Ac 1:8). How should we seek to acquire such an anointing? Before considering the means of acquiring this experience given in Luke-Acts, it is wise to distinguish between the conditions for receiving Spirit anointing and the means for receiving it.

The only real condition given by Luke for receiving Joel's end-time Spirit anointing is repentance. Peter said, *Repent and be baptized, every one of you, in the name of Jesus Christ for the forgiveness of your sins. And you will receive the gift of the Holy Spirit* (Ac 2:38). He appears to include baptism in the name of Jesus as a condition, but context shows that this was not obligatory. There is no record of the apostles being baptized in the name of Jesus. The believers in the household of Cornelius were anointed with the Spirit before their baptism (Ac 10:44-48). And Apollos was not baptized in the name of Jesus (Ac 18:24-26). It is probably best to understand Peter's mention of baptism in the name of Jesus as the usual and recognized expression of repentance adapted from John the Baptist's preaching and not as a second condition. Those who were baptized by John had already repented and did not necessarily need to be baptized in the name of Jesus.[2]

Some may want to consider one other 'condition' a prerequisite for Spirit anointing. Peter told some Jewish authorities that God gives the Holy Spirit "to those who obey him" (Ac 5:32). Even though Peter is clearly drawing a contrast between the disciples who obey God by teaching in the name of Jesus (Ac 5:28-29) and the Jewish authorities who killed Jesus (Ac 5:30), obedience in this sentence probably refers more globally to obedience to the gospel message. One chapter later Luke describes a group of believers as those who *became obedient to the faith* (Ac 6:7). Later on Peter and his Jewish colleagues conclude from the fact that the household of Cornelius had received Spirit anointing that God had granted them *repentance unto life* (Ac 11:18). For this reason, Peter decided to baptize them (Ac 10:47-48). It should not be inferred from Peter's statement that people can somehow merit Spirit anointing by achieving a greater degree of obedience to God than other believers who are not anointed. The contrast is between those who obey God in repentance and faith and those who do not.

The laying on of hands

Luke emphasizes two different means for receiving the Spirit's anointing: the laying on of hands and prayer. Three times in the book of Acts Spirit anointing is associated with the act of laying on hands (Ac 8:17-18; 9:12, 17; 19:6). We will briefly examine six questions to help evaluate the applicability of this gesture today.

What is the origin of the laying on of hands?

Like most of Luke's vocabulary dealing with Spirit experiences, this gesture is probably derived from the Old Testament, where it is used to confer a blessing (Gn 48:13-20) and in the transfer of power or authority (Nb 27:18-23). Of particular interest for our purposes is the conferral of the enabling power of the Holy Spirit associated with the transfer of authority from Moses to Joshua. The writer of Deuteronomy tells us that Joshua *was filled with the*

---

2 It is unclear why the Ephesian disciples were rebaptized in the name of Jesus (Ac 19:5).

spirit [Spirit][3] *of wisdom because Moses had laid his hands on him. So the Israelites listened to him and did what the LORD had commanded Moses* (Dt 34:9). The gesture is used for similar purposes in other books of the New Testament. In Matthew's gospel it is used to confer a blessing (Mt 19:13). It is used frequently in the synoptic gospels and in Acts for healings.[4] Strictly speaking, there is no example of its use for healing in the Old Testament. Naaman, however, expected Elijah to lay his hands on him for healing (2 Kgs 5:11) and, in one Qumran text, Abram recounts how he was asked to pray for the king of Egypt and lay hands on him so that he might live (1 Qap-Gen 20:21-22).[5] The gesture is also used in Acts for the transfer of authority and power in commissioning leaders for ministry (Ac 6:6; 13:3), and in the transfer of the gift of the Spirit (Ac 8:17, 19; 9:17; 19:6). Similarly, in Paul's letters to Timothy, it is used in the transfer of spiritual gifts (1 Ti 4:14; 2 Ti 1:6). In both the Old and New Testaments this tangible gesture appears to represent the transfer of some intangible quality or power.

What is the significance of this gesture?

Do biblical characters attribute some sort of magical power to this gesture? Luke Timothy Johnson believes that it merely "symbolizes the transfer of power."[6] The actual transfer undoubtedly has more to do with the authority of the person making the gesture than with the gesture itself. Certainly there was the possibility that observers could misunderstand the disciples' power in magical terms. Simon the magician knew that he could not simply perform this magical gesture to confer the gift of the Spirit. But, he thought it was possible to purchase this power as you would other magical powers (Ac 8:18-19). Peter's rebuke makes it clear that God's power is not for sale, demonstrating that Peter's "ministry" of conferring the gift of the Spirit was poles apart from the magical dealings familiar to Simon (Ac 8:9-10, 20-23). The gesture probably symbolized the delegated authority of the "hand" of God. The disciples prayed that God would stretch out his *hand to heal*

---

[3] The translation is dependent on context. Most translators prefer the translation "spirit." Nouvelle Edition de Genève translates with "l'Esprit" (Spirit). The translation we choose for Deuteronomy is irrelevant, since it is how the early church and Luke understood this text which counts in our understanding of Luke-Acts. This verse is an excellent and probably the only parallel for understanding Luke's use of this gesture.

[4] Mt 9:18; Mk 5:23; 6:5; 7:32; 8:23, 25; 16:18; Lk 4:40; 13:13; Ac 9:12, 17; 28:28.

[5] Green, p. 226.

[6] *The Acts of the Apostles*, Sacra Pagina Series, vol. 5, ed. Daniel J. Harrington, Collegeville, MN, Liturgical Press, 2006, p. 107.

and perform miraculous signs and wonders (Ac 4:30). In the next chapter we learn that *many signs and wonders* were done *by the hands of the apostles* (Ac 5:12). The repetition of signs and wonders performed by hands in this narrative sequence surely indicates that the *hand* or power of God is extended in ministry through the *hands of the apostles*. Connecting the transfer of power with a physical gesture or point of contact ensures that the chain of delegated authority is correctly interpreted. There was no doubt as to who God used to perform these miracles. In this way, the gesture contributes to Luke's theme of validation through demonstrations of the Spirit's power. Those who saw the miracles performed through the actual hands of Jesus and his Spirit-filled disciples were convinced that God was with them and that God's hand was at work (Ac 4:4, 14-16; 5:14, 33-39; 10:38; 11:21; 14:3).

Was the gesture a fixed practice, or did it take various forms?

Neither Jesus nor his disciples were limited to a specific form for this point of contact. A sick woman was healed when she touched the edge of Jesus' cloak (Lk 8:44). Jesus took Jairus' daughter by the hand to heal her (Lk 8:53). The crippled beggar by the temple was also healed when Peter took him by the right hand and helped him up (Ac 3:7). When Peter cut off the ear of the high priest's servant, Jesus *touched the man's ear and healed him* (Lk 22:51). Jesus made mud with his own saliva and put it on a blind man's eyes to heal him (Jn 9:6). Some were healed through handkerchiefs and aprons touched by Paul (Ac 19:12). Others were healed when Peter's shadow fell on them (Ac 5:15). Though the details of the point of contact may vary from one episode to the next, the laying on of hands appears to be the general description used for summary statements on the healing ministry of Jesus and his disciples (Mk 6:5; 16:18; Lk 4:40; Ac 5:12).

Who had the authority to confer the Spirit through the laying on of hands?

Four characters in Luke-Acts exercise of this authority. Three of them, Peter, John and Paul, had definite positions of authority in the church. However, in the account of Saul's anointing, God sent Ananias to bring healing and Spirit anointing to him. Ananias was a simple *disciple* in Damascus with no apparent role as an authority in the church. His divinely appointed authority to confer these gifts on Saul was clearly communicated in a vision. He was told that Saul had seen him come and lay hands on him in a vision. When

Ananias fulfilled this prophetic vision, Saul received his sight (Ac 9:11-17). Though Saul's anointing is not described in the narrative, it makes perfect sense that his subsequent "powerful" ministry of the word was the result of his newly acquired prophetic anointing (Ac 9:20-22). From these few details it is impossible to determine who might have had the authority to confer the gift of Spirit anointing. But it is clear that God was not limited to working through any particular church authorities. Any disciple could be commissioned by God to do the job (Ac 9:10), and God could confer Spirit anointing on unlikely candidates when church authorities least expected it (Ac 10:45).

When was the laying on of hands used in the book of Acts?

Was this gesture used as frequently in the early church as it is in Pentecostal circles today, with Luke only recording a few of the many occasions? Or was it only used on significant occasions when the Holy Spirit guided them to do so, with Luke recording most of these episodes? There are only 5 episodes in Acts describing the details of initial Spirit anointing: Pentecost (Ac 2:1-4), Samaria (Ac 8:15-17), Saul (Ac 9:11-18), the household of Cornelius (Ac 10:44-47; 11:15-16) and Ephesus (Ac 19:1-6). In three of these episodes believers use the means of the laying on of hands to bring about this Spirit anointing (Ac 8, 9 and 19). In the other two episodes the anointing is a sudden and sovereign act of God (Ac 2:1-4; 10:44-46). This means that every time Luke's characters sought to bring about an experience of Spirit anointing, someone laid hands on the intended recipients. This is probably significant. However, the frequent use of this gesture for various types of blessings and the other forms of touch or points of contact used for some of the same purposes probably indicates that we are looking at familiar patterns of behavior rather than any kind of expected method or formula for acquiring Spirit fullness. In other words, the laying on of hands was probably a familiar way of conferring a blessing and not a prerequisite for acquiring any particular blessing. According to C. K. Barrett, "the laying on of hands was a gesture of blessing whose precise meaning was determined by the context in which it took place."[7]

What implications do these conclusions have for using this gesture as a means of acquiring Spirit anointing today?

We find no teachings on its use in the New Testament, only examples. So, we are obliged to infer principles of use from these examples. We do

---

[7] Barrett, vol. 1, p. 454.

know that the laying on of hands was considered a foundational teaching in the letter to the Hebrews (Heb 6:2). We do not know the content of that teaching, but we do know that it was important by the fact that it is included in this list of foundational teachings. This reference in the book of Hebrews together with the fact that Luke and the other biblical authors feel no need to explain the use of this gesture undoubtedly means that the significance of the laying on of hands was widely understood when these books were written. This means that this gesture was commonly practiced in at least the first thirty years of the early church. The burden of proof rests upon those who desire to eliminate the laying on of hands from current practice. They need to answer such questions as, why the gesture is no longer needed and what has replaced it. If there are no good answers to these questions, it seems biblically appropriate to use the gesture whenever the conferral of any blessing is desired, including Spirit anointing.

On the other hand, the fact that the gesture seems to have been widely used in a variety of contexts in biblical culture and not commonly used in modern cultures introduces some doubt as to whether modern observers will properly understand it. It could even raise the question as to whether the gesture is appropriate in today's context. It is possible that some other more contextualized gesture or means could perform the same function. Without more clear information on the significance and necessity of the gesture in the New Testament, it is difficult to determine if any substitute would appropriately fulfill the same function. Since the historical situation has changed, it is difficult to determine even if the same gesture is fulfilling the same function today. It is probably wise to accept diversity on this issue. We should probably not criticize groups who have no inclination to incorporate this gesture into their practice. But if groups find the use of this gesture practical and edifying, we should rejoice with them. However, great care needs to be taken to keep people from attributing magical powers to this gesture or to those who use it. Those who practice the laying on of hands must continually emphasize that the power to heal and to bless comes from God and is not in any way dependant on the practice of any gesture.

Prayer

The second and more prevalent means of receiving Spirit anointing in Luke-Acts is prayer. Not only do we have examples to follow from the life and ministry of Jesus' disciples, but Jesus himself also gave us an example and specific teaching on the subject. Jesus said that our *Father in heaven give*[s] *the Holy Spirit to those who ask him* (Lk 11:13). This promise, spoken by Jesus and quoted by Luke, is another indication that the Spirit anointing described in Luke-Acts was not immediately and automatically received at conversion. If reception were immediate and automatic, there would be no reason to pray.

The narrative in Acts shows the disciples following Jesus' instructions in this passage. What Jesus did (Lk 3:21) and instructed his disciples to do (Lk 11:13), that is to pray for the reception of the Spirit, is exactly what Luke narrates them doing in practically every episode referring to the reception of prophetic anointing. The only exception is where the reception of the Spirit was totally unexpected in the household of Cornelius (Ac 10:44-45). The disciples *joined together constantly in prayer* before the day of Pentecost (Ac 1:14). The content of their prayers is not described. But, given the facts that Jesus instructed them to pray for the reception of the Spirit (Lk 11:13) and that he told them to wait in Jerusalem to receive this empowering of the Spirit (Lk 24:49; Ac 1:4-8), it is highly probable that this was a major concern in their prayers. A short time later they prayed again for empowering, and were again *filled with the Spirit* (Ac 4:29-31). Considering Luke's tendency to use synonyms, we should not be overly concerned about the use of various expressions in these episodes, since all of these expressions were used to refer to the same experience at Pentecost.

The disciples also prayed for others to receive Spirit anointing. Peter and John prayed for the Samaritan believers and laid hands on them that *they might receive the Holy Spirit* (Ac 8:15-17). Considering the fact that prayer is explicitly linked with the laying on of hands in this passage and on two other occasions in Acts (Ac 6:6; 13:3), it is probably safe to assume that the gesture was accompanied by prayer in the two other episodes where the laying on of hands is used for conferring Spirit anointing (Ac 9:12, 17; 19:6). Luke consistently portrays prayer as a means for acquiring the prophetic anointing of the Holy Spirit.

How should we pray?

Why do we not see more Acts-type manifestations of the Holy Spirit in our churches today? Clearly, Luke and the characters in his narrative expected these types of manifestations to continue providing evidence for the proclamation of the gospel. Were they wrong to expect this? Or is there something wrong in the way we seek and pray for such experiences? The difficulty must be with us. Some simply do not seek God for such empowering. Others may seek and pray for wrong motives or in a wrong manner. I would like to use some instructions from the book of James to outline some of the difficulties in seeking the power of the Spirit.

You do not have because you do not ask God (Jas 4:2)

There are many who *do not ask God* for miraculous power because they believe we should leave miraculous manifestations to the sovereignty of God. They reason that if God wants to manifest his power through miracles and prophetic gifts, he will do it. While it is certainly true that we must entirely depend on God for miracles and that sometimes he performs miracles sovereignly without any prior effort on our part, we do not see Jesus' disciples passively waiting on God's sovereign intervention. If they did not see powerful manifestations of the Spirit, they assumed something was wrong and took steps to remedy the situation. *When the apostles in Jerusalem heard that Samaria had accepted the word of God, they sent Peter and John to them. When they arrived, they prayed for them that they might receive the Holy Spirit, because the Holy Spirit had not yet come upon any of them* (Ac 8:14-16). Paul asked the Ephesian disciples, *Did you receive the Holy Spirit when you believed* (Ac 19:2)? When he discovered that they had not, he continued to work with them until *the Holy Spirit came on them, and they spoke in tongues and prophesied* (Ac 19:6). The disciples in Acts were dissatisfied with a powerless church and sought God for manifestations of his empowering presence. We would do well to follow their example.

Others *do not ask God* for the empowering of his Spirit, because they have already asked. There is the mistaken comprehension that there is no further need to persevere in prayer. Perhaps they prayed once and feel that to continue praying would be a demonstration of their lack of faith. They should just believe that God has answered their prayers. Others feel that they have prayed enough and now need to leave it in the hands of God, adopting a modified version of the sovereignty position above. While the principles of faith and trust in God's sovereignty are both emphasized in Scripture, they do not negate Jesus' instructions to persevere in prayer.

The context of Jesus' instructions underlines the need for perseverance in praying for the gift of the Holy Spirit. When the disciples asked Jesus to teach them to pray, Jesus started with what we call the Lord's Prayer (Lk

11:1-4). In the rest of the passage Jesus encourages his disciples to persevere in prayer. First, he gave the example of a friend who asked his neighbor for bread when a guest arrived in the middle of the night. The friend received the bread only after he persisted in pestering his neighbor until the neighbor got up and gave it to him (Lk 11:5-8).

This illustration is logically connected with the following instructions for his disciples on prayer. Jesus tells his disciples to "ask and keep on asking," "seek and keep on seeking" and "knock and keep on knocking" until they get what they are seeking (Lk 11:9-10). The continuous action expressed in the above translation reflects the meaning of the Greek present tense imperatives used in this text. This translation makes the link with the previous illustration obvious. The disciples are to continuously pester God with their requests in a manner similar to the friend who pestered his neighbor for bread.

Jesus concludes his instructions with a paragraph on the goodness of God. The disciples need not fear pestering God with their requests, because God only gives good things to his children. Just as an earthly father will not give a snake instead of a fish or a scorpion instead of an egg, our heavenly Father will only give good gifts. The culminating answer to prayer given in Luke's version of this episode is the gift of the Holy Spirit. Jesus says, ...*how much more will your Father in heaven give the Holy Spirit to those who ask him* (Lk 11:13). The words *to those who ask* are a translation of a present participle. While participles can have a variety of meanings, the context of this passage leads to the conclusion that continuous action is also implied. Coming directly after an illustration on persevering prayer and instructions to ask and keep on asking, we must conclude that the disciples are to ask and keep on asking for the gift of the Holy Spirit, with the implication that they must keep on asking until they receive it.

Jesus' instructions are reminiscent of an old Pentecostal practice called "tarrying for the Spirit." This expression is taken from the King James translation of some of Jesus' final instructions for his disciples. Jesus said, "... tarry ye in the city of Jerusalem, until ye be endued with power from on high" (Lk 24:49, KJV). If Jesus appeared to his disciples *over a period of forty days* (Ac 1.3) and Pentecost occurred after fifty days, Pentecostals reasoned correctly that the disciples probably persevered in prayer for at least a week before the Holy Spirit came upon them at Pentecost (Ac 1:14). Pentecostals reasoned further, that if the disciples needed to pray for a week or more before receiving the gift of the Holy Spirit, we might also need to pray for a long period of time. This concept is definitely consistent with Jesus' teaching on prayer.

When you ask, you do not receive, because you ask with wrong motives (Jas 4:3)

Some may ask God for Spirit anointing with a motive for self aggrandizement. They may want to prove to themselves or to others that they are more spiritual than, or just as spiritual as other believers. If God were to grant such a request, it might actually contribute to a false sense of pride and cause spiritual harm to the recipient. Those who desire spiritual gifts for such reasons are missing the point entirely. The manifestations of the power of the Spirit are not given primarily for our benefit. We receive the power of the Spirit so that we may be effective witnesses (Ac 1:8). Luke's focus is not on our personal growth in spirituality, but on the proclamation of the gospel to all nations. The early church prayed accordingly. They did not ask to receive spiritual gifts. They prayed that God would enable them to speak the word of God with boldness, by stretching out his hand to *heal and perform miraculous signs and wonders* (Ac 4:29-30). Signs and wonders are not the goal, but a means of enabling the bold proclamation of the gospel. If we make them the goal, God may not want to grant our request.

Some may ask God for Spirit anointing with a competitive motive. This motive is similar to the first in that they are both selfish motives and probably interrelated. However, it is possible for someone to ask for manifestations of the Spirit for the right purpose of evangelism but with the motive of doing it better than others. Those requesting the Spirit with this motive are still seeking to enhance their own reputations rather than God's. If God were to grant this request, he might be contributing to disunity in the body of Christ as well as to increased spiritual pride among the recipients.

It is probably not possibly to eliminate spiritual pride, but it can be greatly reduced if we consider prophetic gifts from the standpoint of the community of believers rather than from the standpoint of individual believers. Luke's narrative emphasizes prayer for the community of believers and the reception of Spirit anointing for the entire community. The first disciples *were all filled with the Holy Spirit* (Ac 2:4; 4:31). The Samaritan believers *received the Holy Spirit* as a group (Ac 8:17). The Holy Spirit *came on all who heard the message* in the household of Cornelius (Ac 10:44), and upon the group of believers in Ephesus (Ac 19:6). This emphasis on "all believers" corresponds as well with Peter's prophetic words that the gift of the Spirit is *for all who are far off* (Ac 2.39). The only exception to this principle in Acts is Saul. His anointing appears to have been an individual experience (Ac 9:17). This is probably because the rest of the believers in Damascus were already anointed with the Spirit.

This same emphasis on community is also evident in Paul's letters. In his letter to the Ephesians he exhorted the entire community to *be* (second person plural imperative) *filled with the Spirit* (Eph 5:18). He did not say, "Let each of you be filled with the Spirit." In his first letter to the Corinthians he emphasized the fact that *the manifestation of the Spirit is given for the common good* (1 Cor 12:7).

Discovering the Spirit in the early church and today

I began this book with a testimony of how I discovered the overwhelming power of the Holy Spirit in my life. We have now come full circle and returned to the notion of needing to discover this overwhelming power of the Spirit in our churches today. This process of discovery does not have to be haphazard. We have been given examples to follow and specific instructions on how to acquire the fullness and power of the Spirit. The following is a summary of some of the concepts we have examined in this book and some of the implications of these concepts for discovering the Spirit today.

Jesus' disciples did not fully understand the activity of the Spirit all at once. They went through a process of discovering the power of the Spirit. First, they witnessed the Spirit at work in the life and ministry of Jesus, the Messiah. They were forced to undergo a paradigm shift in their understanding of the Spirit's end-time role. Jesus was not anointed with the Spirit to enable him to overwhelm nations and reestablish the kingdom of Israel, according to popular expectations (Ac 1:6). Instead, he was anointed with the Spirit to proclaim good news through prophetic words and deeds (Lk 4:18-19; 7:22).

The disciples discovered this same power of the Spirit for themselves on the day of Pentecost. Their initial understanding of this experience came from their comprehension of Old Testament passages, especially Joel's prophecy that God would anoint all his servants with the Spirit, enabling them to 'prophesy' (Ac 2:16-18; Jl 2:28-29). All of Luke's metaphors describing the disciples' experiences with the Spirit are synonymous and were designed to emphasize the fulfillment of this prophecy. According to the logic of Joel's prophecy, the disciples knew they were anointed by the Spirit because of the powerful prophetic gifts they were able to exercise. Having no knowledge or understanding of the immediate reception of the Spirit at conversion, they did not recognize the presence of the Spirit without some tangible phenomenal effect. This understanding of Spirit reception at conversion was probably discovered by Paul, perhaps during his long stay in Ephesus, as he meditated on Ezekiel's end-time promise of Spirit reception (Ez 36:26-27; 2 Cor 3:3; Rom 8:4).

If our reconstruction of the disciple's discovery of the Spirit is correct, we need to update some of Luke's conclusions. Believers, such as those in Samaria, probably had 'received' the Spirit in the Pauline sense of Spirit reception. They simply had not 'received' Spirit anointing like the disciples on the day of Pentecost. This update does not diminish the need for the experiences described by Luke. Phenomenal encounters with the Spirit characterized, inspired and empowered the early church for its evangelistic task. Since that task is not finished, the church still needs empowering. Paul recognized this same need for Spirit empowering in his evangelistic endeavors (Rom 15:18-19; 1 Cor 2:4; 1 Thes 1:5). In the light of Paul' teachings, we should probably refrain from referring to these encounters as receptions of the Spirit. Spirit baptism, Spirit filling and especially Spirit anointing are all better, more up-to-date expressions for describing these phenomenal experiences. Luke reserved the use of this last term for Jesus, probably to emphasize his identity as the Messiah (Anointed One). However, prophetic anointing best represents the meaning implied in all of Luke's Spirit-experience expressions, since it summarizes the message of Joel's prophecy.

Another necessary update concerns the expected effects in a Spirit-influenced or Spirit-filled individual or group. Luke emphasized the tangible prophetic gifts produced by the Spirit, such as prophecy, signs and wonders. He probably did not recognize the influence of the Spirit in other domains. From Paul's teachings we understand that the Spirit also produces godly qualities in the life of the believer (Gal 5:22-23). For Paul, to be Spirit-filled or Spirit-influenced implies more than just the presence of phenomenal prophetic gifts. The Spirit is also active in producing Godly character (Eph 5:18-6:9). The Spirit was undoubtedly active in producing some amazing godlike characteristics in the early church. The church's tremendous concern for the poor and her willingness to make enormous sacrifices in terms of personal wealth to meet their needs was surely inspired by the Spirit, even if the early disciples were unaware of it (Ac 2:44-45; 4:32-37). Luke does not attribute these effects directly to the Spirit's influence because they are not as clearly associated with the Spirit as prophecy and miracles. Individuals can show concern and make sacrifices for the poor apart from the influence of the Spirit. They cannot perform miracles apart from the influence of the Spirit.

Growth in godly character was not and is not an automatic effect produced by the Spirit. Believers can be influenced by sources other than the Holy Spirit (Ac 5:3). They can even grieve the Spirit (Eph 4:30). This is undoubtedly why Paul felt it necessary to teach on walking by the Spirit, emphasizing a continuous submission to the Spirit's will (Rom 8:4; Gal 5:16). Thus, those who have had powerful encounters with the Spirit should exhibit godly characteristics as well as exercise prophetic gifts, but one is not a guarantee of the other. We must not neglect either aspect of the Spirit's influence. However, these two aspects of the Spirit's influence, godly character and prophetic gifts, are not acquired in the same manner. Godly character is the result of progressively submitting to the Spirit's leading (Rom 8:4-14; Gal 5:16-25). Prophetic anointing and prophetic gifts are given, usually in response to prayer. No process is described or implied in the reception of these gifts.

The narrative of Luke-Acts clearly demonstrates that Joel's prophetic Spirit anointing is not automatically received at conversion, even though it is promised to all God's servants (Ac 2:17-18). Nor is it acquired through a process of submitting to the Spirit's influence. Probably because of Joel's prophecy, a church which did not exhibit the powerful tangible effects of the Holy Spirit was unacceptable to early church leaders. Whenever tangible evidence was not forthcoming, the early disciples made every effort to bring it about. Joel's prophecy is still valid today. The last days have not yet come to an end. A powerless church is still unacceptable. If a community of believers is not visibly endowed with the power of the Spirit and not reaching out to the ends of the earth with overwhelming power, every effort should be made to remedy the situation.

According to the clear teachings of Jesus and the examples given in Luke-Acts the effort to be made is in prayer. Jesus taught us to persevere in prayer for the gift of the Holy Spirit (Lk 11:1-13). We find the disciples doing just that before the day of Pentecost. With one mind they persevered in prayer (Ac 1:14).[8] They did not even stop with Pentecost. We find them still praying for Spirit empowering three chapters later, after they have been persecuted and threatened by Jewish authorities (Ac 4:29-30). They later prayed for others to receive this gift (Ac 8:15; cf. 9:17; 19:6). The disciples learned to persevere in prayer until they and their converts were empowered by the Spirit.

It is precisely this emphasis on persevering in prayer until the overwhelming influence of the Spirit empowers our witness which is desperately

---

[8] English translations typically use the word "continue" to translate *proskarteroûntes* instead of the word persevere. Both words imply persistence.

missing in the life and ministry of most churches today. Most Pentecostals are convinced they have what is needed if they speak in tongues. Non Pentecostals feel they have everything they need from the moment of conversion. Yet our churches remain feeble. The average Christian finds it difficult to witness. We are not seeing the crowds overwhelmed by powerful manifestations of the Spirit and cut to the heart with the conviction of sin, who come imploring us with the question, *What shall we do?* (Ac 2:37). But the greatest tragedy of all is that this enfeebled condition of the church does not really bother us that much.

Obstacles to seeking the Spirit

Why do we allow these conditions to persist rather than persisting in prayer to change them? From the Pentecostal perspective, it is often easier to 'help God out' rather than waiting in prayer for God to intervene. For instance, there are some Charismatic enthusiasts who actually coach people in how to receive the gift of speaking in tongues. They might tell them to start out by breathing deeply. Then, they can add some sort of sound to their breathing. Finally, they tell them to speak whatever sounds or syllables might come to mind.

I have heard others instruct seekers in how to be slain in the Spirit. This phenomenon, which occurs frequently in charismatic circles, is loosely based on a few examples in Scripture, where individuals fell down as a result of the overpowering presence of almighty God (Dn 8:17-18; Mt 28:4; Ac 9:4; Rv 1:17). Rob Mitchell, whose healing is narrated in the opening chapter of this book, fell unconscious as he was being healed by the power of God. I once prayed for an inebriated young man who collapsed at my feet and got up a few moments later completely sober. I was witnessing to a group of young people hanging out in a parking lot when the young man came up to me and asked for prayer. After seeing this demonstration of the power of God, the whole group listened attentively as I shared the gospel and several of them gave their lives to Christ. Some enthusiasts, who sincerely desire to help others experience the power of God in this manner, tell seekers that, if they feel like falling down, they should just go ahead and give in to that impression and fall down. Sometimes they may push gently or even violently on the person's chest or forehead as they pray for them.

Others instruct people in how to receive prophecy. They tell us to ask God for a prophetic word and then speak whatever comes to mind. Many of the resulting 'prophecies' from such promptings are not intrinsically bad.

I like to think of them as 'fortune cookie prophecies.' They are worded in Scriptural language in such a way as to be relevant in a thousand and one situations. I once had someone prophesy over me saying that my ministry was going to be like a wedding. I prayed and asked God what the implications of this prophecy might be. When I got no answer, I asked the 'prophet' about its meaning. He informed me that only I could discern the meaning, but that he "got the idea" for this prophecy while he was reading adds in the newspaper that morning.

Others instruct believers in how to receive healing. They tell people to claim their healing, even when visible symptoms would seem to indicate that they are not well. They reason that by Christ's wounds on the cross we "have been healed" or "are healed" (1 P 2:24; Is 53.5), interpreting these passages to indicate the precise moment of our healing rather than the source of our healing. They encourage believers to make positive declarations of their healing, even when all empirical evidence indicates that they are still sick.

The real harm in all the 'help' we give God is that these self-generated 'miracles' diminish the impact of clearly divine interventions. Outsiders observe more questionable 'miracles' than undeniable manifestations of God's power. They see sick Christians who claim they are healed, speaking unintelligible sounds and calling it unknown languages, falling down and calling it the power of God, saying all sorts of things and declaring that their words come from God. We are not denying that God may be at work producing some of these phenomena. But there appears to be a lot of cheap imitation. The results are a far cry from what we read in the gospels and Acts.

All of this cheap imitation reduces our credibility and casts doubt on the undeniable miracles which clearly and overwhelmingly demonstrate the power of the Holy Spirit. When my friend Rob was healed of asthma and emphysema, everyone present knew that God had performed a miracle. We were all struck with a sense of overwhelming awe. Not everyone responded in obedience to Christ, but everyone knew that God had intervened! However, when I tell the story of this healing to people who were not there, and they have already heard many stories about questionable miracles, they may be inclined to skepticism. Miracles in the early church were more like the healing I witnessed. When Peter and John healed a crippled beggar outside the temple courts in the sight of all the people, the leaders of the Jewish Sanhedrin did not know what to do to curb the success of these disciples. They were forced to admit that *Everybody living in Jerusalem knows they have done an outstanding miracle, and we cannot deny it* (Ac 4:16). We need to ask and keep on asking God for such convincing proofs of his presence and power and resist the temptation to 'help God out.'

This does not mean that we must be absolutely certain of divine inspiration before we act. Once, I was asked to pray for a close friend. After spending some time alone with God in prayer, certain very specific thoughts about my friend's need came into my mind. It concerned events in his past of which I had no knowledge. I even knew how old he was when the events occurred. I was excited and scared at the same time. Had God given me a specific answer to my prayers? Or was I just making it up? After more agonizing prayer and much reflection, I felt that I could not have made this up. But I was still afraid that this prophetic revelation might just be the product of my own imagination. I went to my friend and very hesitatingly told him what I *thought* God had revealed to me. My friend wept before God, amazed that God could care enough about him to reveal the specific details of what he needed to hear. His life was changed through this powerful encounter with God's Spirit.

Undeniable miracles, signs and wonders such as those found in Acts are not that unusual in churches around the globe. They are not that well-known because they are buried in a mountain of questionable miracles which constantly come to our attention. I have to admit that, even though I have personally seen and experienced God's miracle producing power in my life and ministry, I am often plagued with doubts, suspicions and skepticism concerning many of the so-called signs and wonders I hear about. If an eye-witness to a miracle like me is skeptical, how can we expect to convince an unbelieving world? I plead with Pentecostal and Charismatic leaders to persevere in prayer for more undeniable manifestations of God's power and avoid trying to 'help God out.'

Non Pentecostal leaders, confronted with so many abuses in Pentecostal and Charismatic circles, are afraid to start the ball rolling. If they were to encourage active prayer for manifestations of the Spirit's power, would they be opening the proverbial Pandora's Box? Would all the abuses present in Pentecostal and Charismatic movements simply reproduce themselves in their congregations? This is a legitimate concern. However, the answer is not to ignore the issue. Charismatic practices and beliefs will most likely manifest themselves anyway. Pastors who try to prevent it will probably end up throwing out the baby with the bath water. They may not have abusive practices in their congregations, but they will also miss out on some of the wonderful and powerful experiences God might want to use to transform their church, and they will probably lose some of the more spiritually hungry members of their congregation. They will be left with those who are satisfied with the status quo.

A better strategy is to develop a determination to seek God and to train one's congregation in seeking God. We need to warn our congregations about abuses and not permit them to be satisfied with cheap imitations. But we also need to stir up the desire for the real thing. There are a lot of abuses in preaching. The text of Scripture has been taken out of context to make it say just about anything. This does not mean that we should stop preaching or stop preparing pastors to preach. God has given us the means of preaching to communicate his love and abiding principles to a needy world. Rather than throwing out preaching, we need to train pastors to *correctly handle the word of truth* (2 Ti 2:15).

In the same way, God has provided the means for confirming his Word to the world with overwhelmingly powerful prophetic words and deeds. It is unthinkable that we should settle for less than what God has provided. A needy and dying world needs us to step up to the plate and, with the Spirit's help, knock it out of the ball park. This is what it will take to bring in all the runners. There are too many people out there, who are skeptical like I was and who need clear and undeniable evidence of God's love and power. This is especially true in areas where there has been very little Christian witness. Among my students in West Africa, almost all who were converted through a verbal witness alone grew up in Christian families. Almost invariably, those who converted from animism or Islam have some sort of vision, dream, healing or miracle which God used to convince them to give their lives to Christ.

The final obstacle to seeking God for manifestations of his miraculous power in our lives and ministries is our own busyness. We want to get all our praying done in seven-minutes a day or less. This is hardly enough time for us to speak 'to' God and tell him what we want. We also need to hear and receive 'from' God. Most congregations spend even less time in seeking God in prayer. Persevering prayer is time consuming. It involves not only asking God to give us what we think we need, but seeking him until we discover what he wants and then knocking on the door until it opens (Lk 11:9-10). Our modern schedules leave very little time for seeking God. Jesus got up to pray *very early in the morning, while it was still dark* (Mk 1:35). On one occasion he spent the night in prayer (Lk 6:12). Jesus told his disciples to wait for the promise of the Father (Ac 1:4) and they persevered in prayer more than a week until Pentecost (Ac 1:14). How can we expect God's empowering when we spend less time in seeking God than either Jesus or his disciples? Are our prayers more efficient or more effective than theirs? If we are serious about reaching the world for Christ and receiving God's prophetic anointing for that task, then we must set aside time for prayer. We must do this again and again until we see heaven's doors opened and the Spirit of God poured out on his servants enabling them to do what God promised they would be able to do. We need to pray until our congregations are overwhelmed by the Spirit and proclaiming the gospel to the nations with powerful words and deeds.

ABBREVIATIONS

Bible versions

NIV	*New International Version.*
JB	*Jerusalem Bible*
NJB	*New Jerusalem Bible*
KJV	*King James Version*
NKJV	*New King James Version*
NAB	*New American Bible*
NASB	*New American Standard Bible*
RSV	*Revised Standard Version*
NRSV	*New Revised Standard Version Bible.*

Works cited

Antiquities	*The Antiquities of the Jews* (Josephus)
Aune	David E. Aune, *The New Testament in Its Literary Environment*, Library of Early Christianity, ed. Wayne A. Meeks, Philadelphia, Westminster, 1987
BAGD	Walter Bauer, *A Greek-English Lexicon of the New Testament and Other Early Christian Litterature*, trans. and adapted by William F. Arndt and F. Wilbur Gingrinch, 2nd ed., revised and augmented by F. Wilbur Gingrinch and Frederick W. Danker, University of Chicago, 1979
Barrett	C. K. Barrett, *A Critical and Exegetical Commentary on The Acts of the Apostles*, The International Critical Commentary on the Holy Scriptures of the Old and New Testaments, ed. J. A. Emerton, C. E. B. Cranfield and G. N. Stanton, Edinburgh, T & T Clark, 1994
Brooks	James A. Brooks and Carlton L. Winbery, *Syntax of New Testament Greek*, Lanham, MD, University Press, 1979
Brown	R. E. Brown, *The Birth of the Messiah: A Commentary on the Infancy Narratives of Matthew and Luke*, New York, Doubleday, 1977
Bruce	F. F. Bruce, *Commentary on the Book of Acts: The English Text with Introduction, Exposition and Notes*, Grand Rapids, Eerdmans, 1955
Cadbury, *Features*	Henry J. Cadbury, "Four Features of Lucan Style," *Studies in Luke-Acts*, ed. Leander E. Keck and J. Louis Martyn, Philadelphia, Fortress, 1980
Cadbury, *Preface*	Henry J. Cadbury, "Commentary on the Preface of Luke," *The Beginnings of Christianity Part I: The Acts of the Apostles*, vol. 2 Prolegomena II, Criticism, ed. F. J. Foakes Jackson and Kirsopp Lake, Grand Rapids, Baker, 1979
Carson	D. A. Carson, Douglas J. Moo and Leon Morris, *An Introduction to the New Testament*, Grand Rapids, Zondervan, 1992

Clark	Andrew C. Clark, *Parallel Lives: The Relation of Paul to the Apostles in the Lucan Perspective*, Paternoster Biblical and Theological Monographs, Carlisle, Cumbria, UK and Waynesboro, GA, Paternoster, 2001
Dana	H. E. Dana et Julius R. Mantey, *A Manual Grammar of the Greek New Testament*, New York, Macmillan, 1955
Darr	John A. Darr, *On Character Building: The Reader and the Rhetoric of Characterization in Luke-Acts*, Louisville, KY, Westiminster/John Knox, 1992
Dunn	James D. G. Dunn, *Baptism in the Holy Spirit: A Re-examination of the New Testament Teaching on the Gift of the Spirit in Relation to Pentecostalism Today*, Studies in Biblical Theology, 2nd Series 15, Naperville, IL, Allenson, 1970
Ervin, *Baptism*	Howard M. Ervin, *Spirit Baptism: A Biblical Investigation*, Peabody MA, Hendrickson, 1987
Ervin, *Conversion*	Howard M. Ervin, *Conversion-Initiation and the Baptism in the Holy Spirit: A Critique of James D. G. Dunn, Baptism in the Holy Spirit*, Peabody, MA, Hendrickson, 1984
Evans	C. F. Evans, *Saint Luke*, Trinity Press International New Testament Commentaries, ed. Howard Clark Kees and Dennis Nineham, London/Philadelphia, SCM/Trinity, 1990
Fitzmyer	Joseph A. Fitzmyer, *The Gospel According to Luke I-X: Introduction, Translation and Notes*, Anchor Bible 28, New York/London, Doubleday, 1981
Green	Joel B. Green, *The Gospel of Luke*, N ICNT, Grand Rapids, Eerdmans, 1997
Harrison	Randall A. Harrison, *L'Esprit dans le récit de Luc: Une recherche de cohérence dans la pneumatologie de l'auteur implicite de Luc-Actes*, Doctoral Dissertation presented at the Faculté Libre de Thélogie Evangélique, Vaux sur Seine, Feb. 2007
Hull	J. H. E. Hull, *The Holy Spirit in the Acts of the Apostles*, Cleveland/New York, World Publishing, 1967

Johnson, *Function*	Luke Timothy Johnson, *The Literary Function of Possessions in Luke-Acts*, SBL Dissertation 39, ed. Howard C. Kee and Douglas A. Knight, Missoula, MT, Scholars, 1977
Johnson, *Luke-Acts*	Luke Timothy Johnson, "Luke-Acts," *The Writings of the New Testament: An Interpretation*, Minneapolis, Fortress, 1999
Kuen	Alfred Kuen, *Baptisé et rempli de l'Esprit*, 2nd edition, Saint Légier, Emmaüs, 1993
Ladd	George Eldon Ladd, *The Presence of the Future: The Eschatology of Biblical Realism*, Grand Rapids, Eerdmans, 1974
Marguérat	Daniel Marguerat and Yvan Bourquin, *La Bible se raconte: Initiation à l'analyse narrative*, Paris/Geneva/Montreal, Cerf/Labor and Fides/Novalis, 1998
Marshall, *Luke*,	I. Howard Marshall, *The Gospel of Luke: A Commentary on the Greek Text*, New International Greek Testament Commentary, ed. I. Howard Marshall and W. Ward Gasque, Grand Rapids, Eerdmans, 1978
Marshall, *Historian*	I. Howard Marshall, *Luke: Historian and Theologian*, Downers Grove, IL, InterVarsity, 1988.
Menzies	Robert P. Menzies, *Empowered for Witness: The Spirit in Luke-Acts*, JPTSS 6, ed. John Christopher Thomas, Rick D. Moore and Steven J. Land, Sheffield, Academic, 1994
Moessner	David P. Moessner, "Dionysius's Narrative 'Arrangement' (οἰκονομία) as the Hermeutical Key to Luke's Re-Vision of the 'Many' " *Paul, Luke and the Graeco-Roman World: Essays in Honour of Alexander J. M. Wedderburn*, ed. Alf Christophersen, Carsten Claussen, Jörg Frey and Bruce Longenecker, JSNTSS 217, Sheffield, Academic, 2002
Oulton	J. E. L. Oulton, "The Holy Spirit, Baptism, and Laying on of Hands in Acts," *Expository Times*, Vol. 66, no. 8, May 1955
PssSol	R. B. Wright, "Psalms of Solomon," *The Old Testament Pseudepigrapha*, vol. 2, ed. James H. Charlesworth, New York, Doubleday, 1985, p. 639-70

Ravens	David Ravens, *Luke and the Restoration of Israel*, JSNTSS 119, Sheffield, Academic, 1995
Robertson	A. T. Robertson, *A Grammar of the Greek New Testament in the Light of Historical Research*, Nashville, Broadman, 1934
Scott	Ernest F. Scott, *The Spirit in the New Testament*, New York, Doran, 1923
Shepherd	William H. Shepherd, Jr., *The Narrative Function of the Holy Spirit as a Character in Luke-Acts*, SBL 147, Atlanta, Scholars, 1994
Stott	John R. W. Stott, *The Baptism and Fullness of the Holy Spirit*, Downers Grove, IL, InterVarsity, 1974
Tannehill	Robert C. Tannehill, *The Narrative Unity of Luke-Acts: A Literary Interpretation*, Volume two: *The Acts of the Apostles*, Minneapolis, Fortress, 1994
Turner	Max Turner, *Power from on High: The Spirit in Israel's Restoration and Witness in Luke-Acts*, JPTSS 9, ed. John Christopher Thomas, Rickie D. Moore and Steven J. Land, Sheffield, Academic, 1996
Wallace	Daniel B. Wallace, *Greek Grammar Beyond the Basics*, Grand Rapids, Zondervan, 1996

The bibliographic information for other sources is provided in the footnotes.

Seeking

Perservering prayer

Seeking in community - like minded believers

Purpose in outreach - evangelism
   - not just personal fulfillment